Lawyers of the Old Left

Morris Hillquit, Seymour Stedman & Charles Recht

Eric B. Easton
University of Baltimore School of Law

Series in Law
VERNON PRESS

www.vernonpress.com

In the Americas:
Vernon Press
1000 N West Street, Suite 1200,
Wilmington, Delaware 19801
United States

In the rest of the world:
Vernon Press
C/Sancti Espiritu 17,
Malaga, 29006
Spain

Series in Law

Library of Congress Control Number: 2025940185

ISBN: 979-8-8819-0302-2

Cover design by Vernon Press. Background image by Freepik. Photographs of Morris Hillquit, Seymour Stedman & Charles Recht, Public domain, via Wikimedia Commons.

Table of Contents

List of Figures

Introduction

This is the story of three lawyers who represented the radical left at the beginning of the twentieth century. They were arguably the most important lawyers of their respective movements, and they were involved in some of the most significant cases of the tumultuous era that surrounded World War I. While all three are relatively unknown today, they all commanded the respect of both their contemporary colleagues and their adversaries, inside and well beyond the courtroom.

Morris Hillquit was practically synonymous with the socialist movement that flourished on the East Coast, particularly New York City, at the end of the nineteenth and beginning of the twentieth century. Not only was he a prolific chronicler and theorist of the movement, but he also ran for political office several times under the Socialist Party banner. Hillquit took a leadership role in the defense of anti-war activists during wartime and the repression that followed, even while managing a thriving law practice. In time, he would become one of the nation's preeminent labor lawyers.

Seymour Stedman might be called the Morris Hillquit of the Midwest. Stedman was a leader, with Eugene Debs and Victor Berger, of the homegrown socialist movement that prevailed in Chicago, Milwaukee, and other midwestern cities. He rose to prominence at the national level, ultimately becoming the party's vice-presidential candidate in Debs's campaign for the presidency in 1920. An ill-advised business venture in the 1930s led to his conviction for violating banking laws; his conviction was reversed, but his career never fully recovered.

Charles Recht was unquestionably the most important American lawyer representing the Soviet Union, both before and after that country was recognized by the United States. Although he also participated in many important civil liberties cases that had little or nothing to do with communism, his advocacy on behalf of Soviet Russia and its U.S. interests formed the core of his legal career. Recht also pursued a second, wholly unrelated career as a novelist, poet, and theatrical translator.

I first encountered these three men while writing a biography of Gilbert E. Roe, a Progressive Republican lawyer who championed left-wing causes during the same period. Roe had represented the socialist magazine *The Masses* in the unsuccessful defense of its mailing privileges, which the government sought to withdraw under the Espionage Act for criticizing the war effort. Hillquit, Stedman, and Recht, along with Dudley Field Malone and Walter Nelles, represented *The*

Masses editors, staff, and contributors in the criminal prosecutions that followed Roe's case.

The "Old Left" in the title refers to the radical ideologies, movements and organizations that captured the attention of many Americans during the last years of the nineteenth century and the first quarter or so of the twentieth. Among them were anarchists, socialists, and communists, with multiple strains of each, as well as suffragists, unionists, pacifists, and others who challenged the establishment from the left. I use the term "Old" merely to distinguish these movements from the so-called "New Left" of the 1960s and 1970s, including Vietnam War protesters and civil rights activists.

Beyond simply reintroducing these lawyers to contemporary readers, this book asserts that the phenomenon of skilled and dedicated American lawyers representing radical causes neither began nor ended with these three and their World War I-era colleagues. Rather, I submit that these lawyers fit comfortably within a long-standing American tradition that has persisted from colonial times to the present day. Accordingly, I am book-ending these three professional profiles with a prologue and epilogue that illustrate this larger proposition.

A second point that I wish to make is that all of these men were lawyers' lawyers. All were leading advocates for their principal clients, all had extensive civil liberties practices, and all had successful commercial practices. The legal and historical literature concerning this period largely focuses on judicial opinions and ideological conflicts; the role of the lawyer is often underplayed. I've tried to remedy that oversight without neglecting the broader context.

For the body of the text, I initially wrote three biographical profiles of the three men, but a perceptive reader of the manuscript found that it obscured the issues these lawyers faced and suggested that a thematic approach would help draw the connections between individual cases and broader legal, political, and social trends. As one reader put it, "This would provide readers with a clearer understanding of how these lawyers' work intersected with the era's defining challenges." I am grateful for the suggestion, and I hope that this organization does its job.

I also wish to thank Jennifer Andruzzi, a marvelous copyeditor who saved me from countless errors of spelling, grammar, punctuation, and style. If any such errors remain, you can be sure they are because I overruled Jennifer's better judgment.

Prologue

The radical impulse in America can be traced to the earliest colonial period. Religious radicals like Roger Williams and Anne Hutchison challenged the authoritarian church; political radicals like Nathaniel Bacon and Jacob Leisler challenged the authoritarian governments.[1] The emergence of lawyers to defend those who embraced radical ideas can also be traced to colonial times.

The most notable case of a practicing lawyer defending antiestablishment interests in those early days was surely that of Andrew Hamilton, who famously defended the printer John Peter Zenger in his 1735 seditious libel trial. Hamilton himself was no radical, though he may have been involved in the Jacobite movement in Scotland as a young man. Hamilton studied law in Virginia and was admitted to the bar there in 1703. He had moved to Maryland by 1708, establishing a thriving law practice, and was called to the English bar in 1714. On his return to America, he was appointed attorney general of Pennsylvania and was soon elected to the Pennsylvania Assembly.

Zenger was a German immigrant who came to America as a teenager. He was apprenticed to New York City's leading printer, William Bradford, then struck out on his own at age 21. After working in Maryland for about four years, he returned to New York as Bradford's partner. As it happened, the colony got a new governor, William Cosby, who could best be described as a political hack whose wife was well-connected and whose purpose in the colonies was to make his fortune.[2] Cosby sacked Lewis Morris Sr., chief justice of the colony, and appointed his own man, young James DeLancey, as chief justice.[3]

Morris did not take this lying down and, with his son Lewis Morris Jr. and a very bright lawyer named James Alexander, started his own political faction, virulently anti-Cosby. They wanted an outlet for their own political ideas, but Bradford was too afraid of losing his government contracts to print them. So they financed Zenger, who left Bradford and set up shop on his own. Zenger became the chief propagandist for a new anti-Cosby, Morrisite party. Alexander became the behind-the-scenes editor of Zenger's newspaper, the *Journal*, which competed with Bradford's pro-Cosby *Gazette*.

---

[1] *See* SIDNEY LENS, RADICALISM IN AMERICA 11-18 (1969).

[2] Eban Moglen, *Considering Zenger: Partisan Politics and the Legal Profession in Provincial New York*, 94 COLUM. L. REV. 1495, 1503-04 (1994).

[3] *Id.* at 1506.

DeLancey tried and failed to get an indictment against Zenger, then offered rewards for proof that Alexander, Morris and the others (who wrote anonymously) were responsible for the attacks on Cosby in the *Journal*, all to no avail. Finally, the *Journal* went too far, publishing a thinly disguised attack on Cosby for jeopardizing the people's liberty and property by bringing cases against colonists in equity or chancery courts instead of common law courts whenever he could get away with it. Equity courts had no juries, only Cosby-appointed judges. In common law courts, juries were safeguards for colonial defendants with whom jurors often identified. Zenger was arrested and prosecuted on a criminal information.[4]

Zenger was prosecuted by Richard Bradley, attorney general of New York, and DeLancey, now Gov. Cosby's new chief judge, presided at the trial. When Zenger's lawyers, Alexander and William Smith, objected to DeLancey's trying the case, they were struck off for contempt[5] and, against their will, John Chambers was appointed to undertake the defense.[6] Chambers planned to argue that the *Journal*'s satirical articles were too indefinite for a conviction and hoped for a favorable jury.[7] But when the trial began on August 4, 1735, it was Andrew Hamilton who took over the defense. Hamilton had been secretly engaged, presumably on the advice of Alexander's wife, Mary Spratt Alexander, a prominent merchant in her own right. She had traveled to Philadelphia to persuade Hamilton to take Zenger's case.[8]

Following the line of argument proposed by Alexander, Hamilton attempted to argue the truth of the *Journal* articles as a defense. English law at the time admitted no such evidence, so Hamilton resorted to jury nullification. He urged the sympathetic colonial jurors that "the facts which we offer to prove were not committed in a corner; they are notoriously known to be true; and therefore, in your justice lies our safety.

> And as we are denied the liberty of giving evidence to prove the truth of what we have published, I will beg leave to lay it down as a standing rule in such cases, that the suppressing of evidence ought always to be taken for the strongest evidence ....
>
> [T]he question before the Court and you gentlemen of the jury is not of small nor private concern, it is not the cause of a poor printer, nor of

---

4 *Id.* at 1507 (citing JAMES ALEXANDER, A BRIEF NARRATIVE OF THE CASE AND TRIAL OF JOHN PETER ZENGER, PRINTER OF THE NEW YORK WEEKLY JOURNAL (1736)). *See also* Moglen, *supra* note 2, at 1514.

5 Moglen, *supra* note 2, at 1515.

6 *Id.* at 1516.

7 *Id.* at 1518.

8 JOAN N. BURSTYN, PAST AND PROMISE: LIVES OF NEW JERSEY WOMEN 6 (1996).

> New York alone, which you are now trying: No! It may in its consequence affect every freeman that lives under a British government on the main of America. It is the best cause. It is the cause of liberty; and I make no doubt but your upright conduct this day will not only entitle you to the love and esteem of your fellow citizens; but every man who prefers freedom to a life of slavery will bless and honor you as men who have baffled the attempt of tyranny; and by an impartial and uncorrupt verdict, have laid a noble foundation for securing to ourselves, our posterity, and our neighbors that to which nature and the laws of our country have given us a right, the liberty, both of exposing and opposing arbitrary power (in these parts of the world at least) by speaking and writing truth.[9]

The jury returned a verdict of not guilty. Zenger went free and lived another decade or so. Cosby died within months. DeLancey eventually grew to be a respected jurist and champion of political rights. Morris Senior became the royal governor of New Jersey, and Alexander Hamilton returned to Pennsylvania, where he later prosecuted a printer for seditious libel. But the law did not change. On the very eve of the American Revolution, the formal law of England and the colonies was still little different from that enforced by the Court of Star Chamber. It was not until 1792 that English law changed to allow juries to consider both fact and law in libel cases, and it was 1843, some 50 years later, that truth became a defense in a criminal libel case.

It would be quite a stretch to call the Morrisites "radicals." These men were not revolutionaries, but loyal English subjects locked in a highly partisan political dispute with the royal governor. Still, Hamilton's invocation of a right to speak and write the truth has resonated with succeeding generations down to the civil libertarians almost 200 years later. There is good reason for tracing the American tradition represented by the three subjects of this book to the Zenger trial. As Moglen puts it, with Zenger's acquittal:

> [The] lawyers of New York had reached an important stage in their political development. For all the agile cynicism of the Morrisite propaganda for law and liberty, the crowd was cheering something real. The willingness of lawyers to defend the subject's liberty under law, if necessary, at the hazard of their lives, their fortunes, and their sacred honor, was now an important force in North America. William Cosby would not be the last Imperial Executive who would be able to read that message without his spectacles.[10]

---

[9] ALEXANDER, *supra* note 4.

[10] Moglen, *supra* note 2, at 1521 (with a nod to King George III and John Hancock).

There was no shortage of radical thinking—and action—in the Revolutionary War period. Patrick Henry, Thomas Paine, and, perhaps most important, Samuel Adams are all well known to any school child today. After the revolution, radicals forced the addition of a Bill of Rights to the Constitution as a condition of ratification, only to see the civil liberties it guaranteed eroded by a Sedition Act enacted by the Federalists in anticipation of a war with France. While the Congress had adopted Andrew Hamilton's view of truth as a defense, that provided little comfort to the Democratic-Republican editors prosecuted under the act. At least 14 of them spent some time in jail.[11]

As in the Zenger case, most of the Republican editors caught up in Sedition Act prosecutions were defended by establishment lawyers of the same party. For example, Matthew Lyon and Anthony Haswell, two Republican editors from Vermont, were advised by attorney Israel Smith, who was serving in the Vermont legislature at the time. Notoriously anti-Jefferson journalist James Callender was represented by three prominent lawyers: William Wirt, who would serve as U.S. Attorney General under James Monroe; George Hay, who became a U.S. Attorney for Virginia and a member of the Virginia House of Delegates; and Philip Nicholas, who served as Virginia's attorney general. One of the editors, Charles Holt of the New Haven *Bee*, was even defended by prominent Federalist lawyers David Daggett and Stephen Hosmer, who were paid by the Republican party leadership.[12]

At least one of the Sedition Act defense lawyers, Thomas Cooper, can be said to have transcended mere partisanship to embrace the radical ideology of his client. No surprise there: Cooper represented himself in *United States v. Cooper*, in which he was charged under the act with libeling President John Adams and tried before Justice Samuel Chase, the act's most prolific enforcer. Simply put, Cooper had written that Adams, among other things, was raising a standing army at great expense to the nation during a time of peace. Chase instructed the jury that these allegations, and others, were false and defamatory: "the boldest attempt I have known to poison the minds of the people." [13] The jury agreed, and Cooper was sentenced to six months in jail, fined $400, and forced to post a bond to ensure his good behavior after his sentence was served.

For our purposes in demonstrating the American tradition of lawyers defending radical causes, the most interesting part of the trial record involved Cooper's response to Chase's question as to whether he was supported in his writing and,

---

[11] JEFFREY L. PASLEY, THE TYRANNY OF PRINTERS: NEWSPAPER POLITICS IN THE EARLY AMERICAN REPUBLIC 129 (2001).

[12] *Id.* at 142. Pasley notes that Holt's prosecutor was Republican District Attorney Pierpont Edwards.

[13] 25 F. Cas. 631, 642 (C.C.D. Pa. 1800).

more importantly, indemnified for pecuniary loss by the Democratic-Republican Party.

> Sir, I solemnly aver, that throughout my life, here and elsewhere, among all the political questions in which I have been concerned, I have never so far demeaned myself as to be a party writer. I never was in the pay or under the support of any party; there is no party in this, or any other country, that can offer me a temptation to prostitute my pen. If there are any persons here who are acquainted with what I have published, they must feel and be satisfied that I have had higher and better motives, than a party could suggest. I have written, to the best of my ability, what I seriously thought would conduce to the general good of mankind. The exertions of my talents, such as they are, have been unbought, and so they shall continue; they have indeed been paid for, but they have been paid for by myself, and by myself only, and sometimes dearly. The public is my debtor, and what I have paid or suffered for them, if my duty should again call upon me to write or to act, I shall again most readily submit to. I do not pretend to have no party opinions, to have no predilection for particular descriptions of men or of measures; but I do not act upon minor considerations; I belong here, as in my former country, to the great party of mankind.[14]

As Eugene Volokh has pointed out, Cooper supported democratic reform in England and France even before emigrating to the United States in 1793–94, along with fellow radical (and discoverer of oxygen) Joseph Priestley. Here, he would become a newspaper editor, a Pennsylvania judge, and a college professor, as well as a prolific scholar.[15] At the time of his trial, however, he depended primarily on his law practice for his living,[16] as would all three of the lawyers profiled in this book.

If democratic revolution and civil liberties, especially freedom of speech, were the animating forces behind eighteenth-century "radicalism" and the lawyers (or at least their arguments) who defended the radical activists of the day, the nineteenth century would add industrialization and cotton plantation as the stimuli of radical activism.[17] The early twentieth-century lawyers profiled in this book were far more closely associated with industrialization and the

---

[14] *Id.* at 643-44.

[15] Eugene Volokh, *Thomas Cooper, Early American Public Intellectual*, 4 N.Y.U. J. L. & LIBERTY 372, 374-75 (2009).

[16] 25 F. Cas. at 643.

[17] LENS, *supra* note 1, at 60.

various ideologies it spawned, but it behooves us to take at least a brief look at the expansion of slavery and abolitionist lawyers.

According to Sidney Lens, the South was dramatically transformed by the invention of the cotton gin, which forever altered the economics of cotton plantation. By the Civil War, annual cotton production had increased thousands of times over the output of the Revolutionary War era, from two million to two billion pounds. The number of African slaves grew from 700,000 to four million to keep this production going. While slavery existed in the North as well, there was no comparable economic justification, and persons of conscience were unconstrained by financial reward or public opinion to adopt an abolitionist ethos. Thus, many abolitionist lawyers were full-fledged members of the northern political establishment—including one former president of the United States.

In the *Amistad* case, Portuguese slave hunters abducted a large group of Africans from Sierra Leone and shipped them to Havana, Cuba, in violation of international law. Two Spanish plantation owners purchased the Africans and put them aboard the Cuban schooner *Amistad* to ship them home. On July 1, 1839, the Africans seized the ship, killing the captain and cook, and ordered the slavers to sail back to Africa. Instead, they sailed north and were seized off Long Island by the United States brig *Washington.* The ship, its cargo, and everyone on board were taken to New London, Connecticut, where the plantation owners were freed and the Africans imprisoned and charged with murder. [18]

The murder charges were dismissed, but the Africans remained in prison while the rights of the plantation owners, the government of Spain, and the captain of the *Washington*—all of whom sought possession of the Africans as slaves or compensation for their "property"—were resolved by trial at the federal district court in Connecticut. Although President Martin Van Buren favored extraditing the Africans to Cuba, abolitionists led by Lewis Tappan raised the money to defend them, motivated by the desire to expose the evils of slavery and generate opposition to the practice. [19]

Roger S. Baldwin of New Haven, Seth Staples and Theodore Sedgewick III of New York, were hired to represent the Africans. Baldwin was a signer of both the Declaration of Independence and the Constitution, who went on to serve as governor of Connecticut and a United States senator. Staples was a lawyer who had previously practiced in Connecticut and represented New Haven in the state legislature. He also founded what would become Yale University's law

---

[18] United States v. Libellants & Claimants of the Schooner Amistad, 40 U.S. 518 (1841). *See also The Amistad Case,* National Archives, https://www.archives.gov/education/lessons/amistad#background.

[19] *Id.*

school. Sedgwick came from a long line of abolitionist lawyers, including his grandfather, who successfully defended escaped slaves in Massachusetts.[20] Sedgwick himself was a member of the New York Antislavery Society and a prolific legal writer who later became United States District Attorney for the Southern District of New York.

The decree issued by the district court held that the Africans

> were born free, and ever since have been, and still of right are free, and not slaves, ... that they were never domiciled in the Island of Cuba, or the dominions of the Queen of Spain, or subject to the laws thereof; that they were severally kidnapped in their native country, and were, in violation of their own rights, and the laws of Spain, prohibiting the African slave trade, imported into the Island of Cuba ... and were there unlawfully held as slaves.[21]

Nevertheless, the court ordered that the Africans be delivered to the United States for deportation to Africa. The circuit court largely affirmed the decree, and the United States appealed to the U.S. Supreme Court.

At the Supreme Court, the defense team was led by former President John Quincy Adams, then serving as a member of the House of Representatives and himself an ardent abolitionist. Adams had previously advised the *Amistad* lawyers but never took a formal role in the case until abolitionists visited him at his home on October 27, 1840, and he reluctantly accepted their entreaties. Adams's opening speech on February 24, 1841, lasted four-and-a-half hours, emphasizing "the steady and undeviating pursuit of one [fundamental] principle, the ministration of Justice." Adams concluded his argument on March 1, speaking for another four hours, and the Court issued its ruling on March 9. Justice Joseph Story's opinion on the future of the kidnapped Africans followed the district court's reasoning almost exactly as to their status as free men but reversed the lower courts' orders to have them deported. All were "declared to be free, and ... dismissed from the custody of the Court."[22]

Unfortunately, the results were not always so benevolent. A series of lawsuits culminating in the notorious U.S. Supreme Court decision *Dred Scott v. Sandford*[23] was undertaken with the sole purpose of obtaining freedom for the

---

20 Brom and Bett v. Ashley (1781). *See Massachusetts Constitution and the Abolition of Slavery*, https://www.mass.gov/guides/massachusetts-constitution-and-the-abolition-of-slavery.

21 40 U.S. 518 (prior history).

22 *Id.* at 597.

23 60 U.S. 393 (1857).

slaves involved.[24] Dred Scott was an enslaved Negro who filed suit seeking freedom for himself and his wife, Harriet, upon their return to Missouri from Rock Island, Illinois, and later Fort Snelling, in the Northwest Territory, where they had lived for several years with their enslaver, an army surgeon stationed there. The case ultimately reached the U.S. Supreme Court by a highly circuitous route involving both state and federal courts. There, Scott argued that because slavery was illegal where he had resided, he had become a free man and thereafter a citizen of Missouri. In what has become an infamous majority opinion, Chief Justice Roger B. Taney declared that Scott did not become free by living in a so-called free territory, that Scott did not become a citizen, and that the courts could not hear his complaint.

Scott's first lawyer was Francis B. Murdoch, who had served as city attorney for Alton, Illinois, when the abolitionist printer Elijah P. Lovejoy was famously murdered and his printing plan destroyed by pro-slavery zealots. Murdoch had prosecuted violators on both sides of the slavery issue, though he came to have strong antislavery sympathies. Having moved to St. Louis, he was apparently persuaded by Harriet Scott's pastor to file the first papers in Dred Scott's initial proceeding.[25] As the case progressed to the federal courts, Scott was represented by Roswell M. Field, an outspoken abolitionist who had served in the Vermont legislature. Field, in turn, recruited Montgomery Blair, who would become Lincoln's Postmaster General, to handle the case at the U.S. Supreme Court. George Ticknor Curtis, who served in the Massachusetts legislature, also argued Scott's case before the Supreme Court. Curtis's brother, Benjamin Robbins Curtis, was an associate justice of the Supreme Court and one of two dissenters from the majority decision.[26]

Although abolitionism *per se* ended with the Civil War, much of its morality and energy was transferred to the postwar Radical Republicans and, later, to civil rights activists. In both *Amistad* and *Dredd Scott*, the advocates were wholly committed to their clients' abolitionist cause but also well-established lawyers in their own right. These same attributes characterized the lawyers profiled in this book, although their roots are more closely associated with the second source of late nineteenth-century radicalism: industrialization.

The "Gilded Age," so named after Mark Twain's eponymous novel,[27] was, as the name implies, covered by a veneer of gold to hide a truly ugly core. The gold was certainly abundant in those years, lining the pockets of "robber barons"

---

[24] Walter Ehrlich, *The Origins of the Dred Scott Case,* 59 J. Negro Hist. 132, 136 (1974).

[25] *Id.* at 140.

[26] Walter Ehrlich, *Was the Dred Scott Case Valid?* 55 J. Am. Hist. 256, 257 n. 3 (1968).

[27] MARK TWAIN, THE GILDED AGE (1873).

like Cornelius Vanderbilt, Andrew Carnegie, John D. Rockefeller, J. P. Morgan and the like. The gold was evident at the lavish dinner parties of Mrs. Astor and her favored 400, in the mansions on Fifth Avenue and "cottages" of Newport, the tables at Delmonico's, the boxes at the Met, and the sumptuous suites at the Waldorf.

Beneath that veneer, however, was a base of poverty and destitution that only grew larger and more desperate as the wealthy grew wealthier. The poor had always been part of the landscape, but their numbers swelled during the Gilded Age as industrialization pulled rural whites and north-bound blacks into the city's sweatshops, while the rumored "streets lined with gold" lured impoverished immigrants from Europe to the Lower East Side. Exacerbated by recession, political manipulation, and greed, the plight of the working class prompted the *New York Herald* to write:

> The story of destitution prevailing among the poor of New York which we publish today will startle our well-to-do readers in their comfortable homes. It is not pleasant to reflect that there are two New Yorks, the one plunged in the most abject misery, wanting all the necessaries of life, shivering from cold, borne down by disease, crowded into the unwholesome tenement houses of the poor quarters, which are now, in truth, dwellings of sorrow and affliction.[28]

The dark side of the Gilded Age afforded fertile ground for the growth of the American Left, from seeds already established in this country and those that the immigrants brought with them. Some working men and women sought relief in the conservative unionism of the Knights of Labor; others, in the radical Industrial Workers of the World. Politically, some embraced progressive reform, while others adopted various strains of European anarchism or socialism. By the end of the Gilded Age, the framework for the "Old Left" had been erected, to become fully developed in the first quarter of the twentieth century.

If the excesses of the Gilded Age led inexorably to the rise of the Left in America, the rise of the Left led, just as surely, to reaction and repression by those most threatened by the movement: corporations that stood to lose their cheap labor and government officials—at all levels—who stood to lose their corporate patrons. The suppression of strikers—by company goons and desperate scabs, by Pinkertons and police, state militia and federal troops—was well established by the end of the Gilded Age. So, too, was the wholesale persecution of alleged instigators, personified by the four Haymarket anarchists who were tried and hanged in 1887, though they were nowhere near that deadly bombing.

---

[28] N.Y. HERALD, Feb. 9, 1874, quoted in ESTHER CRAIN, THE GILDED AGE IN NEW YORK, 1870-1910 at 58 (2016).

In the chaos that followed the Haymarket incident, a rumor was spread that the fiery anarchist Johann Most was coming to Chicago from New York City to supervise assassinations. Most never arrived, but the rumor was enough to send police detectives rushing to the train station to intercept him.[29] Most would become the first high-profile client of Morris Hillquit, the most senior of the lawyers profiled here. His 1901 trial is the earliest case discussed at length herein and foreshadows the civil liberties efforts of all three attorneys.

Civil liberties practice around the turn of the century focused primarily on defending unionists—especially adherents of the anarchist movement—from prison and deportation under the Immigration Act of 1903, also known as the Anarchist Exclusion Act; and victims of Comstock Act prosecutions, typically for advocating and facilitating contraception. By 1917, however, these causes had been supplemented or even supplanted by loyalty issues related to the drift toward war with Germany, under three important statutes: the Conscription Act, the Espionage Act, and, briefly, the Sedition Act. With the armistice, Germany was replaced as America's archenemy by the new Soviet Union, and the threat of international communism became the justification for persecuting the Left. These lawyers, and others, responded accordingly.

---

[29] Lens, *supra* note 1, at 168-69.

Part I

Chapter 1
Early Days

Morris Hillquit

Fig. 1.1: Morris Hillquit

Morris Hillquit, the oldest of the five lawyers profiled here, was born Moishe Hillkowitz on August 1, 1869, in Riga, now the capital of Latvia, then a part of Russia.[1] He was the lead counsel for the defense of *The Masses* staff and contributors in their first criminal trial and one of the most important attorneys representing the "Old Left."

According to his biographer, Norma Fain Pratt, Hillquit was the second son of Benjamin and Rebecca, "German-speaking, middle-class Jews who owned a factory" in Riga.[2] Moishe attended the secular, Russian-language Alexander gymnasium beginning in 1882. After Benjamin lost his factory in 1884, he decided to emigrate to the United States, taking his eldest son, Jacob, and leaving Rebecca, Moishe, one brother and two sisters behind. They would

---

[1] This is the date given by almost every source except his U.S. passport applications, which all say 1886, the year he arrived in the United States. Passport applications available from Ancestry.com.

[2] Norma Fain Pratt, MORRIS HILLQUIT: A POLITICAL HISTORY OF AN AMERICAN JEWISH SOCIALIST 3 (1979).

follow in 1886.[3] At some point, Hillkowitz adopted the given name Morris, though he would retain the family name for several more years.

The Hillkowitzes lived in a two-room tenement on the Lower East Side of New York City. Morris attended public school for a while, then quit to find work in a variety of jobs, as a cuffmaker in a shirt factory, a waistmaker, and a picture frame maker.[4] Hillquit left his last laboring job around 1888 to take a position as a clerk in the national office of the Socialist Labor Party (SLP), working in the bookstore and publications department known as the Labor News Co.[5]

Hillquit had already considered himself an "emotional and sentimental" socialist by the time he arrived in the United States, but his first serious encounter with organized socialism came on the "roofs on Cherry Street." As he describes in his autobiography, Hillquit came to meet with other—mostly Russian Jewish—immigrants on the rooftops of four tenement houses near the corner of Cherry and Montgomery Streets on the Lower East Side. Here, he became "deeply interested" in the various strains of radicalism, learning from his peers and from lecturers enlisted by the newly formed Russian Progressive Union. But it did not take him long "to choose between the rival social creeds that divided the constituency of the Cherry Street roofs and the Russian Progressive Union," Hillquit wrote. "I allied myself with the Social Democrats almost immediately."[6]

Hillquit worked under the auspices of the Socialist Labor Party on the creation of an entity known as "United Hebrew Trades," which he described as a "central labor body without affiliated labor unions, a mere shell within which we hoped in time to develop a solid kernel." This approach was necessary, he said, because the task of educating, then organizing workers would take decades.[7] He also taught English to other immigrants at the Vandewater Creek evening school.[8]

---

3 *Id.* Pratt's version of Hillquit's immigration is sourced primarily to a memoir by his daughter, Nina, entitled "Morris Hillquit: Pioneer of American Socialism" in the Hillquit Papers. That seems to be reasonably corroborated by information Hillquit gave U.S. census takers in 1900, 1910 and 1920 stating his immigration date as 1887. In four separate passport applications, however, Hillquit himself gave his immigration date as 1884, even noting the ship as the *S.S. Pennsylvania.* Census reports and passport applications from Ancestry.com.

4 PRATT, *supra* note 2, at 6.

5 MORRIS HILLQUIT, LOOSE LEAVES FROM A BUSY LIFE 33 (De Capo Press 1971) (1934) [hereinafter LOOSE LEAVES].

6 *Id.* at 9.

7 *Id.* at 18.

8 *Id.* at 40.

Hillquit became a naturalized citizen on May 21, 1890,[9] and the following year, registered at New York University's law school, where he earned his LL.B. in 1893.[10] On December 31, 1893, he married his first cousin, Vera Levene, who had been born in St. Petersburg, immigrated to the United States in 1891, and attended NYU law school as well. Their daughter Nina was born in May 1895, and their son Lawrence the following year.[11]

After passing the bar exam, Hillquit opened a law practice with his brother, Jacob Hillquit, at 132 Nassau St. By 1897, the firm, Hillkowitz and Hillquit, had moved to 320 Broadway, where it shared an office with the brothers' physician cousin, Dr. Phoebus Levene, who was also Morris's close friend. By the following year, Morris had legally changed his own surname, and the firm became known as Hillquit & Hillquit. Around 1910 or so, Phoebus's younger brother, Alexander Levene, joined the firm. By 1913, the firm of Hillquit and Levene had moved to 30 Church St., then to 19 West 44th St. in the mid-1920s. The firm prospered with a variety of civil cases, and Hillquit was able to move his family several times during the first two decades of the twentieth century, ultimately settling on Riverside Drive.[12]

Early on, Hillquit became deeply involved in the internecine warfare that had come to characterize the socialist movement. In an 1899 article for *The People*, an official organ of the SLP, Hillquit viciously attacked Daniel DeLeon, a far-left leader of the movement in America. DeLeon had joined the party in 1890, and from the outset, Hillquit remembered, "he divided the movement into two antagonistic camps—his devoted admirers and followers and his bitter critics and opponents."[13] When those camps formally split the party in two in 1899, Hillquit joined the "secessionists" and declared good riddance to De Leon. [14]

To Hillquit, DeLeon was a "fanatic," a "perfect American prototype of Russian Bolshevism."[15] He was far more impressed by and compatible with two midwestern Socialists—Eugene V. Debs and Victor Berger—whom he met at the national convention of the Social Democratic Party (SDP) in Indianapolis

---

[9] Passport applications from Ancestry.com.

[10] GENERAL ALUMNI CATALOGUE OF NEW YORK UNIVERSITY 117 (1916).

[11] PRATT, *supra* note 2, at 28. Pratt identifies Hillquit's son as Leonard and notes he was "mentally retarded." She also cites another son, Walter, who died shortly after his birth. The information is attributed to Nina's memoir. All other available records indicate Hillquit's son was named Lawrence.

[12] PRATT, *supra* note 2, at 27-29, 35 n. 7. *See also* U.S. Census Reports for 1900, 1910 and 1920; New York Census Reports for 1905, 1915 and 1925; City Directories for 1902, 1910, 1911, 1912, 1916, 1917, 1927 and 1929. Available at Ancestry.com.

[13] LOOSE LEAVES, *supra* note 5, at 45.

[14] Morris Hillquit, *Farewell to DeLeon*, 9 THE PEOPLE 2 (No. 30, Oct. 22, 1899).

[15] LOOSE LEAVES, *supra* note 5, at 46.

in 1900. The SDP had grown out of the indigenous midwestern "Social Democracy of America," which split in 1898 into two factions that Hillquit labeled "romantic" and "modern." The latter became the SDP and attracted members of the anti-De Leon faction of the SLP such as Hillquit. Debs and Berger were leaders of the new party and "made a deep impression" on Hillquit.[16]

The Indianapolis convention marked a high point of unity between the "modern" Social Democrats and the SLP "secessionists." That unity was not to last, however, and the SDP found itself split between those who opposed union with the SLP, including Debs and Berger, and those who favored it. "Chaos now reigned supreme," Hillquit wrote, but the "logic of the situation finally prevailed," and the factions reunited at another Indianapolis convention in the summer of 1901 to create the Socialist Party of America.[17] But factionalism would continue to plague the socialist movement throughout Hillquit's illustrious career.

Seymour Stedman

Fig. 1.2: Seymour Stedman

To call Seymour Stedman the Midwest's Morris Hillquit would be rather too facile, minimizing their differences and, perhaps, deprecating Stedman's own accomplishments. But the greatest achievement of both men was the conviction and leadership they brought to their respective branches of American Socialism. Stedman was born on July 14, 1871, in Hartford, Connecticut, to Frank Stedman and Henrietta Chamberlain Stedman, with a lineage that went back to the American Revolution, including Edmund Clarence Stedman and William Cullen Bryant. Financial difficulties forced the family to move West, to Solomon, Kansas,

[16] *Id.* at 48.

[17] *Id.* at 53-54.

where a series of droughts put the family in poverty, forcing Seymour to leave school in the third grade[18] and go to work tending sheep for $5 per month. In 1881, the family moved to Chicago, which remained Seymour's base for the rest of his life.[19]

Stedman got a messenger job with the Crane Brothers' Manufacturing Co. for about $3 per week. In 1883, workers at the company went on strike. Stedman said later that they went on strike because the work was too hard. "We went out for shorter hours. I was a uniformed boy and I had to work until 7:00 four nights a week, and to 9:00, 10:00, and 11:00 the other three nights. I knew what I was striking for." Stedman was still a messenger at the time of the Haymarket Riots of 1886; he was on the streetcar at the time, headed to Haymarket Square at Desplaines and Randolph Streets, but got there too late to see the event.[20]

Young Stedman later took a job as a janitor with the firm of Baker & Greeley, where he had plenty of time to read, and became attracted to the views of Henry George and the single-tax movement.[21] Later in life, Stedman would reject that theory in favor of socialism, which he defended in a series of debates against single-taxers.

Despite his lack of formal schooling, Stedman went to the dean of Northwestern University's law school, Henry Booth, to plead for admission. After being quizzed on his reading for an hour or more, the 18-year-old Stedman persuaded Booth to let him matriculate. He continued to work as a janitor during the day, attending classes at night; he graduated and was admitted to the Illinois bar in 1891.[22]

Stedman was powerfully attracted to politics, and he decided to become a public orator for the Democratic Party by 1890. "I knew the tariff thoroughly," he would say later, "from the nursing bottle to the brimstone tax of $10 a ton." He sent his application through a friend to Frank X. Branstetter, chairman of the Cook County Democratic committee on speakers and began getting assignments all over the Chicago area.[23] In June 1891, he became secretary of

---

18 Evidently, young Seymour was an indifferent student anyway. *See* SOLOMON SENTINEL, April 14, 1880, at 1 (untitled).

19 William M. Feigenbaum, *Seymour Stedman: Socialist Candidate for Vice-President*, NEW AGE (Buffalo), June 17, 1920, at 3 (reprint at 1).

20 *Id.*

21 *Id.* (reprint at 2). In 1892, Stedman gave a lecture on the "Single Tax" at a meeting of the Chicago Secular Union. *In Church Circles*, INTER OCEAN (Chi.), Feb. 21, 1892, at 29.

22 Feigenbaum, *supra* note 19 (reprint at 2). *See also Fitted for Their Profession*, CHI. TRIB., June 18, 1891, at 5.

23 One early speaking engagement was a Democratic demonstration and picnic on September 5, 1891, at Willow Springs to discuss national issues. *To Discuss National Issues*, CHI. TRIB., Aug. 30, 1891, at 1; *Democrats at Willow Springs*, CHI. TRIB., Sept. 3, 1891, at 3.

the executive committee of the Democratic Campaign Committee,[24] which was then in "dire" financial distress.[25] He also began handling routine legal chores for unions and political organizations.[26]

In July 1892, following the bloody strike and lockout at the Homestead Steel Works near Pittsburgh, Stedman took part in a mass meeting of some 500 Chicago-area workers called to protest the "interference" of armed Pinkerton men and denounce the mill owners, Andrew Carnegie and Henry C. Frick. The Pinkertons went there to provoke strife, Stedman told the crowd. "During the time that hired assassins were shooting down workmen in Homestead, Carnegie was driving a coach and four through Scotland and preaching the beauties of protection and talking of the glories of living in a free country."[27] Meanwhile, Stedman's law practice continued to grow.[28]

The following year, Stedman, still a Democrat, began working for the mayoral campaign of Republican candidate Samuel W. Allerton. In one speech, he branded the incumbent, Carter Harrison Sr., a traitor to true Democratic principles and a complete turncoat, especially at the time of the Haymarket tragedy.[29] On April 4, 1893, however, Harrison won an unprecedented fifth term by a 54%–44% margin over Allerton.[30]

---

[24] Feigenbaum, *supra* note 19 (reprint at 2).

[25] *They Would Not Accept Good Advice*, CHI. TRIB., July 29, 1891, at 3.

[26] For example, Stedman is listed as one of the incorporators of The Mohicans political club, *New Incorporations*, CHI. TRIB., March 20, 1892, at 13, and of The Real-Estate Clerks' Association of Chicago, *New Incorporations*, CHI. TRIB., Aug. 29, 1892, at 9.

[27] *In Bitter Language*, CHI. TRIB., July 11, 1892, at 2-3.

[28] In August, for example, he was identified as an incorporator of the Amnesty Association of Illinois, an organization seeking pardons for three anarchists being held in the federal prison at Joliet. *Amnesty Association Plans*, CHI. TRIB., Aug. 8, 1892, at 3. And he was named as attorney for several new lawsuits filed during the year. *See Circuit Court—New Suits*, CHI. TRIB., Sept. 14, 1892, at 9, and Dec. 1, 1892, at 9, and *Superior Court—New Suits*, CHI. TRIB., Sept. 17, 1892, at 10.

[29] *Fifth Ward Allerton Club Formed*, CHI. TRIB., March 26, 1893, at 2. For a sampling of Stedman's participation in the Allerton campaign, see *It Is Allerton*, INTER OCEAN (Chi.), March 12, 1893, at 1; *Labor Committee At Work*, CHI. TRIB., March 22, 1893, at 2; *Hot Shot for Carter Harrison*, CHI. TRIB., March 23, 1893, at 2; *Announcements*, CHI. TRIB., March 24, 1893, at 6; *Allerton—Allerton*, INTER OCEAN (Chi.), March 24, 1893, at 11; *Allerton—Allerton*, CHI. TRIB., March 26, 1893, at 3; *Allerton—Allerton*, CHI. TRIB., March 27, 1893, at 6; *Allerton—Allerton*, CHI. TRIB., March 28, 1893, at 6; *Address to Voters*, CHI. TRIB., March 30, 1893, at 1; *Allerton Speaks Tonight*, CHI. TRIB., March 30, 1893, at 3; *Allerton Meeting*, CHI. TRIB., March 31, 1893, at 3.

[30] *Harrison Wins It*, CHI. TRIB., April 5, 1893, at 1.

Stedman was still supporting Democratic candidates in early 1894,[31] but his party affiliation came to an end by July when President Grover Cleveland sent federal troops to quell the great Pullman Palace Car Co. strike that paralyzed the Midwest for most of the summer. The strike had been led by the American Railway Union, which in turn was led by its president, Eugene V. Debs, whose rise in prominence over the years was to be the single greatest influence in Stedman's life.[32] Stedman would not only come to represent Debs before the U.S. Supreme Court but would become Debs's vice-presidential running mate in 1920.

On December 16, 1896, Stedman married Maude Irene Moulton. He was 25, she 24. Stedman's best man was his law partner, Charles H. Soelke.[33]

Charles Recht

Fig. 1.3: Charles Recht

Charles Recht began his career protecting the civil liberties of aliens and ended it as the principal lawyer for the Soviet Union and Soviet interests in America. Along the way, he published two novels, a book of poetry, and several theatrical translations.

Recht was born on April 30, 1887, in Varvazor (Warwaschan), Pisek County, Bohemia, Czechoslovakia, Austrian Empire, to Jewish parents Marcus Recht

---

[31] *See, e.g.*, *New Ally for Mason*, CHI. TRIB., May 18, 1894, at 6 (noting Stedman's support for the congressional campaign of Illinois state senator Edward T. Noonan (D). Noonan lost in 1894 and 1896, won in 1898, and did not run for reelection in 1900, but returned to practice law in Chicago).

[32] Feigenbaum, *supra* note 19 (reprint at 2).

[33] *Seymour Stedman to Wed*, CHI. CHRON., Dec. 16, 1896, at 7; *Marriage Licenses*, CHI. TRIB., Dec. 16, 1896, at 5; *In the Gay Society World*, CHI. CHRON., Dec. 17, 1896, at 3.

and Adele (Adla) Kraus Recht. An older sister, Emily, had been born two years earlier; a brother, Joseph, was born two years later, and a brother, William, seven years later, in 1894. The family emigrated to the United States in September 1901. Marcus, who loved German idealist literature and rebelled against political oppression, died before the emigration, but remained a role model for Charles.[34] At the time of the New York Census of 1905, Adele and the four children were living at 2797 8th Ave.[35]

Recht had studied at the gymnasium in Prague and graduated from New York University Law School in 1910, the same year he became a naturalized U.S. citizen. At the time, he had been working as a librarian, studying law part-time and living at home on East 79th Street with his mother and siblings.

Recht's literary talent had already begun to show, however, in a 1907 pamphlet-length, nonfiction manuscript entitled *The Bohemian in America.*[36] In 1910, the newspapers announced that the press of R. G. Badger would soon publish Recht's translation of *The Clouds,* a Bohemian play in three acts by Jaroslav Kvapil.[37] The play was performed in the U.S. on April 30, 1911, at the Lyceum Theatre in New York City as the first production of a new Theatre League, created to promote the performance of international drama.[38] The following year, Recht's translation of August Strindberg's play *Countess Julia* was published to harsh criticism. Said one reviewer:

> It deals in absolute frankness with an affair between a young woman of good family and one of her father's men servants. There seems to be no good reason for having translated and published the work, and there is no excuse for presenting it on the stage except as a gratification of most unwholesome curiosity.[39]

Recht's love for the literature and the theater notwithstanding, Recht still had to earn a living, and evidence of a workaday law practice appeared in the *Times* in 1912, when he handled the sale of a property on East 71st Street. His office at the time was located at 80 Maiden Lane in the Wall Street area. In late 1913, he

---

[34] FRANCES H. EARLY, A WORLD WITHOUT WAR 31-32 (1997).

[35] Census, selective service, immigration and other records from Ancestry.com.

[36] Biographical sketch from "finder" for Charles Recht papers in the Tamiment Library, New York University; *see also* EARLY, *supra* note 63, at 30-31.

[37] *Plays and Players,* POST-STAR (Glenn Falls, N.Y.), Sept. 28, 1910, at 6. The play was published in 21 POET LORE, No. VI, November-December 1910, and is available today from HardPress Publishing, http://www.hardpress.net, and other on-demand publishers.

[38] *League to Study the Drama,* N.Y. TIMES, April 10, 1911, at 13.

[39] *Metcalfe's Review of New York Stage,* BUFFALO EVENING NEWS, April 13, 1912, at 8.

managed the lease of a corner store and cellars on Avenue A,[40] and in May 1914, he oversaw the lease of a store floor and basement on Second Avenue.[41] Toward the end of 1915, Recht handled a bankruptcy sale as attorney for the assignee.[42]

In his first high-profile case, Recht represented the estate of John Miller against Edgar H. Hazelwood, a lawyer and local Republican politician, to recover money from the estate that Hazelwood allegedly procured by fraud.[43] Recht's complaint alleged that Hazelwood, who had been retained by the estate, made a deal with Miller's disinherited son Benjamin to divide any money that Hazelwood could obtain from the rightful heirs. Hazelwood proceeded to con the rightful heirs—two elderly Scots ladies—into signing the inheritance over to him by representing that Benjamin was going to contest the will and that the women could not afford the legal costs. Hazelwood accused Recht of participating in a conspiracy to bring the lawsuit, a claim that Recht called insulting and scandalous; the claim was stricken from Hazelwood's answer by New York Supreme Court Justice William J. Kelly.[44]

While he was working on the *Hazelwood* case in the summer of 1914, Recht collaborated with Dr. Edward J. Lillien—a linguist and art dealer who had served as a district judge in Austria—on a dramatic play.[45] Frances Early has written that Recht spent much of his prewar years with "literary people," including clients like H. L. Mencken, other lawyers like Edgar Lee Masters, playwrights like Eugene O'Neill and Sherwood Anderson, poets like Edna St. Vincent Millay, and Greenwich Village socialists like Max Eastman and his sister Crystal, John Reed, and Floyd Dell.[46]

On January 2, 1915, Recht married Dr. Aristine Pixley Munn, then 28 and a surgical resident at Volunteer Hospital in lower Manhattan. Dr. Munn-Recht had received a B.A. from Bryn Mawr in 1909 and an M.D. from Johns Hopkins University in 1913. She was appointed director of the New York Beekman Street Hospital in New York City, and she would go on to serve as the first Dean of Women at New York University's Washington Square College, lecturer in anatomy and physiology, and assistant attending physician at NYU and Bellevue Medical

---

[40] *Recorded Leases, Manhattan,* N.Y. TIMES, March 12, 1914, at 16.

[41] *Recorded Leases, Manhattan,* N.Y. TIMES, May 12, 1914, at 17.

[42] *Bankruptcy Sales,* N.Y. TIMES, Dec. 15, 1915, at 21.

[43] *Lawyer Hazelwood is Sued by Heirs,* BROOKLYN DAILY EAGLE, Feb. 26, 1914, at 2.

[44] *Hazelwood's Charges Stricken from Answer,* STANDARD UNION (Brooklyn), April 18, 1914, at 1; *Withdraw Charges,* BROOKLYN TIMES UNION, April 18, 1914, at 1.

[45] *Dr. Lillien Drops Dead Seeking Art,* N.Y. TRIB., July 9, 1914, at 9.

[46] EARLY, *supra* note 34, at 30, citing Recht's unpublished memoir, Objection Overruled, in Tamiment Library.

College. She had one child with Recht, John Munn Recht, on January 17, 1916.[47] The Rechts moved to 331 Van Cortlandt Park Ave., Yonkers, Westchester County, in April 1916; Recht moved his law offices to 110 West 40th St.

Soon after the United States formally entered World War I on April 6, 1917, Recht registered for the draft as a nonreligious conscientious objector, claiming his eligibility was limited by his dependents and an unspecified, but apparently not serious, physical disability. He was 30 years old, 5'5" tall, and of medium build, with brown eyes and slightly balding brown hair.[48] Recht looked back upon the war as a fateful moment in his life: "The America I wanted to belong to, the literary world, was to be ignored. Creative forces were being mobilized for [war] propaganda."[49]

One of Recht's formative experiences had been a trial that occurred when he was a gymnasium student in Prague. In that trial, a young, mentally deficient Jew was convicted of the ritual murder of a peasant girl. "For me," he would write much later, "it was the first glimpse of the fact that in political trials, the accused and his lawyers have a more formidable adversary than the prosecutor, and that is public hysteria."[50]

---

47 Information on Aristine Pixley Munn Recht is available in the James Buell Munn Collection at the New York University Archives, subseries B and C; *see also* EARLY, *supra* note 63, at 30-31; Find a Grave, https://www.findagrave.com. Aristine filed for divorce in 1925, alleging infidelity.

48 EARLY, *supra* note 34, at 31; World War I Draft Registration Cards, June 5, 1917, Ancestry.com.

49 *Id.* at 31.

50 *Id.* at 32.

Chapter 2
Practicing Law

A. Civil Liberties Practice

All three lawyers profiled in this book practiced some form of civil liberties law during the World War I era. This section examines four broad categories of their cases: Conscription Act cases, Espionage Act cases, deportation cases, and labor union cases. One or more of these lawyers practiced extensively in each of these categories, and this section surveys those practices in general. Part II of the book discusses those important civil liberties cases that warrant more detailed discussion.

2.1. Conscription Act Cases

On May 18, 1917, some weeks after the declaration of war on April 6, Congress enacted a statute entitled "An Act to Authorize the President to Increase Temporarily the Military Establishment of the United States,"[1] which came to be called the Conscription Act. Among other provisions, the act subjected all male citizens between the ages of twenty-one and thirty to duty in the national army for the period of the existing emergency. It further authorized the drafting of 500,000 enlisted men, with another 500,000 to be called if the president deemed it necessary.[2]

These goals would be accomplished by requiring all men subject to the call to present themselves for registration. The act explicitly exempted designated federal and state officials, those already in the military service, ordained ministers, and theological students, and provided for local rules for physical disability and other exemptions. Notably, the law also exempted from military service members of religious sects whose tenets prohibited engagement in war, though it required such conscientious objectors to register and perform noncombatant services.[3]

Charles Recht, Seymour Stedman, and Morris Hillquit all represented prospective conscripts.

---

[1] 40 Stat. 76 (1917).

[2] Selective Draft Law Cases, 245 U.S. 366, 375, 62 L. Ed. 349 (1918).

[3] *Id.* at 376.

Charles Recht

Resolving to use his legal skills to support the pacifists opposed to the war, as well as other subversives, Charles Recht joined the executive committee of the newly formed Bureau of Legal Advice. The Bureau had been formally organized on May 22, initially as the New York Bureau of Legal First Aid, to look into civil liberties cases arising from the war and connect prospective defendants with appropriate legal representation. The Bureau was headed by eight women who were active in the suffrage and peace movements, including Marion Cothren, Jessie Ashley, and Fannie May Witherspoon.[4]

Recht's involvement with the Bureau would trigger what he would later call his "first skirmish with the war machine."[5] That "skirmish" began on June 3 with a request for assistance from Martha Gruening, a writer and fellow executive committee member, who had been arrested along with Rise Maria R. Spanier, a student, for distributing anti-conscription literature at the corner of Broadway and 23rd Street. Early writes that Recht argued the case before a magistrate judge, "who agreed to have the charges dismissed when the complainant in the case, Louis Horowitz, confessed that a circular had been handed to him at his own request and that he had not seen the defendants pass out the circular."[6]

As chief counsel for the Bureau,[7] Recht found himself challenging the new Conscription Act of 1917, primarily with respect to its application to aliens in the United States. John Angelus, an immigrant from Austria-Hungary, had been conscripted into service in September 1917 and sent to Camp Upton on Long Island.[8] Upon the local draft board's certification of Angelus's eligibility for service, Recht took the case to U.S. District Judge Julius Mayer, seeking to enjoin the local draft board from certifying Angelus for service on the ground that the law was unconstitutional, and, in any case, Angelus was exempt under the express terms of the act because he had not declared his intent to become a U.S. citizen. Mayer dismissed Angelus's cause for lack of jurisdiction.[9]

Recht appealed to the U.S. Court of Appeals for the Second Circuit, which affirmed the lower court on somewhat different grounds. In a decision written by Judge Henry W. Rogers and joined by Judges Henry G. Ward and Charles M. Hough, the court acknowledged that, if Angelus was indeed an alien who had never declared his intention to become a citizen, then he was exempt from

---

[4] FRANCES H. EARLY, A World Without War 21, 31 (1997).

[5] *Id.* at 28.

[6] *Id.*, citing an NYBLA press release, reel 9, box 12, file 1, Tamiment Institute Library.

[7] *Id.* at 32.

[8] *Id.* at 87.

[9] Angelus v. Sullivan, 246 F. 54, 57 (2d Cir. 1917).

service under the act. But it was not for the courts to decide whether those facts were true. The local board, having rejected Angelus's exemption after a fair hearing, had the last word on that subject. If the board hearing was unfair, Recht might have applied for a writ of habeas corpus, the court said, but the court had no authority to use its equitable powers to issue an injunction since an adequate remedy was available at law.[10]

The court disagreed with Mayer's assertion that the courts could never "interfere" with draft cases.

> We think a decision of the boards is final only where the board has proceeded in due form, and where the party involved is given a fair opportunity to be heard and to present his evidence. But if an opportunity to be heard should be denied, there can be no doubt as to the right of the aggrieved party to come into the courts for the protection of his rights.[11]

On the other hand, the court rejected any suggestion that the law was unconstitutional on its face, noting that Congress has explicit authority to raise and support armies. Delegating implementation to the president did not render the act unconstitutional, nor did the Thirteenth Amendment, which prohibits involuntary servitude, restrict the powers granted to Congress.[12]

Recht and the Bureau took some solace in the court's recognition that the judiciary had a role to play in conscription cases. "Thereafter in dozens of decisions throughout the United States the case of *Angelus v. Sullivan* was cited and jurisdiction taken by the court," according to the Bureau's 1918 yearbook. "This decision therefore stands as the most frequently quoted authority in draft law cases."[13] In fact, the acknowledgement that courts had some role to play in the conscription issue allowed Recht and the Bureau to explore other arguments that might keep alien draftees out of uniform.

In one of these cases, Abraham Pfefer, a Russian immigrant who, unlike Angelus, had declared his intention to become an American citizen, was identified as draft-eligible. In February 1918, notwithstanding the *Angelus* dictum on constitutionality, the Bureau decided to challenge the constitutionality of the draft law by bringing a test case on Pfefer's behalf.[14] Recht mounted an "as applied" constitutional argument, asserting three principal infirmities: first, that

---

[10] *Id.* at 64.

[11] *Id.* at 62-63.

[12] *Id.* at 58-60.

[13] EARLY, *supra* note 4, at 88.

[14] *Id.*

Pfefer, as an alien, could not be impressed into military service without an opportunity to leave the United States, and, therefore, the law must be tested by the law of nations; second, that because Pfefer had been admitted to the United States under certain international agreements that would be violated by a change in his condition through an act of Congress, the draft law as applied was an *ex post facto* law; and third, that Pfefer was deprived of his liberty without due process of law because he was impressed into servitude in violation of the Thirteenth Amendment.[15]

Recht's arguments were utterly demolished by U.S. District Judge Thomas Chatfield. The involuntary servitude argument had already been decided by the U.S. Supreme Court a month earlier. Although that case involved a U.S. citizen,[16] Chatfield said, the nature of the servitude was no different from that imposed on aliens.[17] As for the *ex post facto* argument, Chatfield compared Pfefer's position, as an alien affected by a law enacted after his arrival, to that of a citizen affected by a law enacted after he was born. While Congress could not apply a change in the requirements for admission to Pfefer, his status in all other respects could be changed by Congress. Finally, Chatfield pointed to several cases holding that treaties with foreign nations were repealed insofar as they were contrary to the new draft law.[18]

Chatfield conceded that Recht may have been correct on the law as it once stood, "but under present conditions the arguments which have been heretofore urged against impressing the citizens of a neutral into military service do not apply with the same force and scope in this war, where the various nations whose treaties have been repealed in this respect by the Selective Draft Law are engaged in military service for their own existence, as allies or friends of the United States."[19] Pfefer's case was dismissed, and he was remanded to the military authorities. There was no appeal.

Recht was bitter. "If we ourselves are taught that International Law is a thing to be invoked at will, and only when it is convenient to do so," he asked, "how can we logically protest then against other countries who have so glaringly misinterpreted and neglected it?"[20] Recht not only criticized the court's "dogmatic"

---

[15] Pfefer v. Bell, 248 F. 992, 993 (E.D.N.Y. 1918).

[16] *See* Arver v. United States, 245 U.S. 366 (1918), and text accompanying note 23 *infra*.

[17] Pfefer, 248 F. at 993-94 (E.D.N.Y. 1918).

[18] *Id.* at 994 (citing Ex parte Larrucea, 249 F. 981 (S.D.Cal. 1917), Troiani v. Heyburn, 245 F. 360 (E.D.Pa. 1917), and Ex parte Hutflis, 245 F. 798 (W.D.N.Y. 1917)).

[19] Pfefer, 248 F. at 995. *See also* Warm v. Bell, 248 F. 1002 (1918) (holding that the law was constitutional as applied to an Austrian immigrant who had taken out his first papers toward citizenship).

[20] EARLY, *supra* note 4, at 88.

holding in a newspaper interview but went on to promote the work of the Bureau in related cases and solicit financial support.[21]

The Bureau's support for exempt aliens and conscientious objectors apparently came under investigation by military authorities in early March 1918, when it issued a leaflet describing the work that the Bureau had done in helping men of draft age to present claims of exemption.[22] Although Recht was sympathetic—"a different kind of heroism began to crystallize among those in contact with objectors to the war that the more poignant courage was required from those who stood alone"[23]—he does not seem to have played a leading role in the Bureau's defense of non-alien exemptees.

Seymour Stedman

As the nation moved closer to war, Seymour Stedman repeatedly urged neutrality. When the armed neutrality bill was defeated in the U.S. Senate by a filibuster, Stedman stood nearly alone among prominent Illinois politicians in supporting the filibuster. "I am thoroughly in sympathy with the handful of senators who succeeded in defeating the bill," he said. "The question of war should be left to the incoming congress."[24] The *Tribune* editorialized that Stedman's position indicated that he "has not passed to 'the ultra-violet regions where thought-waves do not register,' but inhabits the thickly-populated region where thought-waves register with a dull thud."[25] Once the U.S. entered the war, on April 6, 1917, Stedman joined a new organization—then known as the Chicago Permanent Conference Committee on Terms of Peace—demanding that the Wilson administration define exactly what it was fighting for and on what terms it would make peace.[26] The group held a mass meeting of about 4,000 in Chicago on Sunday, May 27, with Stedman as principal speaker. He blamed "capitalists and royalty" for forcing the war to further their own selfish interests.[27] In an interview with the *Tribune* the next day, however, Stedman reportedly clarified his position that socialism, rather than peace, was the primary goal of the meeting. "We want to stop the war if possible," he said, "but that doesn't matter so much. We are not so much

---

21 *Legal Aid Bureau Hits at Draft Decision,* N.Y. TRIB., Feb. 22, 1918, at 6.

22 *Draft Aid Bureau Faces Inquiry for Exemption Work,* N.Y. TRIB., March 2, 1918, at 15.

23 EARLY, *supra* note 63, at 95 (quoting Recht's later writings).

24 *Chicago Leaders Divide in Vies on Filibuster,* CHI. TRIB., March 5, 1917, at 3.

25 *A Line O' Type or Two,* CHI. TRIB., March 6, 1917, at 6.

26 *Want to Know What This War is All About,* CHI. TRIB., May 20, 1917, at 1 (the organization later expanded and adopted the name People's Council of America for Democracy and Terms of Peace).

27 *"America" Fails to Thrill 4,000 at Peace Meet,* CHI. TRIB., May 28, 1917, at 4.

interested in stopping the war as we are in bringing socialism home to the American people."[28] The next day, Stedman insisted he was misquoted, a charge the *Tribune* denied.[29]

In June, Stedman took on the case of Adolph Germer, secretary of the Chicago-based National Socialist Party, who had been arrested in Grand Rapids, Michigan, on a warrant charging him with conspiracy to defeat the conscription law. Specifically, the indictment charged that literature opposing the draft law circulated in Grand Rapids originated at the Chicago headquarters. Germer, one of 13 men indicted on similar charges, refused to enter a plea at his arraignment, so the U.S. District Court entered a not-guilty plea for him. He was released on a $1,000 bond, and Stedman said he would file a motion to quash the indictment.[30]

The following month found Stedman defending some of the 117 "slackers" alleged to have participated in a draft riot in Rockford, Illinois, the previous month. Stedman was one of 20 Chicago lawyers retained by the Socialist Party to assist conscripts in claiming exemptions from the draft.[31] Each of the defendants was sentenced by Judge Kenesaw Mountain Landis to a year and a day at hard labor and required to register for the draft. Landis and Stedman got into a verbal sparring match when Landis asked one defendant if he belonged to any party or organization. When the man replied that he was a member of the Socialist Party, Landis turned to Stedman.

"This is the type that damned the Socialist Party," he said. "It's probably a matter of conscience with him," Stedman offered, to which Landis responded, "Why, if this man experienced a spasm of conscience he would have an epileptic fit." When another defendant told Landis he did not hear any talking or speaking at the meeting that night, Landis again turned to Stedman. "Did you hear that, Seymour? That's a rather unusual thing, 150 socialists in the same room and not one of them saying a word. What do you think of that?"[32]

In early September, an attempt by the People's Council of America for Democracy and Terms of Peace to hold a mass national rally—including Germer, Crystal Eastman, and Morris Hillquit—in Chicago's West Side Auditorium was thwarted when Gov. Frank O. Lowden ordered the Chicago police to disperse the gathered pacifists, over the vigorous, but ineffective opposition of Mayor William Hale ("Big Bill") Thompson. Stedman was the last to leave the hall,

---

28 *Socialism, Not Peace, is Aim*, CHI. TRIB., May 29, 1917, at 2.

29 *Beg Your Pardon!*, CHI. TRIB., May 30, 1917, at 15.

30 *Adolph Germer Is Held by U.S. as Draft Foe*, CHI. TRIB., June 14, 1917, at 5.

31 *Socialists Give Cold Welcome to the Draft*, CHI. TRIB., July 21, 1917, at 3.

32 *Sorry Day for Slackers; Meet Up With Landis*, CHI. TRIB., July 6, 1917, at 1.

initially refusing to move and daring police to arrest him. Finally, Stedman was escorted out of the hall by police. Stedman would take charge of a rump meeting of delegates at the nearby Fort Dearborn Hotel, having previously been designated as chairman of the doomed national convention. There, Stedman named a nominating committee that, in turn, was tasked with selecting a "permanent executive committee" for the organization.[33]

The following day, the national meeting was reconvened at the auditorium under police protection ordered by Mayor Thompson. Stedman was formally elected chairman, and the organizing work was completed. As word came that Gov. Lowden was sending state militia troops from Fort Sheridan or Springfield to disperse the meeting again, Stedman urged the delegates not to resist. "If we resist," he said, "it would be playing into their hands. If they come to disperse us, let us disperse. It will be a greater victory if they do come. There are times when courage is only dramatics." The convention adjourned at 7 p.m., before any troops had arrived.[34]

In January 1918, Stedman represented four men seeking to avoid military service before Judge Landis, by now well established as a man with little tolerance for draft dodgers. Three of Stedman's clients were aliens claiming exemption from the draft, while the fourth languished in the Camp Grant guardhouse for refusing to serve in the army. All of Stedman's applications for writs of habeas corpus were denied by Judge Landis.[35] Stedman also represented four men convicted in federal district court in West Virginia for distributing a printed circular opposing conscription. His appeal to the Fourth Circuit failed.[36]

In July 1918, Stedman handled two appeals for Detroit socialist Maurice Sugar, a prominent labor lawyer and fellow People's Council member, who refused to register for and advocated vigorously against the draft. Sugar was arrested in late July 1917 for conspiracy to obstruct the draft, along with four others. The following month, he was arraigned for his own failure to register. Sugar represented himself before Judge Arthur J. Tuttle in the U.S. District Court for the Eastern District of Michigan, moving to quash the conspiracy indictment on the grounds that it charged in a single count two distinct offenses, that the acts recited did not constitute a federal crime, and that the Conscription Act itself was unconstitutional.

---

[33] *Big Bill Defies Lowden*, CHI. TRIB., Sept. 2, 1917, at 1.

[34] *What They Did, How They Did It, With Bill's Aid*, CHI. TRIB., Sept. 3, 1917, at 3.

[35] Ex parte Tinkoff, 254 F. 222 (N.D. Ill. 1918). *See also Landis to Pass on 4 Who Seek to Defy Army*, CHI. TRIB., Jan. 10, 1918, at 8.

[36] Firth et al. v. United States, 253 F. 36 (4th Cir. 1918).

In July 1917, Tuttle quickly rejected the first two arguments, then focused most of his opinion on the constitutional issues that Sugar raised. In a detailed and methodical opinion, Tuttle refuted each of Sugar's constitutional arguments and denied the motion to quash.[37] On December 7, Sugar pleaded guilty to all charges in the indictments. Under a plea agreement with the prosecution,[38] he was fined $500, sentenced to one year in the Detroit House of Correction, and disbarred from practice in the federal[39] and, later, state courts.[40]

Stedman had come to Detroit in August 1917 to join in the successful defense of several other men indicted for anti-draft conspiracy.[41] Immediately following Sugar's guilty plea, Stedman joined Sugar's local attorneys to file a motion in arrest of judgment, a strategic motion that would allow an appeal even after a guilty plea. The motion was overruled, and the lawyers then sued out a writ of error, bringing the case before the U.S. Court of Appeals for the Sixth Circuit. The panel consisted of Circuit Judges John Wesley Warrington and Loyal Edwin Knappen and District Judge Walter Evans, who wrote both opinions.[42]

The first opinion, issued July 8, 1918, dealt with Sugar's refusal to register, and Evans gave the arguments asserted short shrift.

> After an examination of the authorities relied upon by the plaintiff in error, and after the most careful consideration possible of the character of objections made, we have concluded that no one of them was sufficient, and that there can be no force in the motion to arrest the judgment when the record shows that the indictment explicitly charged that there was a willful refusal to register, and when a plea of guilty plainly admitted the charge to be true.[43]

The second opinion dealt with the conspiracy charge, but the reasoning of the opinion and outcome of the case were essentially the same: judgment affirmed.[44] Stedman asked the U.S. Supreme Court to review the case, but his petition for a writ of certiorari was denied on November 4.[45] Sugar entered the

---

[37] United States v. Sugar, 243 F. 423 (E.D. Mich. 1917).

[38] CHRISTOPHER H. JOHNSON, MAURICE SUGAR: LAW, LABOR, AND THE LEFT IN DETROIT 1912-1950 (1988).

[39] *Lawyer Punished as Draft Opponent*, DETROIT FREE PRESS, Dec. 5, 1917, at 9.

[40] *Sugar Disbarred by County Judge*, DETROIT FREE PRESS, Feb. 5, 1918, at 14.

[41] *Five Not Guilty of Fighting Draft*, DETROIT FREE PRESS, Aug. 18, 1917, at 5.

[42] Sugar v. United States, 252 F. 74 and 252 F. 79 (6th Cir. 1918).

[43] 252 F. 74, 78.

[44] 252 F. 79, 85.

[45] Sugar v. United States, 248 U.S. 578 (1918) (denying cert.).

House of Corrections on November 25, two weeks after the war ended, and served 10 months.[46]

Morris Hillquit

Within a month of the conscription law's enactment, Morris Hillquit was representing men who had run afoul of the act. Charles F. Phillips and Owen Cattell, two Columbia University students, were being tried in federal court for conspiracy to violate the Conscription Act by printing and circulating an anti-conscription pamphlet. On direct examination, Hillquit elicited testimony from the defendants that they intended to alter the language of their pamphlet to bring it within the law, but Assistant U.S. Attorney Harold A. Content got the young men to admit that they had never made such a statement when questioned by federal officers. Phillips acknowledged that he had already pleaded guilty to refusing to register, even though he was warned of the consequences, and both defendants said they knew that printing the circular was against the law.[47]

It took the jury about six hours to convict the two men on June 21, 1917, but with a recommendation for clemency. Hillquit moved that the verdict be set aside as not in accord with the evidence. Arguments on the motion were scheduled for June 29, as were the sentencing of Phillips on his guilty plea and of both men on the conspiracy conviction. A few moments after the jury left the courtroom, Emma Goldman and Alexander Berkman entered it for their arraignment for Conscription Act violations. The anarchist icons shook hands with Hillquit, then pleaded not guilty to the charges.[48]

2.2. Espionage Act Cases

Congress enacted the Espionage Acts on June 15, 1917, ostensibly to prevent the obstruction of military conscription or recruitment, or encouragement of insubordination within the armed forces, presumably by enemies of the United States. In fact, the law was used almost exclusively to stifle pacifist and anti-war expression in newspapers and magazines, and among conscientious objectors, public school teachers, and left-leaning politicians. After the war, it would be the principal instrument of prosecution during the so-called Red Scare, when Soviet Russia would replace Germany as the nation's archenemy.

---

[46] JOHNSON, *supra* note 38, at 104-105.

[47] *Columbia Youths Admit They Broke Conscription Law*, N.Y. TRIB., June 20, 1917, at 6.

[48] *Students Guilty in Draft Plot; Jury Recommends Clemency*, N.Y. TRIB., June 22, 1917, at 7.

The socialist magazine *The Masses* was the first victim of the Espionage Act, but many more victims—publications and individuals—would soon follow. Several of the more prominent cases appear in Part II; others are surveyed below.

Morris Hillquit

In mid-October 1917, Morris Hillquit appeared at a Washington hearing before Assistant Postmaster General Alexander M. Dockery to defend *The New York Call* in "show cause" proceedings initiated by the government to deprive the socialist newspaper of its second-class mailing privileges. The grounds for revoking those privileges were articles perceived to criticize the war and the government more broadly that rendered the newspaper unmailable under the Espionage Act. In that, *The Call* was in a situation similar to that of *The Masses* magazine and other socialist organs, although this was an administrative hearing rather than a trial.

Beginning with the August 1917 issue, *The Masses* magazine was declared unmailable by the Post Office Department on the grounds that certain articles and cartoons violated the Espionage Act. The magazine's legal challenge to that ruling was led by Gilbert E. Roe and met with initial success when Judge Learned Hand restored the magazine's mailing privilege with a landmark opinion in defense of freedom of speech. That success was short-lived, however, as the Second Circuit quickly reversed Hand's decision, and the magazine was forced out of business.[49]

Hillquit's defense of *The Call* did not reference *The Masses*, except indirectly, although his argument resembled Judge Learned Hand's opinion in that case. Since that opinion, handed down in July, was promptly reversed in August, it is not surprising that Hillquit would avoid any direct reference. Hillquit made several arguments, beginning with the fact that *The Call* was the "organ and spokesman" of the Socialist Party, which was "frankly, unequivocally, opposed to war." Even assuming that position was erroneous, he said, Congress could not, and did not, enact any law prohibiting criticism of government policies in the war.

Taking pertinent provisions of the Espionage Act line by line, Hillquit sought to show that none of them applied to articles in *The Call*, including prohibitions against the dissemination of false information, willful obstruction of recruiting services, and treason. He also argued that the Post Office Department regulations went far beyond the language of the law, including substitution of the word "tends" for "intended," and asserted that only articles constituting a crime

---

[49] *See* ERIC B. EASTON, DEFENDING THE MASSES 178 (2018).

under the law could be excluded from the mail. Finally, he argued, there are no provisions in any law depriving a newspaper of second-class privileges on the spurious ground that it once contained "unmailable" matter and was likely to do so in the future.[50]

Nevertheless, *The Call* lost its second-class privileges and, beginning December 3, 1917, began handling its own distribution through door-to-door sales by carriers and newsstands inside New York City and through first-class mail outside New York City. Its second-class mailing privileges were not restored until June 1921.[51]

Soon afterward, Hillquit was asked to represent another publication caught up in an Espionage Act sanction, *Pearson's Magazine.* In this case, the magazine was alerted by a *New York Times* article entitled "Watch on *Pearson's,*" which alleged that the January 1918 issue of *Pearson's* came to the attention of federal authorities because it "contains many articles sympathetic to Germany, laudatory references to Trotzky and Lenin, the Russian Bolshevik leaders, adverse comment on the peace attitude of President Wilson and uncomplimentary references to Premier Lloyd George of England." *Pearson's* publisher and editor, Frank Harris, denied the accusations and demanded a retraction. When the *Times* refused, Harris reported that the magazine's directors had instructed Hillquit to file a libel suit.

Before that could happen, however, *Pearson's* received an official order to show cause why its second-class mailing privileges should not be revoked under the Espionage Act. So Hillquit and Harris journeyed to Washington for the requisite hearing. When the Assistant Postmaster General asked Harris if he supported the war effort, Harris responded, "Passionately, sir, passionately," much to Hillquit's surprise. The magazine's privileges were not revoked, though several issues were delayed and, according to Hillquit, "the magazine ... was well-nigh ruined."[52]

Charles Recht

Enactment of the Espionage Act and Selective Service Act kept Charles Recht and other volunteer lawyers of the New York Bureau of Legal Advice busy, so much so that Recht described his 40th Street law office as the "clinic" of the

---

50 Morris Hillquit, *The Call Answers Postoffice Attempts to Apply Gag; Hillquit Makes Stirring Address for Free Press,* N.Y. CALL, Oct. 21, 1917, at 8.

51 *The New York Call, 1908-1938,* MARXIST INTERNET ARCHIVE, https://www.marxists.org/history/usa/pubs/the-new-york-call/index.htm.

52 MORRIS HILLQUIT, LOOSE LEAVES FROM A BUSY LIFE 217-20 (De Capo Press 1971) (1934) [hereinafter LOOSE LEAVES].

NYBLA. Many of his cases involved convictions for "disorderly conduct," code words for the soapbox oratory relied upon by the radical movement at the time.[53]

In August 1917, the American Defense Society, led by pro-war agitator Cleveland Moffett, declared "war" on "all public utterances that had an unpatriotic tinge."[54] The ADS board of trustees adopted a manifesto calling for radical suppression of seditious talk on August 14, and the first target of its attack was a speaker on behalf of home rule for Ireland. Many of these speakers were virulently anti-British and therefore, with some justification, deemed pro-German. That night, Moffett attempted to disrupt the pro-Irish speech of one William J. Robinson, a 33-year-old unemployed stenographer, on West 37th Street, near Broadway. Robinson was arrested when William W. Hines complained to police about the now-disorderly gathering. Hines denied that the substance of Robinson's speech prompted his complaint, but rather the gathering itself.

The rhetoric that preceded Robinson's arrest, on display at a hearing the previous day, was indicative of the spirit of the times. Moffett opened the hearing by saying that drastic steps would be taken to prevent seditious speech by the soapbox speakers. Police authorities promised that permits for soapbox orations would be carefully investigated in the future. Even a representative of the Friends of Irish Freedom seemed cowed by the situation. Protesting that Irish Americans were just as patriotic as anyone else, John E. Moore caved: "If the American Defense Society decides that the orator which Mr. Moffett has objected to has given vent to traitorous utterances, I will abide by its decision."[55]

The soapbox orators of 1917 represented many diverse causes—pro-Irish, anti-Jewish,[56] Wobblies, and suffragists[57]—but it was the anti-war speakers who prompted the Manhattan District Attorney to convene an investigative grand jury to look into the incidence of seditious soapbox oratory and the steps being taken to control it.[58] The problem was that sedition was not an offense under New York law, only federal law, and the grand jury returned no indictments.[59] For its trouble, the grand jury was excoriated for disloyalty, with

---

[53] *Id.* at 34.

[54] *Patriots To Fight Soap Box Sedition,* N.Y. SUN, Aug. 15, 1917, at 4.

[55] *Id.* Robinson was replaced by another speaker, who fled the scene when a truckload of soldiers on a recruiting mission arrived and were cheered by the crowd that had gathered. A lieutenant who led the soldiers mounted the soap box and scored 35 recruits. *Id.*

[56] *See, e.g., Donne Sentenced; 2 Attach Justice,* N.Y. SUN, Aug. 29, 1917, at 6.

[57] Mary Anne Trasciatti, *Athens or Anarchy: Soapbox Oratory and the Early Twentieth-Century American City,* 20 BUILDINGS & LANDSCAPES 43, 60 (Spring 2013).

[58] *Grand Jury Widens Sedition Inquiry,* N.Y. SUN, Sept. 11, 1917, at 5.

[59] *Swann Warned Jury of Disloyalty,* N.Y. TIMES, Sept. 16, 1917, at 7.

District Attorney Edward Swann telling the foreman that any public statement to that effect would be tantamount to sending "a cable message addressed to Berlin," and "putting bullets in the backs of our men at the front."[60] An editorial cartoon in *Life* magazine advocated hanging soapbox speakers from the lampposts under which they stood.[61]

Such was the atmosphere when Recht defended Harry Letaner, a 22-year-old soapbox orator who, on November 15, 1917, was railing from a soapbox at Madison Square against the large costs of the war and the Allies' inability to repay their loans from the United States.[62] Letaner drew an angry mob and was arrested and haled before a magistrate. He was freed pending trial on $500 bail and promptly returned to Madison Square to speak on freedom of speech. Again, he drew a hostile crowd, and again, he was arrested, but this time, Magistrate Joseph Corrigan dismissed the charges.[63]

Early writes that Recht also handled cases of defendants whose conduct or belief was different from the prevailing attitudes. She notes that he won an easy victory in the case of Ranislaw Javanovitch, a vaudeville actor who failed to remove his cap when the national anthem was played. Recht also saved Moische Samet from the workhouse when Samet was wrongly accused by a fellow streetcar rider of shouting, "To hell with America!" Samuel Nikition's crime was refusal to buy a Liberty Bond, for which he served nearly nine months before his case was finally thrown out.[64]

Recht was also deeply involved in the representation of New York City public school teachers who had come under attack during the early months of the war for questionable loyalty. Among the first to be dismissed were Thomas Mufson, A. Henry Schneer, and Samuel D. Schmalhausen of DeWitt Clinton High School in Manhattan, following a "trial" that began in late 1917. The three were represented by Gilbert E. Roe, a well-known progressive lawyer who had represented many radical clients before and during the war years.[65] Recht took on the case of Gertrude Pignol, a German teacher at Manual Training High School in Brooklyn. Roe and Recht would later work together defending Comintern agent Agnes Smedley.[66]

---

[60] *Id.*

[61] Trasciatti, *supra* note 57, at 60.

[62] EARLY, *supra* note 4, at 34-35.

[63] *Id.*

[64] *Id.* at 35-37.

[65] EASTON, *supra* note 49, at 178.

[66] *Id.* at 170.

Pignol had emigrated from Germany to the United States as a young woman and became an American citizen in 1910.[67] She had been teaching German and French at Manual for nearly a dozen years when, in October 1917, an anonymous group of her fellow teachers sent a written complaint to the Board of Education denouncing Pignol as pro-German. Questioned by her principal, Horace M. Snyder, and increasingly harassed by her coworkers, she took a three-month leave of absence beginning January 1, 1918.[68]

Upon her return from leave on March 15, she was again interrogated by Snyder and reportedly told him that the United States had no good reason for entering the war and that she did not consider it a true democracy.[69] "If we were at war with Mexico or any other country," Snyder said later, Miss Pignol would be accepted as a teacher.

> But her war attitude is such that her presence in an American school is intolerable. She speaks her pro-German opinions freely; she quite frankly declares that she loves Germany, and that the Prussians are not fighting a war of aggression.[70]

Assistant Superintendent Dr. John S. Tildsley, who also interviewed Pignol, offered similar remarks, and the case was turned over to Gustave Straubenmuller, the acting superintendent. Straubenmuller sent Pignol a formal notice of suspension,[71] which became effective as a dismissal by the Board of Education on March 27.[72] On May 17, Pignol had an opportunity to testify before the board at a trial; represented by Charles Recht, Pignol took a more conciliatory position than she had previously.

"I certainly do pledge my loyalty to the United States," she said. "I love this country. I love its institutions. That is why I became a citizen." As to her feelings for Germany, Pignol admitted, "I have a double sympathy, perhaps, but not a double allegiance." Pignol went on to say that the German invasion of Russia had convinced her of Germany's guilt and that she had bought a Liberty Bond within the past two weeks. She also testified that she had subscribed to the Red Cross and had become convinced of the desirability of an American victory over Germany.[73]

---

67 EARLY, *supra* note 4, at 39.

68 *Id.*

69 *Teacher Accused of Disloyal Views*, N.Y. TIMES, March 20, 1918, at 6.

70 *Teacher Loves German, Faces Loss of Place*, N.Y. TRIB., March 20, 1918, at 1.

71 *Teacher Accused as Disloyal Gets Another Chance*, N.Y. TRIB., March 22, 1918, at 6.

72 *Brooklyn Teacher Dropped for Her German Leanings*, N.Y. TRIB., March 28, 1918, at 8.

73 *Loves America And Germany Too, Teacher Asserts*, N.Y. TRIB., May 18, 1918, at 7.

Recht contended that Pignol's conscientiousness was the chief reason for her difficulties with the school authorities.[74] Later, Recht said that Pignol's permanent dismissal was inevitable. Her decision to buy a war bond "did not affect the decision of the Board, nor was it expected that it would," Recht said. "It was clear by this time, that Miss P. was slated for dismissal and any excuse would serve to accomplish that purpose."[75] Recht cited one portion of transcript to prove his point:

> Mr. McIntyre (Corporation Counsel): Are you willing to take part in the crushing of Germany?
>
> Miss Pignol: I have stated that I am willing to do all in my power to further the United States in this war.
>
> Mr. McIntyre: Even to the point of crushing Germany?
>
> Miss Pignol: I cannot prevent the crushing of Germany if that is the result of the war.
>
> Mr. McIntyre: Do you wish to see Germany crushed if the purposes of the United States cannot be accomplished in any other way?
>
> Miss Pignol: I do not wish to see Germany crushed, no sir.[76]

Pignol was Recht's only client from the ranks of teachers accused of disloyalty, but there were many caught up in the war frenzy. As Stephen Brumberg wrote:

> Teachers who would not actively support the war or participate in war work in the schools, and those suspected of questionable loyalties, were suspended and often dismissed on charges of "conduct unbecoming a teacher." At least ten teachers were fired (and many more transferred to less desirable posts).[77]

Recht explained the situation in the Bureau's 1918 yearbook by quoting Dr. John Finley, the state's Commissioner of Education: "A school-teacher must be absolutely loyal and do with her mind what the soldier does with his body, namely, give it without reserve to the Government."[78]

In 1921, Recht challenged New York's refusal to allow the Lithuanian Workers' Literature Society to amend its corporate charter to provide for admission of

---

[74] *Id. See also M.T.H.S. Teacher Changes Mind,* BROOKLYN TIMES UNION, May 18, 1918, at 2.

[75] EARLY, *supra* note 4, at 40.

[76] *Id.*

[77] Stephen F. Brumberg, *New York City Schools March Off to War,* paper presented at the annual meeting of the American Educational Research Association (April 6, 1988) (available through Educational Resources Information Center [ERIC]).

[78] EARLY, *supra* note 4, at 41.

members not opposed to the "Marxian principles approved by the majority of the members." He lost at both the trial and appellate levels on the ground that Karl Marx had, at times, advocated the violent overthrow of governments, which was deemed criminal under the New York Penal Law.[79]

Seymour Stedman

In April 1918, Seymour Stedman led the defense team in the second prosecution of Jacob O. Bentall, the Socialist Party candidate for governor of Minnesota in 1916. Bentall had been charged with making seditious remarks in a speech at Hutchinson, Minnesota, in July 1917. Typical of the Espionage Act indictments, Bentall was charged with an "attempt to cause insubordination and mutiny among the military and naval forces of the United States." Witnesses testified that nine men who had been drafted were in the audience when Bentall advised against sending "our soldiers across to be killed and have their bodies [d]ried out for the oil that is in them and the remainder to be used for fertilizer." Abe Sugarman, another convicted Minnesota socialist, sat at the table with Bentall and Stedman.[80] Bentall was found guilty on two of the three counts in the indictment, after the jury deliberated for nine-and-a-half hours, and was released on a $10,000 bond.[81] On April 19, he was sentenced to five years' imprisonment at Fort Leavenworth by U.S. District Judge Page Morris.[82]

Stedman represented Bentall on appeal and won a reversal of his conviction. Two of the three Eighth Circuit judges who heard the appeal adopted Stedman's argument that the trial judge erred in charging the jury that "A man cannot say he did not intend to do a certain thing, when the natural consequence of his act is bound to be so and so." Such a charge, they wrote, would effectively negate the evidence that Bentall introduced to show he had no intent to obstruct the draft or incite mutiny in the military.[83]

In August 1918, Stedman unsuccessfully represented Walter Ragansky, a Lithuanian, sentenced by Judge Landis to serve three years for threatening the life of President Wilson, before the U.S. Court of Appeals for the Seventh Circuit in Chicago.[84] Ragansky allegedly declared, "I can make bombs and I will make

---

[79] In re Lithuanian Workers' Literature Soc., 187 N.Y.S. 612 (N.Y. App. Div. 1921).

[80] *Witnesses Relate Seditious Remarks Made by Bentall,* STAR TRIB. (Minneapolis), April 5, 1918, at 15. See Part II for Sugarman's case.

[81] *J.O. Bentall Found Guilty; Peterson is Facing Jury,* MINNEAPOLIS J., April 11, 1918, at 1.

[82] *Bentall Gets Five Years in Federal "Pen,"* The Pioneer (Bemidji, Minn.), April 19, 1918, at 1.

[83] Bentall v. United States, 262 F. 744 (8th Cir. 1919).

[84] *Appeals from Threat Conviction,* CHI. TRIB., May 2, 1918, at 5; Ragansky v. United States, 253 F. 643 (7th Cir. 1918).

bombs and blow up the President," and other words to the same effect. He was arrested and tried before Judge Landis in January 1918, where he claimed that he was only joking and did not intend to kill the president. In his instructions to the jury, however, Landis said that was no excuse. "[The] claim that the language was used as a joke, in fun" is not a defense, Landis said.[85] Ragansky was convicted on three counts[86] and sentenced to three years in prison—the length of time Landis predicted the war would last.[87]

On appeal, the Seventh Circuit panel rejected Stedman's argument that, to constitute a crime, the language in question must be used with an evil or malicious intent—not necessarily to carry out the threat, but to create a sense of hostility toward the President. The court said all that was necessary was to utter words that would naturally be understood by the hearers as a threat and affirmed the judgment below.

In addition to the federal Espionage Act cases, Stedman would handle a number of cases under similar state laws. On October 30, 1919, C. E. Ruthenberg, a leader of the left-wing socialists who would become national executive secretary of the Communist Party of America, was indicted by a Cleveland grand jury on the charge that Ruthenberg advocated "industrial and political reforms, sabotage and unlawful methods of terrorism" in violation of the Ohio criminal syndicalism law.[88] By the time the trial began in mid-November, the charge against Ruthenberg was assault with intent to kill a police officer during the May Day riots in the city. At one point during jury selection, Stedman asked a prospective juror if he was a member of any organization "to preserve the patriotism of all socialists by shooting them." Within the week, however, Common Pleas Judge Dan B. Cull granted Stedman's motion for a directed verdict of acquittal, stating there was no evidence to show that Ruthenberg had anything to do with the assault.[89]

In November 1919, Stedman represented three socialists—Charles W. Steene, Frank Lincoln Preston, and William Hotze—who had been arrested in Syracuse for violating the Espionage Act, as amended by the Sedition Act, by distributing allegedly seditious handbills depicting the torture of conscientious objectors and extending an invitation to a mass meeting on that issue. The men were brought before a United States commissioner, who freed them on bond. At the time, Steene admitted he had received the handbills from Socialist Party

---

[85] Ragansky v. United States, 253 F. 643 (7th Cir. 1918).

[86] *"Speak Not, Even in Jest,"* KANSAS CITY STAR, Jan. 22, 1918, at 4.

[87] *3 Years for Man Who Threatened Wilson*, S.F. CHRON., Feb. 27, 1918, at 3.

[88] *Ruthenberg Is Indicted*, COSHOCTON (Ohio) TRIB., Oct. 30, 1919, at 2.

[89] *Former Socialist Leader on Trial*, MARION (Ohio) STAR, Nov. 13, 1919, at 1; *Ruthenberg Is Freed*, SANDUSKY (Ohio) STAR-JOURNAL, Nov. 18, 1919, at 1.

headquarters in Chicago.[90] They were indicted by the grand jury at Utica in early December and arraigned in U.S. District Court there on December 16. Represented by radical lawyer Eustace Reynolds, Steene and the others pleaded not guilty, and their trial was set for January.[91]

At that point, Stedman took over the case, filing a demurrer to the indictment. Judge Edwin L. Garvin summarily rejected most of Stedman's objections but considered the question of whether the handbills at issue violated the law.

> When a mass meeting is assembled as a result of an invitation of this character, we may expect that resistance to the United States itself will follow. … [Its] form was well calculated to have the effect of arousing the contempt, scorn, contumely, and disrepute which Congress sought to prevent, and under the well-settled principle that one is presumed to intend the natural consequences of his act the indictment charges a crime. Demurrer overruled.[92]

Following a three-and-a-half-hour trial on January 15,[93] all three men were found guilty[94] and were sentenced to serve 18 months in the federal penitentiary at Atlanta.[95] Their story did not end there, however. In June 1920, the new American Civil Liberties Union sent a letter to President Wilson specifically pointing to the *Steene* case as one containing not a "scintilla of evidence of guilt other than the expression of opinion on political questions." The letter transmitted a detailed report purporting to demonstrate the "high-handed and illegal methods" of the Justice Department in *Steene* and other similar cases.[96] On March 21, 1921, the U.S. Supreme Court reversed Steene's conviction on the government's confession of error.[97]

Stedman was also on the brief to the Supreme Court in the appeal of an Espionage Act decision that deprived the publisher of the *Milwaukee Leader*, a Socialist newspaper, of its second-class mailing privileges. Postmaster Albert S. Berleson's decision that the newspaper violated the act had been upheld by the

---

90 *Legion Members Block Syracuse Radical Meeting*, BUFFALO TIMES, Nov. 22, 1919, at 5.

91 *Judge Rebukes Buffalo Lawyer*, BUFFALO COURIER, Dec. 17, 1919, at 16.

92 United States v. Steene, 263 F. 130, 133 (N.D.N.Y. 1920).

93 Untitled, BUFFALO TIMES, Jan. 15, 1920, at 9.

94 *Find 3 Socialists Guilty of Sedition*, ITHACA J., Jan. 16, 1920, at 2.

95 *Utica Radicals Sent to Prison*, STAR-GAZETTE (Elmira, N.Y.), Jan. 19, 1920, at 11.

96 Federated Press, *Civil Liberties Union Challenges Statement of Wilson on Repression*, BUTTE (Mont.) DAILY BULLETIN, June 25, 1920, at 1.

97 Steene v. United States, 255 U.S. 580 (1921).

Court of Appeals of the District of Columbia,[98] and Stedman's contribution to the Supreme Court brief had no effect on the outcome.[99] It may have been some help, however, in shaping the voluminous dissent of Justice Louis D. Brandeis[100] or the more limited dissent of Justice Oliver Wendell Holmes.[101] In 1920, Stedman filed an *amicus curiae* brief in the Espionage Act appeal of John M. Becker, whose conviction was reversed on the ground that his allegedly violative speech was innocuous.[102]

2.3. The Deportation Cases

Of the three lawyers featured in this book, only Charles Recht devoted a substantial portion of his practice to pure deportation cases. Recht's work with prospective deportees for the Bureau of Legal Advice dominated his practice before and even after he began representing Soviet interests in the United States. Most of the Bureau's "clients" were members of the Industrial Workers of the World, the "Wobblies." Recht's most important deportation case, that of Soviet "Ambassador" Ludwig Martens, is discussed in detail in Part II.

Charles Recht

In the fall of 1918, Recht had prepared a pamphlet entitled *American Deportation and Exclusion Laws*, which was published in January 1919 as a report to the Bureau of Legal Advice and reprinted by the National Civil Liberties Bureau.[103] By then, it had become clear that the deportation of radical aliens—especially members of the Industrial Workers of the World—required the Bureau's attention, adding to the Bureau's task of securing the release of conscientious objectors and other political prisoners.[104] As Frances Witherspoon explained,

---

98 United States ex rel. Milwaukee Social Democrat Pub. Co. v. Burleson, 258 F. 282 (D.C. Cir. 1919).

99 United States ex rel. Milwaukee Social Democrat Pub. Co. v. Burleson, 255 U.S. 407, 416 (1921).

100 *Id.* at 417.

101 *Id.* at 436.

102 Becker v. United States, 268 F. 195 (7th Cir. 1920). According to an "exclusive" story in the *Los Angeles Times*, Stedman's *amicus* brief in the Becker case was designed primarily to establish some legal principles that would be helpful in his representation of Berger. Both convictions were ultimately reversed. *Try to Free Berger*, L.A. TIMES, Oct. 12, 1919, at 101.

103 CHARLES RECHT, AMERICAN DEPORTATION AND EXCLUSION LAWS, title page (1919) [hereinafter American Deportation].

104 EARLY, *supra* note 4, at 148.

> everything here in New York has had to give way to the deportation situation, which as you know is the latest and perhaps most exaggerated of all the high-handed things this country has perpetrated in the name of law and order. Our office has been altogether tied up with, first, a series of Chinese deportation cases, and now that of the fifty-four I.W.W.s brought from the West and held at Ellis Island.[105]

In a 1919 article for *Pearson's Magazine*, Recht tells the story of the I.W.W. deportations, beginning on November 5, 1916, with an incident in Everett, Washington, that became known as the "Bloody Sunday" of the "Free Speech Fight."[106] As recounted by Elizabeth Gurley Flynn, a well-known Wobbly organizer, the I.W.W. had distributed a flyer calling for an open-air meeting in Everett on the afternoon of November 5.[107] "Come and help maintain your own and our Constitutional privileges," the flyer read, as part of an effort to organize the lumber industry centered in Everett. The campaign had been a bloody one, as a "reign of terror, led by drunken Sheriff McRae" and an employers' organization called the Commercial Club broke up meetings and beat up speakers.[108]

On the day of the meeting, Flynn wrote in her autobiography, a delegation of 250 Wobblies left Seattle for Everett on the excursion steamer *Verona*.

> The Everett authorities were tipped off by two Pinkerton detectives who were stool pigeon passengers on the *Verona*, pretending to be IWWs. As it proceeded, one of them raised his hand in a signal and the little boat was ambushed from three sides in a deadly fusillade from the dock and the adjoining piers. It listed and some men fell overboard. It then backed out into the stream and, bullet-scarred and bloody, with a grim load of dead, dying and wounded men, returned to Seattle.[109]

Six men on the excursion steamer *Verona* were killed by a sheriff and his officers, more were drowned, and dozens were wounded, Recht wrote. "During the subsequent trial, it developed that some of the deputy sheriffs had been

---

105 *Id.* (citing Letter from Frances M. Witherspoon to Theodore Lunde, Feb. 14, 1919, reel 3, box 4, file 16, NYBLA, TIL).

106 Charles Recht, *The Deportation of the I.W.W.—1919* [hereinafter *Deportation*], PEARSON'S MAGAZINE, May 1919, at 295-98, available at GG Archives, https://www.gjenvick.com/Immigration/Deportation/DeportationOfTheIWW-1919.html. For more on the *Verona* incident, *see* LOWELL S. HAWLEY AND RALPH BUSHNELL POTTS, COUNSEL FOR THE DAMNED 183 (1953).

107 ELIZABETH GURLEY FLYNN, THE REBEL GIRL 222 (1955).

108 *Id.*

109 *Id.*

well supplied with liquor. As a result, they became infuriated and began shooting wildly."[110]

During the shooting, one of the deputy sheriffs, Jefferson Beard, was killed, and 74 members of the union were indicted for his murder—although Recht wrote that, according to the I.W.W., Beard was killed by one of the other deputies. In any event, the workers' trial began on March 5, 1917. They were all acquitted on May 5. "This incident must be borne in mind to realize the strength of the prejudice which was created and still prevails in the Northwest," Recht wrote.[111]

By May 1919, when Recht wrote that description of the *Verona* incident, he had become deeply involved in the deportation proceedings involving I.W.W. members from the Pacific Northwest. Early sets his initial involvement with the Wobblies in the fall of 1917,

> when a nationwide raid of IWW locals by Department of Justice officials and American Protective League volunteers resulted in mass arrests and subsequent espionage trials of IWW members .... In the months following the raids, Recht—whose name was almost daily in the news defending 'undesirables'—came to represent a number of the eastern Wobblie locals.[112]

In 1919, however, Recht's focus had shifted to the deportation of I.W.W. members from the Northwest, who were being shipped to Ellis Island as a first step in the process. Recht was joined by Caroline Lowe, a socialist lawyer from Kansas City who was sent to New York by the I.W.W. national headquarters in Chicago. She had been one of the lawyers who assisted in defending William D. "Big Bill" Haywood and the Wobblies at the April 1918 trial in Chicago following the September 5, 1917, raids on I.W.W. offices around the country.[113]

Recht wrote that the industrial unrest that followed the *Verona* incident "became acute in the general strike in Seattle in 1919." Toward the end of 1917, the lumber branch of the I.W.W. called a general convention in Seattle. "As some of the delegates arrived," Recht wrote, "they were seized by the local police, the Seattle Minutemen, and the sheriff and turned over to the Immigration authorities for deportation." After more than a year, the 38 detainees were herded into a

---

[110] *Deportation, supra* note 106.

[111] *Id.*

[112] EARLY, *supra* note 4, at 155-56.

[113] *Id.* at 156. *See also* HAWLEY & POTTS, *supra* note 106, at 230.

train—known as the "Red Special"—and brought to Ellis Island on February 10, 1919.[114]

On February 12, Recht and Lowe sought a writ of habeas corpus from Judge John C. Knox, sitting in the U.S. District Court for the Southern District of New York, for 49 of the 54 aliens awaiting deportation on Ellis Island. Knox signed the writs as a matter of course but scheduled a hearing for the following day. The move followed a series of meetings among socialist and I.W.W. leaders, including Seymour Stedman—who had led the second criminal defense of *The Masses* staff—and Elizabeth Gurley Flynn, who announced a mass protest meeting on Sunday, February 16. Remarkably, the activists and their lawyers knew none of the names of the deportees, and even accounts of the numbers are sometimes conflicting.[115]

Following lengthy arguments on February 13, focusing on whether the attorneys—Recht and Sidney R. Fleisher for the socialists, Lowe for the I.W.W.—had the authority to represent the deportees. Ultimately, Knox dismissed the writ without prejudice, but admonished the lawyers that, if they contemplated further action, they must be prepared to present evidence that some law was violated. "I would suggest," he said, "that Mr. Recht and Mr. [Ben A.] Matthews [Chief of the Criminal Division of the Federal District Attorney's Office] arrange so that the records of each case can be investigated."[116]

Thus, the lawyers did gain access to the deportees' records, and Recht and Lowe left for Washington that night to review them. The Bureau of Legal Advice also issued a formal statement asserting "that the order for their deportation is invalid and should be annulled by the courts."[117] Following their review of the records, Recht and Lowe submitted a 200-page brief—largely written by Recht—to Labor Secretary William B. Wilson, berating Wilson for failing in his mandate to represent labor. Recht also wrote an analysis of the economic conditions in the Northwest that had led to I.W.W. activism in the region.[118]

---

114 *Deportation, supra* note 106. Early notes that 54 individuals were shipped out on the "Red Special," but only 39 of them had been arrested for I.W.W. activities. The other 15, including one woman, were not members of any radical organization. Recht's work focused on the Wobblies aboard the train. EARLY, *supra* note 4, at 162.

115 *Federal Judge Grants Habeas Corpus Writs on Socialists' Plea,* N.Y. TRIB., Feb. 13, 1919, at 1; *49 'Reds' Get Writ of Habeas Corpus,* N.Y. HERALD, Feb. 13, 1919, at 14; *Habeas Corpus Writs Issued,* BUFFALO COMMERCIAL, Feb. 13, 1919, at 2.

116 *Writs for Reds Vacated,* N.Y. TIMES, Feb. 14, 1919, at 4.

117 *I.W.W. Suit for Liberty of Deportees Fails,* N.Y. TRIB., Feb. 14, 1919, at 18.

118 EARLY, *supra* note 4, at 163.

Wilson's views on the matter were expressed in a letter to the International Association of Machinists.

> Those you refer to as radicals are being sent out of the country because they have been found advocating the overthrow of our government by force. They have had every possible opportunity, both at the places where they were originally arrested some time ago and at the department at Washington, to defend themselves against the charges made under the immigration law.[119]

On his return from Washington, however, Recht declared that none of the aliens would be deported. "Forty-three of the I.W.W.s will be released by the government within the month," Recht told reporters. "The only two who will be deported are an Englishman and an Irishman who desire to return to their own countries." Recht said that his examination of the records revealed that the "only basis for deporting the men is that they are members of the I.W.W., and Anthony Caminetti, Commissioner General of Immigration, told me Tuesday night [February 18]: 'I'm not going to deport anybody because he is a member of the I.W.W.'"[120]

Caminetti also authorized Recht and Lowe to meet with the prisoners for the first time, which they did on February 19. According to Recht,

> We have found evidence that all these men were arrested and held for more than a year until the October 1918 amendment to the immigration law was passed. This gave the Seattle authorities some basis for getting rid of them. The records show plainly that both Secretary Wilson and Commissioner Caminetti have been deceived by the local officials in the West, who are using the immigration amendment as a basis for breaking strikes. The entire case of the government is based on statements sent to Washington by Fisher and Callahan, two local immigration inspectors in Seattle. [121]

On March 15, Secretary Wilson granted paroles to 12 of the 54 western I.W.W. members on Ellis Island. In 19 cases, the deportation orders were affirmed, while in 23 cases, no applications for reopening the hearings were pending. Informed of the decision by telegram from Caminetti, Recht declared a great victory.

> When the men got here on the so-called 'Red Special' about a month ago, they were to be deported immediately. Every application for stay

---

[119] *Secretary of Labor Justifies Action of Deporting Radicals*, N.Y. TRIB., Feb. 20, 1919, at 18.

[120] *Lawyer Insists Radicals Won't Be Deported*, N.Y. TRIB., Feb. 20, 1919, at 18.

[121] *Id.*

> was denied and we were not even allowed to see the men upon their arrival. Now, however, the Bureau of Immigration virtually confesses and admits that it would have deported unjustly at least twelve of the men. We were not really prepared for so large a measure of success. I regard it, too, as an indictment of the "railroading" methods adopted in this case.[122]

Still, Recht and Lowe continued their efforts on behalf of the deportees. Lowe obtained writs of habeas corpus from Judge Learned Hand on March 27 on behalf of 21 detainees, with hearings scheduled the following day.[123] Ultimately, 14 of the men were unconditionally released from the island. Nineteen of the 38 remained on the island when Recht published his account, five men having submitted to deportation a few days after arrival.[124]

For most of the remaining 19 Wobblies, Early wrote,

> Recht and Lowe secured writs of habeas corpus, which were argued before Judge Augustus N. Hand on April 10 and 15. Hand sustained one writ on April 10 (the deportee was discharged), and on April 14, 11 of the writs were withdrawn with no prejudice (mutual consent) and returned to the Department of Labor for reconsideration. Of these, warrants for deportation were canceled for three and three others were released on parole. [125]

On June 10, Hand denied seven writs sought by Recht and Lowe, with the following admonition:

> Most members of the I.W.W. organization may at the present time, either on grounds of principle or expediency, disbelieve in destructive sabotage, but those who distribute I.W.W. songs, the pamphlet of St. John, and the Book of Walter C. Smith on "Sabotage" for the purpose of familiarizing prospective members with the doctrines and spirit of those publications, are open to a charge of advocating or teaching the destruction of property.[126]

Recht's article for *Pearson's* goes on to detail the suffering of the men, then incarcerated for 14 months. He pointed out that these workers had lived in the

---

[122] *U.S. Paroles 12 of 54 'Reds'; Rest Must Go,* N.Y. TRIB., March 16, 1919, at 6.

[123] *Woman Starts Fight to Free 21 I.W.W.'s Held at Ellis Island,* N.Y. TRIB., March 28, 1919, at 10.

[124] *Deportation, supra* note 106.

[125] EARLY, *supra* note 4, at 163-64.

[126] *I.W.W. Aliens Lose in Federal Court,* N.Y. HERALD, June 11, 1919, at 20; *Court Refuses to Stay Deportation,* DAILY SENTINEL (Rome, N.Y.), June 12, 1919, at 10.

U.S. for many years, some for more than 30 years, and one was actually a native-born American, slated for deportation because the immigration inspector has plenary authority to determine who is an alien, whence he came to this country, and whether he is an anarchist. Recht accused powerful lumber interests in the Northwest of colluding with the government in these deportations.[127]

In addition to the "Red Special" cases, Recht handled several other unsuccessful deportation cases involving Wobblies and other anarchist or socialist activists. Three such cases are briefly reported in Recht's *American Deportation and Exclusion Laws*: Joseph Komes, John Meehan, and Frank R. Lopez.[128]

Joseph Komes, an alien resident of Wisconsin, was incarcerated for threats against the United States and public officials when, on January 25, 1918, an immigration inspector visited the jail to question him. During the examination, the sheriff stood by in a threatening manner, according to Komes's affidavit, putting Komes in fear of assault. Denying that he had ever said marshals and judges should be shot, Komes requested legal counsel. Once the examination ended and the inspector left, the sheriff reportedly assaulted Komes, threatening to kill him rather than let him leave jail.

Subsequently, the Immigration Department conducted a hearing in Hurley, Wisconsin, where Komes again denied threatening public officials. Nevertheless, he was ordered deported and shipped to Ellis Island. When Recht won a hearing on a habeas corpus writ before Judge Learned Hand, the Immigration Department canceled the warrant of arrest and deportation. Komes was released from Ellis Island on January 10, 1919, after being imprisoned for more than a year. As Recht described the situation, Komes was "set adrift in the city of New York, penniless, and without a job."[129]

John Meehan was arrested in Everett, Washington, on May 21, 1917, for violating a local anti-billboard act. On finding that Meehan was an I.W.W. member, he was ordered deported to England, whence he had emigrated 25 years earlier. Recht endeavored to have Meehan deported to Saskatchewan, where he had a brother, but, ultimately, the Canadian government objected. It was illegal in Canada to belong to the I.W.W. In December 1918, after nearly 19 months' incarceration, Meehan was deported to England, where he had no relatives, without money or adequate clothing.[130]

Finally, Frank R. Lopez, a native of Spain, was arrested in Boston, charged with anarchy, and ordered deported through Ellis Island. Lopez had lived in the

---

[127] *Deportation*, *supra* note 106.

[128] AMERICAN DEPORTATION, *supra* note 103, at 7.

[129] *Id.* at 7-9.

[130] *Id.* at 9, 30.

United States since 1904, when he arrived here at age 19. Lopez described himself as a "philosophical anarchist," and there was no allegation that he was ever violent or engaged in criminal conduct. Lopez owned a house in East Dedham, Massachusetts, where he lived with his wife and 10-year-old son. He was a highly skilled cabinetmaker and a member of the American Federation of Labor.[131]

Recht argued Lopez's habeas petition before U.S. District Judge John C. Knox, whose December 9, 1918, opinion is instructive as to the contemporary interpretation of the Immigration Act.

> [Lopez] objects to his deportation upon the ground that since he is a "philosophical anarchist" rather than the type which believe in assassination and other violence for the accomplishment of their ends, he does not come within the class of persons denounced by the Immigration Act of February 1917. The theory of anarchy and that of government must at all times be in conflict, and I cannot believe that the philosophical anarchist, at least so far as his ultimate purpose is concerned is any less dangerous than is the advocate of violence .... The conclusion that [Lopez] has been found advocating and teaching anarchy is amply sustained by the record and the writ of habeas corpus will accordingly be dismissed.[132]

Recht appealed Lopez's case to the U.S. Court of Appeals for the Second Circuit, but fared no better at the appellate level. Recht argued that Lopez could not be deported under the Immigration Act because he had been in the country for 15 years. In an opinion by Judge Henry W. Rogers, joined by Judges Charles M. Hough and Martin T. Manton, the court held that the statute applied to Lopez because the statute did not limit the time of deportation for anarchists. Because it found sufficient evidence that Lopez was an anarchist, based on his teaching, speaking and distribution of literature, the court dismissed the appeal and remanded him to the commissioner.[133]

While his case was being further appealed, Lopez was released on bond, whereupon he returned to Boston. According to Elizabeth Gurley Flynn, Lopez became secretary of the Sacco-Vanzetti Defense Committee,[134] working on behalf of two Italian anarchists wrongly accused and later executed for murdering a guard and a paymaster during the April 15, 1920, armed robbery of the Slater and Morrill Shoe Co. in Braintree, Massachusetts. In January 1921, U.S. Attorney

---

[131] *Id.* at 10; FLYNN, *supra* note 107, at 219.

[132] AMERICAN DEPORTATION, *supra* note 103, at 31.

[133] Lopez v. Howe, 259 F. 401 (2d Cir. 1919).

[134] FLYNN, *supra* note 107, at 219.

Francis G. Caffey notified Recht that the U.S. Supreme Court had dismissed Lopez's appeal[135] and ordered that he surrender into the custody of the Commissioner of Immigration at Ellis Island on or before January 20, 1921, at 10:30 a.m. Recht sent a copy of the letter to Lopez on January 14 and, the same day, asked Caffey to postpone the surrender until January 27.[136]

With the trial of Sacco and Vanzetti due to begin soon, one of their lawyers, Fred H. Moore, took a deposition on January 18 from Robert Reid, a constable of the city of Boston, who had been helping Moore with Vanzetti's defense. The deposition—filed in Lopez's case against Frederic C. Howe, Commissioner of Immigration at the Port of New York—asserted that deporting Lopez on January 20 would "deprive defendant Bartolomeo Vanzetti of essential and material testimony on the trial of his cause." To protect Vanzetti's interests, Reid asked that the execution of the deportation order be extended for at least 90 days from the January 20 deadline.[137] According to Flynn, the Department of Labor finally agreed to postpone his departure until after the Sacco-Vanzetti trial, where he was an important witness for the defense.[138]

In his memoirs, Recht wrote that he won 90% of the 80 deportation cases he handled in 1919, including the Wobbly cases that he and Caroline Lowe worked on together.[139] But, overall, the Red Scare and hostility to the new Soviet government was too hard to overcome. "All of our troubles were due to foreigners—the cry for social equality is inspired by agitators—all agitators are foreigners—all radicals are agitators—the Bolsheviks are the most radical—every radical is a Bolshevik."[140]

Nearly a year later, on April 27, 1920, a subcommittee of the Committee on Immigration and Naturalization of the U.S. House of Representatives, held a three-day subcommittee hearing to review reports in the cases of many of the aliens transferred from Seattle and elsewhere to Ellis Island for deportation—and thereafter released. Many, if not most, of those mentioned in the committee's

---

[135] Lopez v. Howe, 254 U.S. 613 (1920).

[136] Letter from Francis G. Caffey to Charles Recht, undated; letter from Charles Recht to Frank Lopez, Jan. 14, 1921; letter from Charles Recht to Francis G. Coffey, Jan. 14, 1921, in Boston Public Library, available at https://ark.digitalcommonwealth.org/ark:/50959/k0 699x97p.

[137] Deposition of Robert Reid, in *Lopez v. Howe*, Jan. 18, 1921, in Boston Public Library, available at https://ark.digitalcommonwealth.org/ark:/50959/k0699x97p.

[138] FLYNN, *supra* note 107, at 219.

[139] EARLY, *supra* note 4, at 170.

[140] *Id.*

report were clients of Charles Recht, and the report shows that Recht was still involved with these cases well into 1920.[141]

For example, the last entry in the compendium of reports presented to the subcommittee involved the case of one David Horvath. Horvath emigrated from Hungary to the United States in 1908. In September 1919, the 18-year-old was being detained at Fort Oglethorpe, Georgia, on the grounds that he was an alien anarchist, that he believed in and advocated the overthrow of the U.S. government by force or violence, and that he did not believe in any organized government. According to Commissioner Caminetti, Horvath was a member of the I.W.W. and believed in industrial democracy whereby an organization, such as the I.W.W., takes control of the industries and runs them to suit itself. "His idea is to take the industries away from the capitalists without pay … regardless of the manner in which it has to be done."[142]

Recht wrote Caminetti on October 10, asserting his representation of Horvath and asking for a hearing. On October 23, Caminetti advised Abercrombie that Recht's associate, Rose Weiss, was in Washington to review the records. Caminetti noted that Horvath and four other aliens had waived representation by counsel and that he had so advised Weiss. He also advised Abercrombie that it would be inadvisable to permit Recht to represent these clients at this late stage in the proceedings and recommended denying his request to view the records.[143] Two days later, Recht reiterated his request, pointing out that Horvath's waiver of counsel occurred because he could not afford to pay for a lawyer or obtain one who was willing to take the case *pro bono.*[144] Again, the Commissioner's office recommended against letting Recht reopen the case.[145]

The correspondence continued along these lines through November, then paused until April 1920, when Recht formally requested to appear on behalf of

---

141 *I.W.W. Deportation Cases, Hearings Before a Subcommittee of the Committee on Immigration and Naturalization,* 66th Cong. 56 (1920).

142 Letter from A. Caminetti to John W. Abercrombie, Acting Secretary [of Labor], Sept. 19, 1919, in *I.W.W. Deportation Cases, Hearings Before a Subcommittee of the Committee on Immigration and Naturalization,* 66th Cong. (1920) at 86.

143 Letter from Caminetti to Abercrombie, Oct. 23, 1919, in *I.W.W. Deportation Cases, Hearings Before a Subcommittee of the Committee on Immigration and Naturalization,* 66th Cong. (1920) at 87.

144 Letter from Recht to Caminetti, Oct. 25, 1919, in *I.W.W. Deportation Cases, Hearings Before a Subcommittee of the Committee on Immigration and Naturalization,* 66th Cong. (1920) at 87.

145 Letter from Alfred Hampton, Assistant Commissioner General, to Abercrombie, Nov. 1, 1919, in *I.W.W. Deportation Cases, Hearings Before a Subcommittee of the Committee on Immigration and Naturalization,* 66th Cong. (1920) at 87.

Horvath, who had just been sent to Ellis Island from Fort Oglethorpe.[146] On April 23, Recht sent Caminetti a "special plea" to reopen the Horvath case, blaming his predicament on youthful indiscretions and asking that he be paroled to his family in Cleveland. This time, it appears, Recht was successful. The letter bears a notation that Recht's application for a rehearing was granted the following day.[147]

Recht's legal work for the many Ellis Island detainees in the fall of 1920 was complicated by the government's announced decision to ship 100 or so prospective deportees to the Deer Island Immigration Station in Boston Harbor. Recht said he would not oppose the transfer but would go into federal court there to demand that his clients be deported or released.[148] When 34 of the Ellis Island detainees were actually transferred to Deer Island, Recht dispatched Rose Weiss to begin the fight in federal court there. As a test case, Weiss was to represent Ephrim Kertz, a Russian arrested in January 1920, in Seattle, and charged with I.W.W. activities. She would ask the authorities to release or deport Kertz, who remained in detention because there was no transportation available to Russia.[149]

Acting under the auspices of the newly formed Deportees' League, which operated out of the Bureau's building at 110 W. 40th St., Recht and Weiss were finally able to arrange for the deportees to reach Russia by way of the new Republic of Latvia.[150] On December 22 and 23, at the behest of Recht and Weiss, 23 deportees surrendered themselves to immigration authorities at Ellis Island and boarded the steamship *Imperator*, which sailed December 23 via Libau (Liepāja) and Riga. Recht and Weiss were present at the departure, with Weiss telling reporters that the majority of Russians remaining under deportation orders would be glad to leave the country if permitted to do so.[151]

---

[146] Letter from Recht to Commissioner General of Immigration, April 17, 1920, in *I.W.W. Deportation Cases, Hearings Before a Subcommittee of the Committee on Immigration and Naturalization*, 66th Cong. (1920) at 88.

[147] Letter from Recht to Commissioner General of Immigration, April 23, 1920, in *I.W.W. Deportation Cases, Hearings Before a Subcommittee of the Committee on Immigration and Naturalization*, 66th Cong. (1920) at 88.

[148] *Ellis Island 'Reds' to be Shipped Away to Jail Off Boston*, BROOKLYN DAILY EAGLE, Sept. 28, 1920, at 1.

[149] *Deportees' League Formed to Free Reds*, N.Y. TIMES, Oct. 3, 1920, at 25.

[150] *Id.; 23 Reds, Against Their Wills, Must Go Back to Russia*, N.Y. TRIB., Dec. 19, 1920, at 11.

[151] *23 Deportees Put Aboard Imperator*, BROOKLYN DAILY EAGLE, Dec. 23, 1920, at 3; *Six Brooklyn Radicals in Party Deported Today*, BROOKLYN STANDARD UNION, Dec. 23, 1920, at 5.

As for the 34 Russian deportees at Deer Island, Recht said it was

> not at all certain that the arrangement with the Latvian Government will apply to all Russian deportees from the United States. In the case of the twenty-three who left today, we secured passports from Ludwig C. A. K. Martens, which assure the Latvian Government that the deportees will be received in Russia when they get to the border. It does not appear that the arrangement with Latvia and the Soviet Republic by which these deportees are sent back is a permanent thing.[152]

In addition to the mass deportation cases, Recht represented several individual detainees with special circumstances. For example, in April 1920, Recht secured the release of an alleged anarchist and I.W.W. member named John Johnson, who had been arrested in Pittsburgh and detained for more than a year on Ellis Island pending deportation.[153] And in July 1920, Recht represented Martin Abern, secretary of the Communist Party of Minnesota, a post to which he was elected while serving 14 months in prison for draft evasion. Born in Romania, Abern was being held at Ellis Island awaiting deportation, but Recht secured his release on a $1,000 bail.[154] Recht even represented a real estate broker seeking the release of an indigenous Peruvian named Victor Lizarrago, who arrived in the U.S. as a stowaway on a United Fruit Co. steamship.[155] Apparently, there was nothing political about it.

2.4. Labor Union Cases

Once again, only one of the lawyers profiled here devoted a substantial portion of his practice to representing labor unions: Morris Hillquit. Hillquit was the principal counsel to the International Ladies Garment Workers' Union during the latter part of his life, but represented many other unions throughout his long legal career. Seymour Stedman played a prominent role in the 1914 Calumet copper miners' strike and the 1916 Westinghouse strike in Pittsburgh, and those cases are also recounted here.

Charles Recht also represented members of the International Workers of the World. Recht's work generally involved deportation cases and is discussed above under that heading.

---

152 *23 Willing "Reds" Deported to Russia*, N.Y. TIMES, Dec. 24, 1920, at 4.

153 *Held as Anarchist, Is Released on Writ*, N.Y. HERALD, Apr. 8, 1920, at 22.

154 *Communist, Ordered Deported, Granted Bail*, N.Y. TRIB., Jul. 24, 1920, at 14.

155 *Broker to Aid Stowaway*, N.Y. TRIB., Mar. 14, 1920, at 12.

Morris Hillquit

Hillquit's involvement with the labor unions began early and accelerated throughout his legal career, culminating in his nearly full-time representation of the International Ladies Garment Workers' Union. In April 1906, the U.S. Circuit Court in Manhattan handed a victory to Hillquit's client, the Mason Builders' Association of the City of New York, when it refused to grant a fireproofing contractor a preliminary injunction to avoid the union's New York City work rules.[156]

In 1907, Hillquit represented organized labor in an immigration case involving alien lithographers detained at the Port of New York. The workers had been imported by manufacturing lithographers due to a scarcity of skilled workers in that field. Despite Hillquit's protestation that admitting the workers would violate the alien contract labor law, Commerce and Labor Secretary Oscar S. Strauss ruled that the men were entitled to admission based on an earlier attorney general opinion.[157]

The following year, Hillquit unsuccessfully represented a Cigarmakers' Union local on a deceased member's insurance claim.[158] He successfully defended an unincorporated union against a damage claim brought by an expelled member.[159] And he successfully defended a union client against a claim for insurance proceeds during a period when the decedent member was ineligible for benefits.[160]

In late 1909 and early 1910, he represented striking shirtwaist makers in their negotiations with the manufacturers' association. In mid-December, those negotiations had foundered on the question of recognition of union shops, which the manufacturers steadfastly refused to consider. Ultimately, with the assistance of state arbitrators, the strike produced union contracts in almost every shop—except for Triangle Shirtwaist, where disaster would strike the following year. Hillquit's involvement with the garment workers foreshadowed the path his legal practice would follow until the end of his career.[161]

---

156 National Fireproofing Co. v. Mason Builders' Ass'n, 145 F. 260, 265 (S.D.N.Y. 1906).

157 *Lithographers Come In*, N.Y. TRIB., Nov. 5, 1907, at 4.

158 Munch v. Albrecht, 111 N.Y.S. 209 (N.Y. App. Div. 1908).

159 Schmidt v. Weyell, 113 N.Y.S. 630 (N.Y. City Ct. 1908).

160 Taufer v. Brotherhood of Painters, Decorators & Paperhangers of Am., 122 N.Y.S. 527 (N.Y. App. Div. 1910).

161 *See Hitch in Arbitration*, N.Y. SUN, Dec. 8, 1909, at 2; *Arbitration Hitch*, N.Y. TRIB., Dec. 8, 1909, at 3; *No Chance of Arbitration*, N.Y. SUN, Dec. 12, 1909, at 7; *Standing by Union*, N.Y. TRIB., Dec. 14, 1909, at 9; *Church Shirtwaist Debate*, N.Y. SUN, Dec. 27, 1909, at 5; and *To Fix Shop Terms*, N.Y. TRIB., Jan. 4, 1910, at 13.

In the summer of 1910, some 50,000 to 70,000 cloak makers went out on strike. Early on, notables such as Louis D. Brandeis tried to settle the strike, resulting in the Perpetual Protocol of Peace, which Hillquit would call the "most advanced and enlightened code of labor relations."[162] In his autobiography, Hillquit never mentions his own role in that settlement, but his biographer says he was again part of the arbitration team on behalf of the workers.[163] In any event, Hillquit would become one member of the three-member Board of Arbitration, created by the protocol and empowered to issue binding decisions to resolve disputes that could not be settled by a Grievance Committee of workers and management. Hillquit represented the workers on the board, Brandeis the public, and Hamilton Holt the Cloak, Suit, and Skirt Manufacturers' Protective Association. In a full-page story two years later, the *Times* touted the protocol as a "model for labor disputes the country over."[164]

In May 1915, eight leaders and members of the Cloak and Skirt Makers' Union were indicted for the 1910 murder of Herman Liebowitz, a strikebreaker in the 1910 strike. One of the defendants was Morris Sigman, general secretary and treasurer of the parent International Ladies' Garment Workers' Union, and the union hired Hillquit as chief defense counsel. Hillquit would say later that no case he ever handled caused him greater anxiety and concern.[165]

Liebowitz was apparently lured to the union hall—or perhaps, as Hillquit suggests, he had come to change sides—when he was caught up in a melee and struck on the head; he then fell and hit his head on the pavement. The case was investigated at the time, then dropped and generally forgotten. Hillquit indicates that the reopening of the case was "presumably" related to some "underworld gangs" that operated under the guise of labor unions but actually furnished cheap nonunion labor to unscrupulous employers.[166]

In fact, that spring and summer had seen a major crackdown on East Side gangs whose crimes included assaulting strikebreakers, allegedly at the behest of corrupt union leaders. In addition to the eight union members arrested for murder, another 22 persons were charged with assault, extortion and other crimes. Included were many members and leaders of notorious East Side gangs, nearly all "fingered" by a mobster with the colorful moniker of "Dopey Benny" Fein.

---

[162] LOOSE LEAVES, *supra* note 52, at 130-31.

[163] NORMA FAIN PRATT, MORRIS HILLQUIT: A POLITICAL HISTORY OF AN AMERICAN JEWISH SOCIALIST 103 (1979).

[164] *This Conciliation Plan May Solve Strike Problem*, N.Y. TIMES, June 16, 1912, at 10 (48).

[165] LOOSE LEAVES, *supra* note 52, at 133.

[166] *Id.* at 134.

Fein had been arrested for extortion the previous September, later confessing to his own crimes and exchanging information for more lenient treatment. "If the unions wanted a scab beaten or killed, or a non-union shop proprietor intimidated," police told the *Tribune*, "they came to Benny for handling the job. He got $12 a day for himself, and the union had to pay $8 apiece a day for each operative he supplied." It was Fein who named the union leaders as responsible for the death of Herman Liebowitz,[167] and at least eight witnesses testified before the grand jury that they saw Sigman strike Liebowitz with an iron pipe. Hillquit expressed skepticism as to this version of the story, but he conceded that the defense team had neither witnesses of their own nor alibis for their clients.[168]

At least one judge, Justice John Ford, seems to have been skeptical as well. Ford sustained a writ of habeas corpus sued out by the defense team and released all eight men on bail aggregating $135,000. "These defendants are all married, have families and reside in the City of New York," Ford said. "None of them appears to have anything in the nature of a criminal history. The evidence against them, as shown by the minutes of the grand jury which found against the defendants, is, to say the least, inconclusive as to all and of questionable probative force as to most."[169]

In fact, one of the defendants was dismissed before the trial because the evidence against him before the grand jury was deemed insufficient. Still, the defense had no coherent theory of the case. "Then, almost on the eve of the trial, the answer came to me in a flash," Hillquit wrote. Recognizing that his belief in the innocence of the accused men was not based on the particular facts in the case, but on his intimate knowledge of the whole background and surroundings, Hillquit determined that "our best chance to win was to impart that knowledge to the court and the jury, to make them see the case as I saw it."[170]

The trial began on September 23, 1915, before Justice Arthur S. Thomkins.[171] In his opening statement, Hillquit took the jury step by step through the causes and circumstances of the 1910 strike and, afterward, had the "distinct feeling of

---

167 *Thirty Indicted in Record Raid on Gangsters*, N.Y. TRIB., May 12, 1915, at 16; *Gunman Bares Plot by Labor to Slay Foes*, N.Y. SUN, May 12, 1915, at 1.

168 LOOSE LEAVES, *supra* note 52, at 135.

169 *Eight Union Men Give $135,000 Bail*, N.Y. TRIB., Aug. 8, 1915, at 6; *Union Leaders Quit Tombs*, N.Y. SUN, Aug. 8, 1915, at 3; *Grants Bail to 8 Accused of Murder*, N.Y. TIMES, Aug. 8, 1915, at 9.

170 LOOSE LEAVES, *supra* note 52, at 135-36.

171 *Seven 'Workers' Tried in Block for a Murder*, N.Y. Eve. World, Sept. 23, 1915, at 1; *7 Labor Leaders Face Murder Jury*, N.Y. TIMES, Sept. 24, 1915, at 22.

a friendly court atmosphere." Each defendant took the stand to explain his part in the strike. "The economic and social education of the jurors thus continued for another week," he wrote. [172]

At the close of the evidence, two more defendants were dismissed from the case on the motion of the prosecutor. The jury deliberated for two or three hours, then advised Justice Thomkins that they had agreed upon a verdict of acquittal for all five remaining defendants.[173] Hillquit's lessons on the history of organized labor and the causes of the 1910 strike might have had some influence on the jury; more likely, the jurors simply did not believe the prosecution witnesses.

Hillquit's involvement with the labor movement, and the ILGWU in particular, deepened during 1915. In May, for example, Hillquit and Levene successfully defended the ILGWU from a charge that the union illegally caused a nonunion worker to be discharged from a union shop simply because the union had informed the employer that the worker was not a union member.[174] In July, he represented the ILGWU before the Council of Conciliation, winning a promise from the manufacturers that action would be taken against any of their members who demanded wage kickbacks from their workers on pain of discharge.[175] And in August, as the union representative to the Council, he helped negotiate a settlement agreement with the clothing manufacturers that avoided a strike.[176]

Hillquit's 1916 opened with a major change on the Council of Conciliation due to the appointment of Louis Brandeis to the United States Supreme Court. Hillquit and his opposite number, Julius Henry Cohen, counsel for the manufacturers, prepared a telegram of congratulations from both of them.[177]

In late April, the Cloak and Suit Manufacturers' Protective Association had voted to lock out some 60,000 workers in 400 shops in an effort to break the closed-shop principle that the unions had won in 1910. ILGWU president Benjamin Schlesinger had vowed to "fight to the bitter end," and Hillquit had predicted that fight would be a long one.[178] The unions' reaction was a strike by

---

[172] LOOSE LEAVES, *supra* note 52, 138-40.

[173] *Id.* at 140-41; *Acquit Union Men of Murder Charge,* N.Y. TIMES, Oct. 9, 1915, at 15.

[174] Cusumano v. Schlessinger, 152 N.Y.S. 1081 (N.Y. App. Div. 1915).

[175] *Wage Schedules to be Argued To-Day,* N.Y. TRIB., July 16, 1915, at 9.

[176] *Get Day's Truce to Bring Peace in Cloak Trade,* N.Y. TRIB., Aug. 5, 1915, at 9; *A Happy Ending,* N.Y. TRIB., Aug. 6, 1915, at 6; and *Mayor Thanks Dr. Adler,* N.Y. TIMES, Aug. 7, 1915, at 14.

[177] *Praised for Aiding Labor,* N.Y. TIMES, Jan. 29, 1916, at 3.

[178] *Employers Decide on Cloak Lockout,* N.Y. TIMES, April 28, 1916, at 22.

some 200,000 workers in the clothing, transportation, construction, and other industries.[179] All attempts at conciliation failed.

As the strike intensified, Hillquit won an unrelated case in the New York Court of Appeals, where he defended the National Brotherhood of Painters, Decorators and Paperhangers against a claim for damages from a union member who had been expelled by his local. The court held that the national union was not licensed in New York and that its affiliation with its locals did not subject it to jurisdiction in the New York courts.[180] But the ILGWU strike continued unabated.

On July 20, President Wilson ordered the departments of Commerce and Labor to investigate the strike, to which the warring factions responded by agreeing to appoint an outside expert to try to settle the issue of wages. But Hillquit's statement was far from sanguine: "The conference today has not changed the situation. The strike is still on .... The union still believes that the only way to solve the difficulties is to submit the entire controversy to arbitration. We will welcome the government mediators."[181]

Those mediators were appointed on July 31 and began their work the next day.[182] The strike officially ended on August 3, with a large majority of the workers voting to accept the proposed terms.[183] In fact, very little was changed by the strike, though the union considered it a great success and the workers paraded through Union Square to celebrate their victory.[184]

In January 1918, several New York newspapers raised their prices from one cent to two, claiming wartime exigencies as the reason. News dealers feared that their sales would be dramatically lower, despite a higher commission on each paper sold, and went out on strike. Hillquit represented the news dealers in talks with Mayor John Francis Hylan, but the strike began to fail in February with the growth of alternative means of distribution.[185]

Hillquit would learn in January 1919 that he had lost his final appeal on behalf of an Amalgamated Clothing Workers union local for ownership of $7,000 on deposit in a New York bank. The dispute arose in 1915 when about three-fourths of

---

179 *200,000 Strikers Likely by Monday*, N.Y. SUN, April 29, 1916, at 22.

180 People ex rel. Solomon v. Brotherhood of Painters, Decorators & Paperhangers, 112 N.E. 752 (N.Y. 1916).

181 *Wilson Orders Strike Inquiry*, N.Y. TRIB., July 21, 1916, at 6.

182 *New Federal Move in Clothing Strike*, N.Y. TIMES, Aug. 1, 1916, at 5.

183 *Garment Workers' Strike Officially Declared at End*, N.Y. EVE. WORLD, Aug. 3, 1916, at 1.

184 *Garment Workers Parade*, N.Y. TRIB., Aug. 8, 1916, at 6.

185 *Some Newsdealers Resume Deliveries*, N.Y. TIMES, Feb. 1, 1918, at 18; *Newsdealers Strike in New York*, Tumblr, https://tmblr.co/Zq0s6n2Ul66oT; *Paper Sale Biggest Since Strike Started*, N.Y. TRIB., Feb. 5, 1918, at 9.

the membership voted to leave Amalgamated and affiliate with the United Garment Workers union, leaving ownership of the bank accounts in doubt. Hillquit and Levene represented the remaining one-fourth of the Amalgamated local's membership against the breakaway local. The New York Court of Appeals ultimately affirmed the decisions below that the fund comprised dues, fines and assessments paid by the members of the United affiliate and awarded ownership to the United local.[186]

Appellate Division gave Hillquit a victory in April 1921 when it reversed the trial court's granting an employer, G.M. Piermont & Co., an injunction to prevent its International Ladies Garment Workers' Union-affiliated employees from picketing. Both Piermont and the ILGWU alleged the other side violated the union contract, and the employees went out on strike. When Piermont retained nonunion employees to keep its factory open, the union began picketing and allegedly interfered with the factory's operations. Piermont sued and initially won an injunction against the picketing at trial. Hillquit appealed for the union and, on April 29, Appellate Division reversed, holding that the union was conducting the strike peaceably and without resort to lawless acts.[187]

Toward the end of 1921, Hillquit became embroiled in the legal battle accompanying a massive garment workers' strike. The strike began in mid-November when some 40,000 garment workers walked off the job to protest the manufacturers' plan to introduce a piece-work payment system, contrary to their May 1919 contract, which required payment by weekly wage and was not due to expire until June 1922.[188] As chief counsel for the ILGWU, Hillquit recruited attorney Samuel Untermyer as *pro bono* associate counsel, who recommended in a letter to Hillquit that a lawsuit should be initiated against the manufacturers' association to enjoin them from violating the contract.

For their part, the manufacturers were adamant that the 1919 contract had been abandoned by the union, that the week-work pay system was destroying the industry, and that new mechanisms for determining workers' pay and resolving disputes had to be found immediately.[189] Hillquit filed his lawsuit on November 29, and Justice Charles L. Guy immediately issued a preliminary injunction to prevent the manufacturers from establishing an industry-wide piece-work system or otherwise conspiring to violate the contract. According to both sides, this was the first known instance of an international union seeking enforcement of an agreement alleged to have been violated by an

---

[186] Brownfield v. Simon, 121 N.E. 858 (N.Y. 1919).

[187] Piermont v. Schlesinger, 188 N.Y.S. 35 (N.Y. App. Div. 1921).

[188] *50,000 to Strike in Needle Industry*, N.Y. TIMES, Nov. 11, 1921, at 1.

[189] *Untermyer Backs Garment Strikers*, N.Y. HERALD, Nov. 21, 1921, at 4; *The Garment Strike*, N.Y. DAILY NEWS, Nov. 21, 1921, at 33.

association of manufacturers. Even Justice Guy noted that courts that had issued injunctions in similar cases against unions "welcome this opportunity to demonstrate that the same rules of law and justice apply to everyone."[190]

A series of legal maneuvers on both sides ensued, including the union's filing a civil lawsuit seeking millions of dollars in damages for violating the contract[191] and the manufacturers obtaining an injunction barring at least some of the striking workers from receiving strike benefits.[192] On January 11, 1922, the New York Supreme Court granted the union's motion to permanently enjoin the manufacturers from violating the 1919 contract during the pendency of all the litigation on the issue, at least until June 1, 1922, when the contract would expire by its own terms.[193] Appellate Division affirmed Justice Robert Wagner's ruling on May 26, but by then, the strike had long since ended. Based on Justice Wagner's decision, the manufacturers dropped their demands for a piece-work system and agreed to take the workers back under the terms of the 1919 contract. The strike had lasted nine weeks, costing the union more than a million dollars and imposing uncounted costs on the manufacturers.[194]

Labor unrest returned to the garment district in 1923 when Charles Maisel & Co., a coat manufacturer, sought to reorganize its business by drastically reducing the number of employees and farming much of the work out to subcontractors. The ILGWU alleged the reorganization was not in good faith and therefore not authorized by the 1919 contract, as modified in 1922. When the union refused to consent to the reorganization, Maisel pulled out of the manufacturers' association, which was governed by the contract, and sought to outsource all of its manufacturing. Maisel's employees went on strike, which lasted 14 or 15 weeks. Efforts to reach a negotiated settlement continued throughout the strike, and an agreement was finally reached on July 5, 1923.

When a subsequent dispute arose, an arbitrator found for the union, but Maisel refused to comply. The employees walked out again, and Maisel went to court, claiming the July 5 agreement was procured by duress or was otherwise legally invalid and seeking to enjoin the new strike. Hillquit represented the

---

190 *Court Enjoins Piece Work and Longer Hours in Cloak Trade,* N.Y. TRIB., Nov. 30, 1921, at 1; *Cloak Trade Piece Work is Enjoined,* N.Y. HERALD, Nov. 30, 1921, at 15; *Union Gets Injunction Against Cloak Makers,* N.Y. DAILY NEWS, Nov. 30, 1921, at 2; *Needle Employers Must Not Conspire,* N.Y. HERALD, Dec. 1, 1921, at 12.

191 *Cloak Workers Sue Employers for Millions,* N.Y. DAILY NEWS, Dec. 4, 1921, at 4.

192 *Strikers Struck Dumb as Court Stops Benefits,* N.Y. DAILY NEWS, Jan. 9, 1922, at 5.

193 Schlesinger v. Quinto, 192 N.Y.S. 564 (N.Y. Sup. Ct. 1921). *See also Strikers Win Big Victory in Garment War,* N.Y. TRIB., Jan. 12, 1922, at 1.

194 *50,000 Garment Makers Return to Work Today,* N.Y. DAILY NEWS, Jan. 17, 1922, at 2; *Garment Makers' Futile Strike Cost $1,046,531,* N.Y. DAILY NEWS, March 19, 1922, at 8.

union, and, on June 5, 1924, won a ringing affirmation of the workers' right to strike. The court held that the contract was not created under duress, since the strike constituted merely a threat to do what the union had a legal right to do. Nor did a clause in the contract giving the union the right to strike if some of the employer's work was done by strikebreakers violate the state's Anti-Monopoly Act.[195]

The *Maisel* decision, welcome as it must have been, was a mere skirmish compared with the industry-wide garment workers' strike that had been threatening since June 1. On June 12, Hillquit delivered an ultimatum to the manufacturers demanding they submit to arbitration within 24 hours or the union would begin strike preparations.[196] When the manufacturers declared there was nothing to arbitrate, Gov. Alfred E. Smith stepped in to appoint a mediation commission to try to reconcile the opposing positions on minimum wages, enlargement of shops, equitable distribution of work, guaranteed work throughout the year, and a label on each garment attesting to its manufacture by union labor.[197]

The underlying problem in the industry, at least from the labor perspective, was the proliferation of sub-manufacturers, contractors, and jobbers far beyond the number of factories that would guarantee employment stability. "The workers can strike and prove that their services are essential to the industry," Hillquit told the governor's commission, "but they will not know against whom they are striking. The employers have built up a wall of irresponsibility between themselves and their employees. The jobber system has proved highly injurious in practical operation and threatens our industry with total demoralization. It is unhealthy and dangerous." Hillquit said these manufacturers, having no reputation to sustain, turn out half-sewn, badly made garments "with the poorest workmanship that will in any way pass muster."[198] The manufacturers responded with accusations that Hillquit was looking to drive thousands of manufacturers out of business.[199]

While there was a brief walkout on June 20, the workers returned to work the following day as negotiations continued.[200] When those negotiations failed by

---

195 Maisel v. Sigman, 205 N.Y.S. 807 (N.Y. Sup. Ct. 1924).

196 *Cloak Workers' Ultimatum Sets Reply in 24 Hours*, N.Y. DAILY NEWS, June 13, 1924, at 21.

197 *Smith to Name Peace Board in Garment Workers' Fight*, N.Y. DAILY NEWS, June 14, 1924, at 29.

198 *Governor Hears Hillquit Arraign Cloak Industry*, N.Y. DAILY NEWS, June 18, 1924, at 2.

199 *Employers' Doom in Union Demands, Commission Told*, N.Y. DAILY NEWS, June 19, 1924, at 11; *Hillquit Accused of Attack on 2,000 Shop Employes*, N.Y. DAILY NEWS, June 19, 1924, at 8.

200 *Garment Strike Starts as Peace Conference Sits*, N.Y. DAILY NEWS, June 21, 1924, at 20.

the end of the month, all 50,000 or so workers went back out on strike and remained out for about two weeks. Management and labor finally reached an agreement with the help of state mediators in mid-July, and the strike ended with the union declaring victory.[201] While the employers accepted the commission's recommendations, at least formally, the settlement would not be the last word on issues.

In January 1925, Hillquit argued his first case before the United States Supreme Court. In *Pennsylvania R. System v. Pennsylvania R. Co.*,[202] a union known as Federation No. 90, purporting to represent some 20,000 employees of the Pennsylvania Railroad Co., had sought to enforce a ruling of the Railroad Labor Board created under Title III of the Transportation Act of 1920 as to how those employees were to choose a union to represent them in negotiations with the company. The company completely ignored the ruling, imposed its own selection process, and reached an agreement regarding wages and working conditions with representatives chosen under that process. Hillquit represented the Federation, alleging the company's conduct constituted a criminal conspiracy to deprive the workers of their lawful rights and asking for an injunction against further promoting that conspiracy.

The federal district judge who heard the case dismissed the Federation's claim, and the circuit court of appeals affirmed that dismissal. Despite broadly agreeing that the company was using every means at its disposal to thwart the Railroad Labor Board's ruling, the U.S. Supreme Court held on March 2, 1925, that the board's ruling was not mandatory under the law, that violations of that ruling could not constitute criminal conspiracy, and that the injunctive relief the Federation requested could not be granted. The Court concluded that the only remedy available to the Federation had to come from the court of "public opinion."[203]

The rail union case must have been a difficult loss, but in 1925, Hillquit faced even more serious problems with his primary client, the ILGWU. As Hillquit biographer Norma Fain Pratt describes it, Hillquit had largely remained on the sidelines as left-wing communists favoring confrontation gained increasing influence in the union. At the ILGWU convention in 1925, however, Hillquit spoke for acceptance of arbitration and against the use of strikes. When the Smith commission's final report was issued on May 20, 1926, the union ignored Hillquit's call for moderation and ordered a general strike on July 1. Pratt called the strike a "disaster," with Hillquit finally negotiating a settlement in November

---

201 *50,000 Needle Workers' Strike Scheduled to End Wednesday*, N.Y. DAILY NEWS, July 12, 1924, at 7.

202 267 U.S. 203 (1925).

203 *Id.* at 217.

1926 on terms "not appreciably better than what had been offered the union months earlier. The strike seriously damaged union morale and depleted its financial resources. Hillquit blamed the communist leadership."[204]

Hillquit's struggle with the communist element in the ILGWU continued through the end of the decade. Pratt opines that he probably could not have changed the leftward direction of the union,[205] but he remained active in the union's legal affairs. In July 1929, for example, he helped to draft an agreement to settle a garment workers' strike involving about 19,000 workers.[206] In February 1930, he helped settle a strike involving garment trade contractors and jobbers,[207] and in October 1932, he worked with a mediator to prevent another strike.[208] The following year, Hillquit submitted a proposed code of wages and working conditions under the National Industrial Recovery Act on behalf of the ILGWU, which became the first union to do so.[209] Pratt concludes that Hillquit "contributed appreciably" to unionization in the garment industry.[210]

Hillquit also fought for various unions in court as well as at the bargaining table. In 1926, for example, Hillquit successfully represented a bakers' union local in fending off an injunction against members' picketing in front of a bakery and attempting to compel the business to employ union labor.[211] That same year, however, Hillquit lost an appeal by another bakers' union local whose picketing of another bakery had been enjoined for disseminating false or misleading information as to the nature of their dispute with the bakery.[212] The following year, Hillquit lost a similar case against the retail grocery workers' union for picketing a group of "mom & pop" butter and egg stores where picketers had committed acts of violence against the stores' customers.[213]

In 1930, Hillquit won a judgment enforcing a painters' union agreement with a Philadelphia contractor to pay higher New York wages on the ground that the

---

204 PRATT, *supra* note 163, at 226-28. *See also 40,000 Striking Cloakmakers Will Vote Tomorrow on Ratifying Peace Accord*, N.Y. DAILY NEWS, Nov. 14, 1928, at 8; *Red Wing Quiet as Garment Men Meet Strikers*, N.Y. DAILY NEWS, Dec. 17, 1926, at 39.

205 PRATT, *supra* note 163, at 231.

206 *Write Peace Pact Today in Cloak Strike*, N.Y. DAILY NEWS, July 15, 1929, at 11.

207 *Peace Dov Roosts in Garment Trade Lofts; Lehman Settles Dress Strike*, N.Y. DAILY NEWS, Feb. 23, 1930, at 6.

208 Untitled photograph, N.Y. DAILY NEWS, Oct. 5, 1932, at 25.

209 *Union Offers F.D. Amended Garment Code*, N.Y. DAILY NEWS, July 20, 1933, at 14.

210 PRATT, *supra* note 163, at 231-32.

211 Public Baking Co. v. Stern, 215 N.Y.S. 537 (N.Y. Sup. Ct. 1926).

212 Wilner v. Bless, 154 N.E. 598 (N.Y. 1926).

213 L. Daitch & Co. v. Retail Grocery & Dairy Clerks' Union, 221 N.Y. S. 446 (N.Y. Sup. Ct. 1927).

agreement was entirely voluntary and absent duress.[214] When the union workers struck for noncompliance, the company won a preliminary injunction against them in federal court, but the injunction was dismissed on the merits. The company appealed to the U.S. Supreme Court, which affirmed the union victory.[215] In Hillquit's last reported union case, his client, a manufacturers' association that had entered into a collective agreement with the garment workers' union, won an injunction to prevent another association from violating the terms of that agreement.[216]

Representation of the ILGWU[217] and other unions,[218] together with labor-focused politics, would dominate the final decade or so of Hillquit's life.

Seymour Stedman

In early 1914, Seymour Stedman became actively involved in the strike of copper miners in the Calumet region of Upper Michigan, addressing mass meetings of union members all over Chicago in support of the Calumet miners.[219] More importantly, he was named to a special committee, with Victor Berger and Charles Edward Russell, by the national Socialist Party to investigate the strike.[220] The committee began its work by meeting with Michigan Governor

---

214 Glicman v. Barker Painting Co., 238 N.Y.S. 419 (N.Y. App. Div. 1930).

215 Barker Painting Co. v. Brotherhood of Painters, Decorators & Paperhangers, 281 U.S. 462 (1930).

216 American Cloak & Suit Mfrs.' Ass'n v. Brooklyn Ladies' Garment Mfrs.' Ass'n, 255 N.Y.S. 614 (N.Y. Sup. Ct. 1931).

217 *See, e.g.*, Altman v. Schlesinger, 198 N.Y.S. 128 (N.Y. App. Div. 1923) (granting employers an injunction restraining ILGWU officers and members from threatening employers' employees, continuing a strike in the employers' factory, and picketing the employers' place of business).

218 *See, e.g.*, *Police Clubbed Strike Pickets, Union Charges*, N.Y. DAILY NEWS, May 13, 1922, at 7 (Hillquit representing Upholsterers Union); *Kosher Bakers Defy Untermyer, Keep Store Open*, N.Y. DAILY NEWS, May 29, 1922, at 3; *Jewish Bakers Issue Defiance to Undermyer*, N.Y. TRIB., May 29, 1922, at 18; *Grand Jury to Act on Bakers' Union*, N.Y. TIMES, May 29, 1922, at 13; *Bakers to Close Shop; Trial Is Postponed*, N.Y. HERALD, June 17, 1922, at 4 (Hillquit representing Kosher Bakers Union); *Poison Pen Hits at Bakers' Union*, N.Y. DAILY NEWS, March 20, 1923, at 5 (Hillquit representing Bakery and Confectionery Workers' Union No. 100); *Golden Silence*, N.Y. DAILY NEWS, Sept. 14, 1923, at 3 (Hillquit representing United Mine Workers of America); N.J. Painting Co. v. Local No. 26, Bhd. Of Painters, etc., 126 A. 399 (N.J. 1924) (Hillquit representing painters' union); Carey v. Int'l Bhd. Of Paper Makers, 206 N.Y.S. 73 (N.Y. Sup. Ct. 1924) (Hillquit representing candidate for office of president of the paper makers' union).

219 *Ferris Will Try to Settle Strike*, CHI. TRIB., Jan. 2, 1914, at 4.

220 *Miners' Committee Wait to Hear from Gov. Ferris*, DAY BOOK (Chi.), Jan. 7, 1914, at 25.

Woodbridge N. Ferris on January 8,[221] and urging the governor to force the mining companies to recognize the Western Federation of Miners. When the governor refused in no uncertain terms, the socialists asked that all mine guards be withdrawn and the miners protected from eviction. Stedman suggested that the state establish tent colonies for the miners, opining that the companies had no legal right to own and rent houses under their charters. The state attorney general disagreed, and the meeting ended with no resolution and no sense of the next steps to be taken.[222]

About a week later, the committee issued its report, starkly condemning the companies for employing and supporting imported gunmen who were responsible for a number of murders and other crime in the strike area. "[The] employment of militia was entirely unnecessary, worked infinite harm and did no good," the report said, "while the use of private guards to supersede, with their rifles and drunken whims, the constituted authorities, has been most clearly demonstrated to be a great, perilous and intolerable evil." The committee pointed out that recognition of the union was all that was needed to return the men to the mines and expressed profound regret that the governor had failed to take advantage of that opportunity to advance the condition of the working class.[223] In a luncheon talk soon thereafter, Stedman asserted that, before the strike, about 10% of the miners were socialists, but that number had grown to 80% as a result of the strike.[224]

Two years later, on May 25, 1916, Stedman and several other lawyers arrived in Pittsburgh to defend labor activists indicted on charges growing out of long-simmering and ultimately explosive strikes in the Braddock area. The strikes began innocently enough in early April 1916, when a thousand tool repairmen employed by the Westinghouse Electric and Manufacturing Plant in East Pittsburgh went on strike for higher pay.[225] In a week or so, the strikers accepted the company's offer of a 10% salary increase and double time on Sundays.[226] But labor unrest continued, with nearly 500 munitions workers at the Westinghouse plant going out on strike a few days later.[227] As the strike spread, workers clashed with police, weapons surfaced, and some injuries occurred. The strike was conducted under the auspices of the American Industrial Union

221 *Troops to be Taken from Strike Region*, INTER OCEAN (Chi.), Jan. 8, 1914, at 5.

222 *Governor Ends Copper Inquiry; Hears Owners*, INTER OCEAN (Chi.), Jan. 9, 1914, at 1.

223 *Report of Calumet Conditions is Made by National Socialist Party Committee*, DAY BOOK (Chi.), Jan. 16, 1914, at 5.

224 *Says Strike Made Socialists*, CHI. TRIB., Jan. 18, 1914, at 14.

225 *Westinghouse Men Demand Higher Pay*, PHILA. INQUIRER, April 1, 1916, at 3.

226 *Strikers Accept Offer*, PITTSBURGH DAILY POST, April 4, 1916, at 8.

227 *Shell Makers Are Making Demand for Higher Pay*, PITTSBURGH PRESS, April 9, 1916, at 11.

(A.I.U.), with one John Hall as principal organizer, and a nonemployee, Fred H. Merrick, as a major agitator. The American Federation of Labor, which would ultimately retain Stedman to defend indicted strikers, expressed support for some, if not all, of the strikers' demands.[228]

Numerous plants closed down in the wake of the strike,[229] police on the scene sometimes outnumbered strikers,[230] and various attempts were made to end the strike peacefully.[231] Some strikers were arrested, including Merrick and socialist Anna Goldberg, but the peace seemed to be holding.[232] Both were released pending further proceedings, and the press reported that April 29 was the "quietest day since the strike began."[233] The peace would come to an abrupt end the next evening, when about 4,000 strikers attended a mass meeting addressed by Hall, Merrick, Goldberg and others.[234] All hell broke loose the following day, May 1, when an estimated 5,000 strikers rioted, invading a number of area plants, attacking police, and destroying property for about three hours.[235] The next morning, ten strike leaders were arrested,[236] but the rioting continued throughout the day. Banner headlines on the front page of the *Pittsburgh Daily Post* screamed:

> TROOPS ARE ORDERED TO STRIKE ZONE;
> 2 KILLED, 30 HURT IN BRADDOCK RIOTS;
> LEADERS ARE JAILED ON MURDER CHARGES[237]

Local attorney William H. Pratt, who represented the strike leaders who were arrested during and after the riots, tried and failed to obtain their release on

---

228 *Westinghouse Employees and Police Clash,* PITTSBURGH POST-GAZETTE, April 25, 1916, at 1.

229 *Plants Closed as a Result of Strikes,* PITTSBURGH POST-GAZETTE, April 27, 1916, at 9; *Westinghouse Plants Closed by Officials,* PITTSBURGH DAILY PRESS, April 27, 1916, at 2.

230 *Government Sends Envoy to Probe Big Strike Here,* PITTSBURGH PRESS, April 27, 1916, at 1.

231 *Strikers Elect Directing Body,* PITTSBURGH DAILY POST, April 28, 1916, at 3; *Strikers Check Fire in Plant,* PITTSBURGH DAILY POST, April 29, 1916, at 2; *U.S. Moves in Westinghouse Labor Trouble,* PITTSBURGH POST-GAZETTE, April 29, 1916, at 1; *Peace Agents in Strike Zone,* PITTSBURGH DAILY POST, April 30, 1916, at 4.

232 *Girl Striker is Arrested; Refuses Bail,* PITTSBURGH PRESS, April 29, 1916, at 1; *Westinghouse Strikers Now Rest on Oars,* PITTSBURGH PRESS, April 30, 1916, at 1.

233 *Mediators Arrive on Scene of Westinghouse Trouble,* PITTSBURGH POST-GAZETTE, April 30, 1916, at 16.

234 *Strikers Hold Mass Meeting,* PITTSBURGH POST-GAZETTE, May 1, 1916, at 3.

235 *Westinghouse Strikers Riot; Damage Results,* PITTSBURGH POST-GAZETTE, May 2, 1916, at 1.

236 *Note to "M'Namara" Found on Prisoner,* PITTSBURGH POST-GAZETTE, May 3, 1916, at 1.

237 PITTSBURGH DAILY POST, May 3, 1916, at 1.

bail from Judge Ambrose B. Reid, pending grand jury action.[238] Following a series of hearings, the grand jury indicted Merrick—the "real leader of the mob element"—for inciting the May 1 riot,[239] but its formal presentment to the court contained more than 30 names altogether, with charges ranging from inciting to riot, to aggravated riot, to destruction of property. Hall was said to have arranged for Merrick's services in inciting the strikers to riot and then to have aided and abetted the rioters.[240] Based on the presentation, Reid issued an order to return indictments against 36 rioters,[241] even as the grand jury prepared to indict Merrick and more than a dozen others for the deaths that occurred on May 2.[242]

Stedman arrived in Pittsburgh just in time to question prospective jurors at the beginning of the trial on the initial indictments. William J. Brennan was the lead attorney for the defense; District Attorney R. H. Jackson was the lead prosecutor.[243] By the time the jury was selected, the number of defendants had been reduced to fewer than 30, resulting from no contest pleas and decisions not to prosecute.[244] The most stunning defection from the defense ranks was union leader John Hall, who pleaded no contest and testified for the prosecution against Merrick. Stedman raised a vigorous objection, but Judge Reid let Hall continue to testify regarding Merrick's incendiary speeches.[245] The prosecution rested on June 1, and the defense began calling defendants to testify on their own behalf.[246] Stedman handled the direct examination of Merrick, who denied that he had encouraged violence at the mass meeting.[247] Surprisingly, there was no cross-examination, and the defense rested.

Stedman closed for the defense, pointing out that the May 1 riots began with a lawful and orderly parade to celebrate International Labor Day. When the parade reached the plant, he said in an hour-long speech, the crowd was forced

---

238 *Court Decree Denies Liberty to Agitators,* PITTSBURGH POST-GAZETTE, May 5, 1916,

239 *Indict Merrick for Riot,* PITTSBURGH PRESS, May 19, 1916, at 12.

240 *36 Are Indicted by Grand Jury for Rioting,* PITTSBURGH PRESS, May 21, 1916, at 11.

241 *Indictments are Returned in Riot Probe,* PITTSBURGH DAILY POST, May 21, 1916, at 1.

242 *Alleged Riot Leaders Held for Grand Jury,* PITTSBURGH PRESS, May 24, 1916, at 13.

243 *Jurors Closely Quizzed,* PITTSBURGH PRESS, May 26, 1916, at 1. Reid's calling for a trial within days of the indictment prompted attorney Pratt to declare that his clients were being "railroaded," an accusation that drew a sharp rebuke from Reid. *Judge Rebukes Attorney for Statement in Court,* PITTSBURGH POST-GAZETTE, May 23, 1916, at 9.

244 *Braddock Riot Trials Open; 29 Accused,* PITTSBURGH DAILY POST, May 27, 1916, at 2; *Jury Selected to Try 26 Men for Rioting,* PITTSBURGH POST-GAZETTE, May 27, 1916, at 9.

245 *Hall Makes Plea of No Defense; Counsel Object,* Pittsburgh Press, May 29, 1916, at 1.

246 *Riot Defense Begins Before Judge Reid,* PITTSBURGH PRESS, June 1, 1916, at 1.

247 *Merrick Denies that He Urged Strike Riots,* PITTSBURGH PRESS, June 2, 1916, at 1.

against the gates, which gave way under the strain. There was no plan to enter the works, nor any speech or meeting that advocated violence.[248] Judge Reid sent the case to the jury on June 2, even as the grand jury was handing up new indictments; eight members of the North Braddock police department were charged with failure to help suppress the riot when requested.[249] In a little over two hours, the jury returned with guilty verdicts for Merrick and ten of the 16 other defendants remaining on trial. Stedman said he would submit a motion for a new trial in a few days, then sought to postpone the trial on the new indictments.[250]

The so-called May 2 riot trial opened on June 8, with Judge T. J. Prather presiding. Stedman was now fully in charge of the defense, Brennan having withdrawn to attend the Democratic national convention. [251] Once again, Hall was the key witness for the prosecution, although he admitted under Stedman's cross-examination that there were no calls for violent action at any of the A.I.U. meetings that preceded the riots.[252] And once again, Merrick was the last witness for the defense, offering testimony that was essentially the same as he had given in the first trial.[253] On June 17, after two hours' deliberation, the jury found Merrick, Goldberg and one other defendant guilty of riot and inciting to riot, but not guilty of aggravated riot or riotous destruction; all other defendants were acquitted on all charges.[254]

On July 1, after denying the defense's futile arguments for new trials, Judges Reid and Prather jointly sentenced the defendants convicted in either or both trials. Reid sentenced Merrick to two years on his first conviction; Prather sentenced him to 18 months on his second. Hall was sentenced to one year, as was Anna Goldberg. Other defendants received sentences ranging from probation to one year.[255] Merrick was released on a $10,000 bond pending appeal to the Superior Court,[256] which heard arguments on a consolidated appeal on November 16. The opinions, published on March 7, 1917, affirmed all of the convictions, finding "the elements necessary to constitute a riot are so

---

[248] *Twenty Others Indicted in Riot Case*, PITTSBURGH POST-GAZETTE, June 3, 1916, at 7.

[249] *Braddock Riot Cases Are Now in Jury's Hands*, PITTSBURGH PRESS, June 3, 1916, at 1.

[250] *11 Rioters Found Guilty; 6 Acquitted*, PITTSBURGH DAILY POST, June 4, 1916, at 1.

[251] *Second Riot Trials Open; 18 Arraigned*, PITTSBURGH DAILY POST, June 9, 1916, at 11.

[252] *Slow Progress Being Made in Riot Trial*, PITTSBURGH PRESS, June 9, 1916, at 8.

[253] *Jury to Get Riot Cases Late Today; Merrick on the Stand*, PITTSBURGH PRESS, June 16, 1916, at 19.

[254] *3 Convicted, 11 Acquitted in Riot Cases*, PITTSBURGH DAILY POST, June 18, 1916, at 1.

[255] *15 Leaders in Braddock Riots Are Sentenced*, PITTSBURGH POST-GAZETTE, July 2, 1916, at 4.

[256] *Merrick Released Under $10,000 Bond*, PITTSBURGH PRESS, July 27, 1916, at 24.

indisputably established in this case by the undisputed testimony, that no other verdict than guilty could have been expected."[257]

B. Earning a Living

All three of the lawyers profiled in this book had extensive commercial practices in addition to their civil liberties endeavors. Hillquit and Stedman seemed to have managed a truly diverse private practice coincident with their political activities. Recht's employment by Soviet-related entities for commercial matters constituted nearly all of his private practice.

Morris Hillquit

During his many years of practice, Morris Hillquit was both a committed socialist and a thoroughly bourgeois attorney. Hillquit rationalized this apparent contradiction: "I can see nothing wrong ... in principle for a socialist to practice law in a capitalist system or to engage in any other capitalist activities."[258] Hillquit's first reported cases are utterly mainstream, without any ideological content. In *Kramer v. Schatzkin*,[259] for example, Hillquit represented the debtor in an action to recover on a promissory note signed by the debtor and his partner. Hillquit persuaded the trial court that his client was protected by the statute of limitations, but that decision was reversed on appeal.[260] And in *Luban v. Simonds*,[261] Hillquit represented the successful plaintiff in an action to recover certain property allegedly taken by the defendant. On appeal, the defendant raised the lack of personal or subject-matter jurisdiction, but the court rejected both arguments.[262]

In 1902, the Hillquits would represent a member of the Social Democratic Party in an election dispute, as well as a private insurance society. In *In re Ward*, Hillquit represented Christopher Ward, the nominee of the Social Democratic Party for the office of congressman from the Seventh Congressional District. Although Ward had been nominated at a party convention, his certificate of nomination was rejected by the Board of Elections on the ground that the party had failed to comply with certain technical requirements of an 1899 election

---

[257] Commonwealth v. Merrick, et al., 65 Pa. Super. 482, 492 (1917). *See also* Commonwealth v. Goldberg, 65 Pa. Super. 482 (1917), and Commonwealth v. Detwiler, 65 Pa. Super. 494 (1917).

[258] PRATT, *supra* note 163, at 28 (citing Morris Hillquit, *Statement*, Paris, June 11, 1931, at 2, in Morris Hillquit Papers).

[259] 57 N.Y.S. 803 (N.Y. App. Term 1899).

[260] *Id.* at 806.

[261] 61 N.Y.S. 697 (N.Y. App. Div. 1899).

[262] *Id.* at 698.

law. The Hillquits sought and won a writ of mandamus forcing the board to put Ward's name on the ballot; the court held that the 1899 law did not apply to the SDP and that the party had complied with an 1896 election law that did apply.[263]

The Workmen's Sick & Death Benefit Fund of the United States was a private society incorporated in 1884 and licensed to issue insurance policies in 1899. In *Kunkel v. Fund*, the Hillquits successfully opposed the payment of death benefits to the executrix of the deceased member's will, notwithstanding provisions of the will to the contrary, on the ground that the executrix was not a named beneficiary of the policy.[264] But in *Gleiforst v. Fund*, the Hillquits were unable to sustain the expulsion of a member who had distributed a circular among other members criticizing officers of the society.[265]

Later in 1902, Hillquit represented Jacob Deshel and a group of creditors of the bankrupt Union Cloak and Suit Co. Before declaring bankruptcy, the company had assigned certain assets to those creditors, who were now being sued by Edward Benedict, th e trustee in bankruptcy, on the ground that the assignment constituted an unlawful preference. Hillquit initially won a jury verdict, which was affirmed by the Appellate Division,[266] but the Court of Appeals ultimately reversed that judgment on the ground that the trial court erred in charging the jury that the trustee had to prove that the bankrupt company intended to give the creditors a preference. The court ordered a new trial,[267] but there are no further reported proceedings. Also during 1903, Hillquit represented the administrator of the estate of Charles Gmaehle, a bricklayer who died after falling from scaffolding on which he was working, in an action against Gmaehle's employers for wrongful death. The reported decisions focused on technical aspects of the case and never reached the merits.[268]

Notwithstanding his busy political schedule, Hillquit's law practice had continued apace, and the winter of 1905–06 saw three more reported appellate opinions, none of them political. In *Bender v. Schatzkin*, the Hillquits won a new trial for their clients in a dispute over the sale of a property in the Bronx.[269] In *Rosenthal v. Reinfeld*, a new trial was awarded to the opponents of the

---

263 In re Ward, 74 N.Y.S. 403, 404-405 (N.Y. Sup. Ct. 1902).

264 75 N.Y.S. 188, 188-89 (N.Y. Sup. Ct. 1902).

265 75 N.Y.S. 44 (N.Y. Sup. Ct. 1902).

266 Benedict v. Deshel, 79 N.Y.S. 205, 208 (N.Y. App. Div. 1902).

267 Benedict v. Deshel, 68 N.E. 999, 1001 (N.Y. 1903).

268 Gmaehle v. Rosenberg, 80 N.Y.S. 705 (N.Y. App. Div. 1903); 81 N.Y.S. 930 (N.Y. Sup. Ct. 1903); 82 N.Y.S. 366 (N.Y. App. Div. 1903); 70 N.E. 411 (N.Y. 1904).

269 1905 N.Y. Misc. LEXIS 513*3 (N.Y. App. Div. 1905).

Hillquits' client because of an evidentiary error below.[270] And in *Dielmann v. Berka,* the Hillquits saved their client, an insurance association, half of a death benefit claim awarded in full by the trial court.[271]

More legal opinions would follow. In May 1906, Hillquit won the reversal of an adverse opinion regarding mechanics' liens.[272] In 1907, the Hillquits lost a case brought against their client, the seller of certain real property, who failed to give a clear title as promised, allowing the buyer to unwind the transaction.[273] And the Hillquits won a new trial after their client, the prospective purchaser of a horse, had been found liable for conversion when the horse died while lawfully in his possession.[274]

From 1908 through 1910, the Hillquit firm's reported cases were all routine civil matters, including

- the unsuccessful pursuit of a wrongful death claim where a bricklayer fell to his death from a scaffold for failing to follow his foreman's direction,[275]
- the successful recovery on a promissory note by holders for value and in due course,[276]
- the successful enforcement of a mechanic's lien,[277]
- the successful appeal of a disappointed claimant to a share of a decedent's estate,[278]
- the unsuccessful defense of a city contractor against the negligence claim of a pedestrian who was injured when he tripped on a board that the contractor left on the sidewalk,[279] and
- the successful appeal of an adverse ruling against a tenant whose use of a cellar coal room was barred by his landlord contrary to the fair construction of his lease.[280]

---

270 96 N.Y.S. 199, 200 (N.Y. App. Div. 1905).

271 97 N.Y.S. 1027, 1028 (N.Y. App. Div. 1906).

272 Mechanic's Lien of Harris H. Uris v. Brackett Realty Co., 99 N.Y.S. 642, 643 (N.Y. App. Div. 1906).

273 Levin v. Hill, 102 N.Y.S. 690, 691 (N.Y. App. Div. 1907).

274 Meise v. Wachtel, 104 N.Y.S. 915, 916 (N.Y. App. Div. 1907).

275 Ripp v. Fuchs, 113 N.Y.S. 361 (N.Y. App. Div. Div. 1908).

276 Mindlin v. Appelbaum, 114 N.Y.S. 908 (N.Y. App. Div. 1908).

277 Uris v. Brackett Realty Co., 88 N.E. 1133 (N.Y. 1909).

278 In re Collins, 116 N.Y.S. 243 (N.Y. App. Div. 1909), *aff'd* 89 N.E. 1098 (N.Y. 1909).

279 Friedman v. City of New York, 116 N.Y.S. 750 (N.Y. App. Div. 1909).

280 Greenblatt v. Zimmerman, 117 N.Y.S. 18 (N.Y. App. Div. 1909).

Hillquit also served as referee for the sale at auction of a Madison Avenue apartment house in early 1910.[281]

In 1912, Hillquit unsuccessfully represented a real estate company in a dispute with an employee over commissions owed,[282] and a foster father seeking an order authorizing him to adopt two minor children in his care.[283] The next year, he successfully defended a fraternal mutual benefit insurance corporation against a claimant for benefits on the death of an ineligible member.[284] All of Hillquit's reported cases for the rest of the decade involved unions and were previously discussed.

In June 1920, the New York Supreme Court ruled against Hillquit's client, the Lithuanian Socialist Federation, which was seeking control of certain funds claimed by the Lithuanian Socialist Home Association, which was represented by Charles Recht, the Soviet Union's leading American lawyer. The Federation, which was affiliated with the Socialist Party, had created the Association for the purpose of building and operating one or more clubhouses in New York and elsewhere for the social, political, cultural and recreational activities of Federation members. The Federation also deposited $10,000 in the Association's accounts.

The Association proceeded to collect an additional $15,000 but never fulfilled the purpose for which it had been incorporated. Instead, it passed a resolution to join the Communist Party, rename itself the Lithuanian Communist Federation, and transfer all its money to that entity. Hillquit appealed the decision allowing that transfer, and, on April 1, 1921, Appellate Division reversed, holding that the original organization had a right to prevent the new organization from diverting the funds to other purposes.[285]

From 1925 until his death, Hillquit's reported commercial cases involved corporate law,[286] trusts and estates,[287] divorce,[288] insurance,[289] negligence,[290]

---

281 *Auction Sales This Week*, N.Y. TIMES, Jan. 23, 1910, at 57.

282 Benequit v. New York & New Jersey Real Estate Improv. Co., 133 N.Y.S. 226 (N.Y. App. Div. 1912).

283 In re Korte, 139 N.Y.S. 444 (Kings Cnty. Ct. 1912).

284 Waltz v. Workmen's Sick and Death Benefit Fund of the United States, 141 N.Y.S. 578 (N.Y. App. Div. 1913), *rev'g* 139 N.Y.S. 1016 (N.Y. Cty. Ct. 1912).

285 Herman v. Brooklyn Sav. Bank, 187 N.Y.S. 738 (N.Y. App. Div. 1921).

286 Hassel v. Pohle, 212 N.Y.S. 561 (N.Y. App. Div. Div. 1925).

287 In re Estate of Wronkow, 216 N.Y.S. 422 (N.Y. Surr. Ct. 1925).

288 Miller v. Miller, 159 N.E. 681 (N.Y. 1927); Rosenthal v. Rosenthal, 173 N.E. 899 (N.Y. 1930).

289 Int'l Union Bank v. Nat'l Surety Co., 157 N.E. 269 (N.Y. 1927); Int'l-Madison Bank & Trust Co. v. Eagle Indem. Co., 178 N.E. 777 (N.Y. 1931); Conway v. North Side Lumber Co., 252 N.Y.S. 476 (Mun. Ct. Manhattan 1931).

290 Gellis v. Ahneman & Younkheere, Inc., 157 N.E. 888 (N.Y. 1927).

banking,[291] real estate,[292] and, of course, politics. Hillquit's last reported case involved the 1932 mayoral election, in which Hillquit ran again, and lost again, under the Socialist banner.[293] On September 1, 1932, Mayor James J. Walker resigned, and the president of the Board of Aldermen, Joseph V. McKee, assumed the rights and duties of the office of mayor. At issue in the case was whether the vacancy was to be filled at the general election on November 8, 1932, or whether the president of the Board of Aldermen should continue to act as mayor for the duration of Walker's term, that is, through the general election of 1933.

Hillquit represented Algernon Lee and others favoring a 1932 election. The trial court ruled the other way, but it was reversed on appeal. On October 6, 1932, the New York Court of Appeals affirmed the appellate ruling,[294] and the election was held on November 8. John P. O'Brien, the Tammany candidate, won the election with just over a million votes. The Republican, Lewis H. Pounds, polled 570,000, and Morris Hillquit, who ran on the Socialist ticket, 290,000.[295] (See chapter 3.)

Charles Recht

Charles Recht would have a long and prosperous legal career. His last reported case was in 1958; he died in 1965 at age 78. The Soviet Union was not only Recht's client for matters pertaining to that country but also a direct and indirect source of his substantial probate practice for private Russian and Eastern European clients, and for a growing caseload of international trade and shipping cases. The Russian Soviet Federative Socialist Republic (RSFSR) was incorporated into the new Union of Soviet Socialist Republics in December 1922, but the USSR would not be recognized by the United States until 1933. At least until then, Recht would remain its most important legal representative in the United States.[296]

---

[291] Silverman v. Nat'l City Bank, 232 N.Y.S. 339 (N.Y. Sup. Ct. 1928); Sokoloff v. Nat'l City Bank, 164 N.E. 745 (N.Y. 1928); Bernhard Ulmann Co. v. Central Union Trust Co., 178 N.E. 796 (N.Y. 1931); Workers Unity House, Inc. v. Internat'l Union Bank, 252 N.Y.S. 1015 (N.Y. App. Div. 1931).

[292] Morrill Realty Corp. v. Rayon Holding Corp., 240 N.Y.S. 38 (N.Y. Sup. Ct. 1930).

[293] *Socialists Name Hillquit for Mayor,* N.Y. Daily News, Sept. 16, 1932, at 48.

[294] MacAdams v. Cohen, 184 N.E. 91 (N.Y. 1932).

[295] *O'Brien Elected, but M'Kee Gets 100,000 Votes,* N.Y. Daily News, Nov. 9, 1932, at 2.

[296] There was some confusion regarding Recht's position between 1922 and 1933. Early reports on his return to the U.S. from Russia in 1922 seemed to indicate that Recht was appointed something of an unofficial ambassador. *See, e.g., New Soviet Envoy Here from Russia,* N.Y. Times, June 4, 1922, at 47; *Reds Make N.Y. Lawyer Their Official Envoy,* N.Y.

Many of Recht's probate cases involved routine questions that might arise in any probate situation.[297] In others, however, Recht represented prospective beneficiaries in the Soviet Union or the Baltic States. These persons were generally prevented from receiving the distribution they were due on the ground that the money would likely be confiscated. A New York law, enacted because of reports of expropriations in Russia, allowed for distribution only when the recipient would enjoy the full benefit of the proceeds. Funds subject to that rule would be held in the city treasury.[298] By 1945, however, the Surrogate's Courts were finding that legatees resident in Russia were receiving the full benefit of their legacies and allowed distributions to be made to them—often through Recht in his capacity as attorney to the Consul General of the USSR.[299]

Recht's Latvian clients had no such luck. Because the United States did not recognize the Soviet regime in Latvia or the incorporation of Latvia into the USSR, the New York Surrogate Courts did not recognize any of the credentials issued by that regime to enable Recht to obtain distributions for his Latvian

---

DAILY NEWS, June 4, 1922. Recht would later claim no special credentials other than attorney for that country. *See Recht Not To Be U.S. Soviet Representative*, BUFFALO COURIER, June 7, 1922, at 1. It is likely that the confusion stemmed from the fact that Recht's instructions included some duties that might be handled by a commercial attaché, including an effort to bring American motion pictures to Russia and to represent the Russian Volunteer Fleet (merchant marine). *See, e.g., New Soviet Envoy Here from Russia*, N.Y. TIMES, June 4, 1922, at 47.

[297] *See, e.g.,* In re Estate of Burnstine, 258 N.Y.S. 438 (Surr. Ct. N.Y. Cnty. 1932) (right to examine witness to will); In re Estate of Rubenstein, 257 N.Y.S. 637 (Surr. Ct. Westchester Cnty. 1932) (application for revocation of letters of administration); In re Estate of Notarius, 266 N.Y.S. 714 (Surr. Ct. Bronx Cnty 1933) (contested accounting of executor involving construction of will); In re Grauds' Estate, 43 N.Y.S.2d 803 (Surr. Ct. N.Y. Cnty. 1943) (determination of death); In re Estate of Paskievitz, 55 N.Y.S.2d 595 (Surr. Ct. N.Y. Cnty. 1944)) (striking objections not timely filed); In re Levner's Estate, 90 N.Y.S.2d 294 (Surr. Ct. N.Y. Cnty. 1948) (construction of will); In re Backman's Will, 89 N.Y.S.2d 459 (Surr. Ct. Bronx Cnty. 1949) (determination of next of kin); In re Brown's Estate, 91 N.Y.S.2d 247 (Surr. Ct. N.Y. Cnty. 1949) (construction of will); Zakatoff Will, 81 A.2d 430 (Pa. 1951); In re Steinreich's Estate, 133 N.Y.S.2d 137 (Surr. Ct. Queens Cnty. 1954) (return of gift items); In re Grossman's Will, 148 N.Y.S.2d 771 (Surr. Ct. Kings Cnty. 1956) (payment to residuary legatee); In re Seidman, 148 N.Y.S.2d 771 (Surr. Ct. Kings Cnty. 1956) (payment to residuary legatee).

[298] *See, e.g.,* In re Estate of Landau, 16 N.Y.S.2d 3 (Surr. Ct. Kings Cnty. 1939) (denying distributive share of estate to Soviet national); In re Estate of Bold, 18 N.Y.S.2d 291 (Surr. Ct. N.Y. Cnty. 1940).

[299] *See* In re Estate of Alexandroff, 61 N.Y.S.2d 866 (Surr. Ct. N.Y. Cnty. 1944) (allowing distributions to residents of Russia, modifying previous orders in *Landau* and *Bold* accordingly). *See also* In re Adzericha's Estate, 61 N.Y.S. 867 (Surr. Ct. N.Y. Cnty. 1945).

clients.[300] Nor was Recht able to apply a bequest to establish a Jewish school in Lithuania when the court held that the legacy was impossible of performance because, "as a matter of common knowledge," religious teaching was not permitted within the U.S.S.R. or the countries absorbed into it.[301]

Recht's Russian clients were sent back to square one in the 1950s when the United States reversed its position again and promulgated a regulation holding that there was no reasonable assurance that Soviet nationals would actually receive checks or warrants drawn against funds of the United States and ordered that delivery of such checks be withheld. Once again, bequests were paid into the New York City treasury.[302]

Occasionally, Recht would have to go to court to fight for his own compensation in these cases. In one case, the court held that Recht was entitled to reasonable compensation for establishing the identity of his principal, a resident of Lithuania.[303] In another, he was denied payment for his services when a distribution to his Czechoslovakian clients was barred for lack of reasonable assurance that the legatees would actually receive the money.[304]

One of Recht's earliest shipping-related cases similarly involved the eligibility of Soviet entities to sue in federal court for claims related to the expropriation of their property by the United States. In January 1917, the Russian Volunteer Fleet, a Russian corporation, became the assignee for the value of contracts for the construction of two ships by the Standard Shipbuilding Company of New York. In August 1917, following the overthrow of the Czar, the United States requisitioned the contracts and the ships being built under them, for wartime purposes, fixing the compensation due at $1.4 million. Volunteer estimated the value at $4 million and, in 1919, filed suit for the balance.

The U.S. Court of Claims found that, by the time that lawsuit was filed, the new Soviet Union had assumed power in Russia, but had not been recognized by the United States. Accordingly, the court lacked jurisdiction to hear the claim. With Recht on the brief for Volunteer, the U.S. Supreme Court reversed,

---

300 In re Keyes, 93 N.Y.S.2d 416 (Surr. Ct. Kings Cnty. 1949). *See also* In re Eckert, 41 N.Y.S.2d 263 (Surr. Ct. N.Y. Cnty. 1943); In re Eckert, 45 N.Y.S.2d 318 (Surr. Ct. N.Y. Cnty. 1943); In re Grauds' Estate, 59 N.Y.S.2d 710 (Surr. Ct. N.Y. Cnty. 1945).

301 In re Estate of Shapiro, 112 N.Y.S.2d 46 (Surr. Ct. N.Y. Cnty. 1952).

302 In re Best, 107 N.Y.S.2d 224 (Surr. Ct. N.Y. Cnty. 1951). *See also* Sobko Estate, 88 Pa. D. & C. 76 (Comm. Pleas Ct. Phil. Cnty. 1954); In re Von der Heid's Estate, 227 N.Y.S.2d 807 (Surr. Ct. Kings Cnty. 1958).

303 In re Aronson, 114 N.Y.S.2d 280 (Surr. Ct. N.Y. Cnty. 1952).

304 In re Estate of Klein, 1223 N.Y.S.2d 866 (Surr. Ct. Saratoga Cnty. 1952).

holding that reading the law so as to prevent the award of just compensation violated the Fifth Amendment.[305]

Several of Recht's other maritime cases involved seeking recovery of or compensation for shipping and other matériel requisitioned by the United States.[306] Others involved breach of contract,[307] arbitration issues,[308] and other compensation claims.[309] His routine civil cases involved partnership fraud,[310] divorce,[311] immigration,[312] illegal picketing,[313] landlord-tenant,[314] insurance,[315] corporate governance,[316] elections,[317] and employment law.[318]

A few of Recht's cases attracted considerable publicity. During the spring or summer of 1921, Recht happened to read an item in a motion picture weekly detailing a lawsuit brought by one Jacques Roberto Cibrario, an Italian national, against Patrick A. Powers, president of the Powers Film Products Co. of Rochester, New York. The article noted that Cibrario was acting on behalf of the Soviet government, but he was unknown to Recht at the time. Recht initiated a discreet investigation of his own, retaining the Burns Detective Agency in the effort. He confirmed that Cibrario was indeed acting with Soviet authority, but not in the way that the government had intended.[319] Cibrario was

---

305 Russian Volunteer Fleet v. United States, 282 U.S. 481 (1931).

306 *See, e.g.*, The Denny, 127 F.2d 404 (3d Cir. 1942); The Florida, 133 F.2d 719 (5th Cir. 1943); The Kotkas, 135 F.2d 917 (5th Cir. 1943); Int'l Aircraft Trading Co. v. U.S., 109 Ct. Cl. 435 (1947); Estonian State Cargo & Passenger S.S. Line v. U.S., 115 Ct. Cl. 815 (1950); Latvian State Cargo & Passenger S.S. Line v. U.S., 342 U.S. 816 (1951).

307 *See, e.g.*, Kulukundis Shipping Co. v. Amtorg Trading Corp., 126 F.2d 978 (2d Cir. 1942); The Wildwood, 133 F.2d 765 (9th Cir. 1943); Ecco High Frequency Corp. v. Amtorg Trading Co., 81 N.Y.S.2d 610 (N.Y. Sup. Ct. 1948).

308 *See, e.g.*, In re Amtorg Trading Corp., 100 N.Y.S.2d 747 (N.Y. Sup. Ct. 1950); Amtorg Trading Co. v. Camden Fiber Mills, 103 N.E.2d 342 (N.Y. 1951).

309 *See, e.g.*, Halpern v. Amtorg Trading Corp., 39 N.Y.S.2d 907 (N.Y. App. Div. 1943); The Regent, 67 F. Supp. 149 (E.D.N.Y. 1946).

310 *See, e.g.*, Troster v. Dann, 145 N.Y.S. 56 (N.Y. App. Term 1913).

311 *See, e.g.*, Radda v. Radda, 167 N.Y.S. 213 (N.Y. App. Div. 1917).

312 *See, e.g.*, Lopez v. Howe, 254 U.S. 613 (1920).

313 *See, e.g.*, Benito Rovira v. Yampolsky, 187 N.Y.S. 894 (N.Y. Sup. Ct. 1921).

314 *See, e.g.*, Bozzuffi v. Darrieusecq, 210 N.Y.S. 455 (N.Y. Sup. Ct. 1925).

315 *See, e.g.*, Sliosberg v. N.Y. Life Ins. Co., 155 N.E. 749 (N.Y. 1927).

316 *See, e.g.*, Herman v. Brooklyn Sav. Bank, 187 N.Y.S. 738 (N.Y. App. Div. 1921); Lenc v. Zicha, 164 N.E. 600 (N.Y. 1928).

317 *See, e.g.*, In re Adler, 173 N.E. 265 (N.Y. 1930).

318 *See, e.g.*, Gaetjens v. Gaetjens, Berger & Wirth, Inc., 151 F. Supp. 701 (S.D.N.Y. 1957).

319 *"Count Cibrario" Held in $800,000 Theft from Soviet*, BUFFALO TIMES, Aug. 4, 1921, at 13.

arrested on August 1, 1921, based on an affidavit filed by Recht and his associate, Rose Weiss, charging him with the theft of $136,000 belonging to the Soviet government. A flamboyant denizen of the Broadway district known as the "Count," Cibrario was arraigned before Judge Alfred J. Talley and held on $10,000 bail for examination on August 4 in Tombs Court.[320]

In July 1918, Cibrario had won a contract from the Cinematographic Committee of the Commissariat of Public Education for the purchase of film, projectors and related materials valued at about $1 million. Cibrario was to receive as commission 6% of the total purchase price, with 1% ($10,000) payable in advance as a guaranty of fulfillment. The advance was paid, and in early August 1918, the Commissariat delivered $1 million to Dr. William C. Huntington, the American commercial attaché in Petrograd, to be deposited in a U.S. bank for Cibrario's use in purchasing the equipment called for in the contract. The funds were duly deposited in the National City Bank of New York.[321]

According to Recht, Cibrario bought inferior goods at prices much lower than those cited in the contract, obtained payment for them from the National City Bank—at the contract price—keeping the difference for his own use. This was accomplished either by buying the goods in the name of one of several dummy corporations and having that corporation send a bill for the contract price, or by having the manufacturers bill the goods at the contract price and rebate the difference to Cibrario.[322] The goods, characterized by Recht as "junk," were stored in warehouses, which issued receipts that Cibrario could take to National City Bank to collect his reimbursement.[323] This practice continued from 1919 well into 1921, making Cibrario wealthy enough to enjoy a luxury apartment and chauffeur-driven automobile and to host lavish parties. One estimate put Cibrario's total theft at $800,000.[324]

The criminal case against Cibrario was based on information in Recht's affidavit of August 1, 1921, to the effect that one of the warehouse receipts Cibrario presented for reimbursement was signed by the corporation Standard Cinemas Machine Co., which Cibrario controlled. Cibrario sent himself a letter from a dummy director saying that a large shipment was being held and would be held until $136,000 was paid. Cibrario, Recht charged, then drew $136,000 from National City Bank on the strength of that document, whereupon the corporation was liquidated. Recht said there were some 30 lawsuits against

---

320 *$136,000 Film Theft Charged by Soviet*, N.Y. HERALD, Aug. 2, 1921, at 1.

321 RSFSR v. Cibrario, 191 N.Y.S. 543, 544 (N.Y. App. Div. 1921).

322 *Id.* at 544-45.

323 *$136,000 Film Theft Charged by Soviet*, N.Y. HERALD, Aug. 2, 1921, at 1.

324 "*Count Cibrario" Held in $800,000 Theft from Soviet*, BUFFALO TIMES, Aug. 4, 1921, at 13.

Cibrario in the civil courts, although this was the first criminal complaint against him.[325]

The Powers case that first led to Recht's involvement was exceptional in that it was actually brought by Cibrario, seeking return of the full purchase price of more than 10 million feet of raw film stock purchased from Powers's company. Powers admitted that he initially agreed to invoice Cibrario for the film at a higher price than the actual purchase price and rebate the difference to Cibrario. According to Powers, the total invoice price amounted to $354,000, from which Cibrario cleared $136,000.[326] Cibrario claimed that the film was defective, but Powers refused to buy it back. It appears that the quality of the film had deteriorated in warehouse storage before it was shipped to Russia, and it was actually worth an estimated $20,000 to $50,000.

In the end, neither the criminal case nor Recht's civil cases on behalf of the Soviet government were successful. All four of the criminal indictments against Cibrario were dismissed on November 29, 1921, by General Sessions Judge Joseph Mulqueen on the ground that the evidence submitted to support them was inadequate. Cibrario's attorneys had argued that the criminal cases were brought merely to embarrass him in defending the many civil cases. They also claimed that the Grand Jury that handed up the indictments had received illegally obtained evidence.[327] The civil case was more complicated, but no more successful in the end.

The case was ultimately styled *Russian Soviet Federative Socialist Republic (RSFSR) v. Cibrario* and was initially heard in the New York Supreme Court by Justice John V. McAvoy. On September 14, 1921, McAvoy found "a good and sufficient cause of action for an accounting, for the appointment of a receiver and for an injunction against the defendant Cibrario" and all of his dummy companies. The receiver was to take possession of all books and papers, property and other assets, and payments on debts due to all of the defendants.[328] Cibrario appealed McAvoy's order,[329] urging the Appellate Division to rule that the RSFSR had no capacity to sue in the federal or state courts because it had never been recognized as a sovereign nation by the United States.[330]

---

325 *$136,000 Film Theft Charged by Soviet*, N.Y. HERALD, Aug. 2, 1921, at 1, 9.

326 *Rebates Alleged on Soviet Films*, N.Y. HERALD, Aug. 3, 1921, at 11. *See also Says Soviet Aid Got $100,000 in Film Deal*, N.Y. TRIB., Aug. 3, 1921, at 18.

327 *Cibrario Charges Dismissed by Court*, N.Y. HERALD, Nov. 30, 1921, at 15.

328 Order Appealed from as Resettled, in Papers on Appeal, at 3, RSFSR v. Cibrario, 191 N.Y.S. 543 (App. Div. 1921) ; *See* New York Supreme Court, Case on Appeal, Google Books.

329 Notice of Appeal, in Papers on Appeal, at 1, RSFSR v. Cibrario, 191 N.Y.S. 543 (App. Div. 1921)). *See* New York Supreme Court, Cases on Appeal, Google Books.

330 RSFSR v. Cibrario, 191 N.Y.S. 543, 545 (App. Div. 1921).

The court's opinion, written by Justice Victor J. Dowling and joined by Presiding Justice John P. Clarke and Justices Alfred R. Page and Samuel Greenbaum, agreed with Cibrario and dismissed the claims against him.

> Whenever the question has been raised in this state, it has been held that the test of the right of a foreign sovereignty to sue in our courts is its recognition by our own government .... In the case at bar, while plaintiff claims to be a de facto government, and its title and right to sue alike rest on that claim, it is unable to show any acts of recognition by the government of this country. On the contrary, the record proves that, so far as this country is concerned, the plaintiff is non-existent as a sovereignty.[331]

Recht applied for leave to appeal the case to the Court of Appeals, and received from that court an order staying the enforcement of Dowling's dismissal. In the meantime, Recht refiled the original case, this time naming one Preobazhenski, a member of the Cinematographic Committee, and other members as plaintiffs. That case, too, was dismissed; Supreme Court Justice Leonard A. Giegerich held in January 1922 that Dowling's ruling applied equally to the committee and its members.[332] Ultimately, the Court of Appeals would affirm Appellate Division's decision,[333] but not until it had dealt with another of Recht's cases on behalf of the Soviets.

In the *Cibrario* case, Recht represented the RSFSR as plaintiff, seeking to recover funds allegedly embezzled by Jacques Cibrario. In the *Wulfsohn* case, Recht represented the RSFSR as defendant, fighting allegations that the Soviet government unlawfully confiscated some $4 million in furs belonging to Max Wulfsohn & Co., a New York City furrier. Notwithstanding the alleged value of the furs in question, Wulfsohn sought $516,785 in damages. On October 13, 1921, Wulfsohn obtained an attachment from New York Supreme Court Justice Vernon M. Davis against RSFSR funds in New York. Copies of the attachment were served on Recht and Rose Weiss, who denied they held any Soviet property or funds.[334]

With respect to Recht, the attachment order also demanded an examination, which Recht proceeded to challenge. On October 29, Justice George V. Mullan vacated the order to examine Recht, relying on his denial in open court that he had any Soviet funds. "The only evidence submitted by the plaintiff to impeach [Recht's denial] was that Mr. Recht has recently acted as attorney for the Russian Government," which he would not likely do without payment in hand,

---

331 *Id.* at 548-50.

332 Preobazhenski v. Cibrario, 192 N.Y.S. 275, 277 (1922).

333 RSFSR v. Cibrario, 235 N.Y. 255, 265 (1923).

334 *N.Y. Firm Sues Bolsheviki for Confiscated Furs*, N.Y. TRIB., Oct. 14, 1921, at 24.

Mullan said. "I think that is altogether too far-fetched and against it is the unequivocal word of an officer of this court." Mullan refused to quash the attachment order, however.[335]

Recht's next step was a motion to dismiss the complaint based on Appellate Division's disposition of the *Cibrario* case. Recht's argument was perfectly logical: Since the Soviet government could not bring a civil lawsuit in the New York courts because it was not recognized by the United States government, it seemed logical that the Soviet government could not be sued in the New York courts for the same reason. Unfortunately for Recht, logic was no match for precedent. "[The] immunity of a foreign government from suit is not based upon any absolute right by virtue of its sovereignty, but upon international comity," Justice Giegerich wrote in January 1922, "and as there is no international comity existing between the United States and the [Russian government], it has no valid claim to such immunity."[336]

Recht had also argued that, even without sovereign immunity, the Soviet government was a "body politic," not a foreign corporation, and if it were not recognized as a sovereign government, it was no legal entity at all and, therefore, not subject to suit. Giegerich made short work of that argument as well, quoting the state's Civil Practice Act to the effect that any corporation that is not a domestic corporation, that is, a New York corporation, is a "foreign corporation." He pointed out that the New York Court of Appeals had previously held that governments were inherently corporate and that even the United States government was a "foreign corporation." Accordingly, the Soviet government could be sued like any other foreign corporation in the New York courts.[337]

Again, Recht appealed to the New York Supreme Court's Appellate Division. In its opinion of July 21, 1922, the court noted that the furs were alleged to have been seized on June 25, 1920, and were valued at $127,935, not $4 million or even $500,000. It made no difference to the court, however, which expressed no interest in the merits of the claim. In an opinion written by Justice Adelbert P. Rich, and joined by Presiding Justice Abel E. Blackmar and Justices William J. Kelly, Walter H. Jaycox, and Addison J. Young, the court affirmed the trial court on essentially the same grounds.[338]

Recht appealed, placing both the *Wulfsohn* and *Cibrario* cases before the New York Court of Appeals. *Wulfsohn* was argued first, on November 22, 1922, and ultimately gave Recht one of his rare victories. Judge Charles Andrews wrote the

---

335 *Russian Soviet Lawyer Scores Court Victory*, BROOKLYN STANDARD UNION, Oct. 30, 1921, at 3.

336 Wulfsohn v. RSFSR, 192 N.Y.S. 282, 283-84 (Sup. Ct. 1922).

337 *Id.* at 284.

338 Wulfsohn v. RSFSR, 195 N.Y.S. 472 (App. Div. 1922).

majority opinion, reversing the decision below on January 9, 1923; only Judge Frederick E. Crane dissented, without a written opinion.

Both parties agreed that the RSFSR was a *de facto* government, that is, it had the power to enforce its authority within its own territory, that it was obeyed by the people over whom it ruled, and it was able to enforce its claims by military force. As such, Andrews wrote, "our courts are not competent to review [its actions]. They may not bring a foreign sovereign before our bar, not because of comity, but because he has not submitted himself to our laws. Without his consent, he is not subject to them."[339]

Andrews asserted that recognition was not a factor here. A recognized state could not be haled into U.S. courts without its consent; an unrecognized state poses the same problem, he wrote.

> In either case the hands of the state department would be tied. Unwillingly it would find itself involved in disputes it might think unwise .... The question is a political one, not confided to the courts but to another department of government. Whenever an act done by a sovereign in his sovereign character is questioned it becomes a matter of negotiation, or of reprisals or of war.[340]

Wulfsohn sought review in the U.S. Supreme Court, but it declined for lack of jurisdiction.[341]

Cibrario was argued on January 9, 1923, the very day that *Wulfsohn* was decided. This time, Recht would not be so fortunate. Again, Judge Andrews wrote the opinion, this time affirming the Appellate Division's holding that an unrecognized state could not bring a lawsuit in the New York courts. The opinion, however, had a very different tone.

Andrews began by pointing out that a recognized state's ability to bring a lawsuit in U.S. courts depended either on treaty or comity. For unrecognized governments, he wrote, the "rule of comity is our only guide." Andrews reasoned that "until such government is recognized by the United States, no such comity exists." Finding no precedent to the contrary, Andrews might have ended his opinion, leaving the Appellate Division's holding intact. But he seemed to go out of his way to hold that the public policy of the United States would trump comity in any event, at least with respect to the Soviets. "[It] is impossible to hold that to-day any such relations exist between the United

339 Wulfsohn v. RSFSR, 234 N.Y. 372, 375-76 (1923).

340 *Id.* at 376.

341 Wulfsohn v. RSFSR, 266 U.S. 580 (1924) (dismissing for want of jurisdiction).

States and Russia as call upon our courts to enforce rules in favor of the latter depending on the comity of nations."[342]

In 1948, Recht brought another high-profile lawsuit on behalf of Russian composers Dmitri Shostakovich, Sergei Prokofiev, Aram Khachaturian and Nicholai Miaskovsky against Twentieth Century-Fox Film Corp. seeking to enjoin the use of their music as background or incidental music in the defendant's film *The Iron Curtain,* which credited the composers for the music. For purposes of the litigation, the composers conceded that all the music involved was in the public domain and not protected by copyright law.

The essence of Recht's complaint was that the use of his clients' music in a motion picture whose theme was objectionable to them implicated such legal issues as libel, false endorsement, and moral or authors' rights. The court held there was no libel, and, anyway, injunctions are not available for libel; there was no endorsement implied by use of the music; and the existence of moral rights under American law was at best questionable. The motion was denied in all respects.[343]

Seymour Stedman

While Seymour Stedman undertook commercial cases throughout his career, that aspect of his practice was not nearly as extensive as was the case with Hillquit and Recht. In 1899, Stedman represented an allegedly corrupt executor in Quincy, Illinois,[344] and was listed as an incorporator for Thompson Ice Cream Co., Chicago, in 1900.[345] The same year, Stedman lost a tort case to recover damages in the death of one Kittie Landgraf, who jumped from a fourth-floor window when the building in which she worked caught fire. A jury found the building owners not liable for negligence, and the judgment was affirmed by the Appellate Court of Illinois.[346]

In 1914, Stedman represented John H. Coyne, one of the campaign managers for State Auditor James J. Brady, against whom Coyne filed a slander suit seeking $20,000 in damages. Coyne had been made a bank examiner upon Brady's appointment, with a comfortable $5,000 per year salary, all of which he lost three months later as a result of Brady's alleged manipulation. Coyne claimed that Brady, in ousting him from office, accused him of misappropriating campaign funds.[347]

---

342 RSFSR v. Cibrario, 235 N.Y. 255, 263-65 (1923).

343 Shostakovich v. Twentieth Century-Fox Film Corp, 80 N.Y.S.2d 575 (N.Y. Sup. Ct. 1948).

344 *Sent to the County Jail,* Grand Island (Neb.) REPUBLICAN, Dec. 28, 1899, at 1.

345 *New Illinois Corporations,* INTER OCEAN (Chi.), Jan. 12, 1900, at 9.

346 Landgraf v. Kuh, 90 Ill. App. 135 (1900).

347 *Coyne Charges Jugglery in Jobs by Auditor Brady,* CHI. TRIB., June 7, 1914, at 1.

Specifically, Stedman's declaration for Coyne alleged that Brady and two confederates circulated a false report that Coyne solicited and accepted $2,500 from the La Salle Street Trust & Savings Bank on behalf of Brady's campaign, but then kept the money for himself. Brady then used the false report as justification for ousting Coyne from his position in favor of a protégé of the bank's president.[348] The $20,000 in damages would be equivalent to four years' salary, according to the declaration.[349]

In the spring of 1915, Stedman represented one J. B. Hogarth in a proceeding before the public utilities commission seeking lower electricity rates.[350] That action was just part of a much larger case that Hogarth, a former superintendent of the Chicago Railway Co., who today might be called a "whistleblower," was trying to make against Sam Insull, head of both Commonwealth Edison and the Elevated Railways Collateral Trust. The essence of the case was that Insull, who also owned coal mines in southern Illinois, sold coal to both utilities at the city's expense. Hogarth, whom Stedman had represented *pro bono*, later withdrew his complaints, saying he was tired of pursuing them.

Stedman's reaction was philosophical. "I don't know a better argument for public ownership of public utilities than our experience the past year," he said. "Any public body capable of intelligent regulation is capable of intelligent management under which the enormous profits of the corporations would go to the people in better service."[351]

In any event, Stedman had yet another high-profile client to represent. Page Waller Eaton, a political lieutenant for Mayor William Hale "Big Bill" Thompson, resigned her position as superintendent of social surveys and charged that her superior, Louise Osborne Rowe, commissioner of public welfare, had been regularly extorting one-third of her $3,000 per year salary as "contributions" at the behest of Thompson's wife, who needed the money to support her sister. Stedman had advised Eaton to have someone witness the alleged payments, and it was one of the witnesses, Socialist Alderman William E. Rodriguez, who broke news of the scandal at a city council meeting.[352]

---

348 *Perjury Threatens Brady; Swore Wife Never Had Wed; Shown by His Affidavit,* CHI. EXAMINER, June 9, 1914, at 1.

349 *Says Banks "Paid for Examiners,"* CHI. TRIB., June 11, 1914, at 10.

350 *Commonwealth Edison Accused of Having "Yellow Dog" Fund,* DAY BOOK (Chi.), April 12, 1915, at 1; *How the Commonwealth Edison Stings the People with High Prices,* DAY BOOK (Chi.), April 28, 1915, at 31.

351 *Insull Enemy Says Good-By to Chicago,* DAY BOOK (Chi.), Jan. 26, 1916, at 1; *Eaglets,* CHI. EAGLE, Sept. 25, 1915, at 6.

352 *City Hall Woman Charges Graft; Names Sister-in-Law of Mayor,* CHI. TRIB., Feb. 22, 1916, at 1.

The *Tribune* covered the scandal as though little else—such as World War I and a presidential campaign—were going on. One front-page banner headline screamed "City Graft War Spreads," with the story below reporting "on seemingly reliable authority" that State's Attorney Maclay Hoyne was preparing a vigorous investigation with a view toward taking the matter to the grand jury. "Steddie" figured prominently in every story.[353] *The Day Book* was even more excited: "Great Stuff in Probe of Alleged Graft" headed its coverage of rival hearings before the Civil Service Commission and the City Council Committee on Civil Service. Testifying before the latter, Stedman opined that city hall should be cleaned out from top to bottom. *The Day Book*'s coverage of the scandal took the first four-and-a-half pages of the tabloid-sized paper; the two-inch story that followed concerned the controversy over warning Americans off armed merchant ships.[354]

The war had begun to compete with the scandal, at least in terms of placement and column inches in the *Tribune*.[355] Still, the "petticoat graft" hearings consumed as much or more space than any other single story in recent years. The question of Stedman's own integrity surfaced subtly at one commission session when commissioners elicited from an alleged eyewitness to a payoff from Eaton to Rowe that he was in business with Stedman and his brother in a firm created to manufacture and sell electrical devices.[356]

The city council committee hearings, however, came to an abrupt end when the committee voted to turn the whole matter over to Hoyne and the grand jury. Hoyne said he would take no action before the primaries coming up in a few days, but that afterward he would jump into the case without fear or favor.[357] Hoyne added the latter, no doubt, because the scandal had become hopelessly entangled in city politics. The *Day Book* reported that two days of hearings by two different bodies had produced no new information and implied some doubt as to whether the grand jury would ever get the case.[358]

Hearings before the Civil Service Commission in the so-called "Petticoat Scandal" continued on March 3, with Stedman making an impassioned plea on behalf of his client. "Salary splitting not only went on in the public welfare bureau," Stedman told commissioners, "but it is going on in many other departments of the City Hall." Chairman Percy Coffin took the testimony under

---

353 *City Graft War Spreads*, CHI. TRIB., Feb. 23, 1916, at 1.

354 *Great Stuff in Probe of Alleged Graft*, DAY BOOK (Chi.), Feb. 24, 1916, at 1.

355 *See Smash on to Verdun* and *Rowe Inquiry Bodies Starts*, CHI. TRIB., Feb. 24, 1916, at 1.

356 *Bank Is Cited To Give Eaton Cash Deposit Facts*, CHI. TRIB., Feb. 25, 1916, at 3.

357 *Women's Charges of City Pay Roll Graft Put Up to Grand Jury*, CHI. TRIB., Feb. 25, 1916, at 1.

358 *Graft Probes Yield Nothing to People*, DAY BOOK (Chi.), Feb. 25, 1916, at 1.

advisement and said a decision would be made in about a week.[359] In the end, the commission took almost two months to reach a verdict in favor of Rowe, concluding that Eaton, Stedman's client, had made up the extortion plot because she was disappointed in not getting Rowe's job.[360]

The next day, a Hoyne aide said Rowe would probably not be prosecuted, based on Eaton's own testimony that she thought the money was a loan. "[It] is obvious nobody can be indicted for giving or receiving a loan," the aide said. Stedman took the defeat philosophically. "You couldn't have expected the civil service commission to render any other verdict, considering they are appointed by the Mayor." Stedman said he was still contemplating a civil suit against Rowe for the return of the loan.[361] If he ever filed such a suit, it did not make the newspapers.

January 1921 found Stedman defending mobster "Mike de Pike" Heitler, who was charged with transporting and selling $200,000 worth of Kentucky bourbon in Chicago, [362] speaking on "Communism in the Middle Ages" at the Washington Park Forum,[363] and appealing the indictment of L. C. Russell before the U.S. Supreme Court.

Russell had been indicted for "unlawfully and corruptly endeavoring to influence" a juror who had supposedly been called for possible jury duty in the forthcoming trial of I.W.W. chief William D. "Big Bill" Haywood. L. C. Russell allegedly offered to pay money to the juror, also named Russell, in return for his vote to acquit. The defense had argued that because there was no evidence that the prospective juror would even be on the jury, the indictment was insufficient. The district court agreed and quashed the indictment, but the Supreme Court reversed, holding that the word "endeavor" was much broader than the technical word "attempt" and that the defendant's conduct satisfied the statutory requirement.[364]

Also in 1921, Stedman's law firm, now styled Stedman, Soelke & Johnson, won a reversal of the conviction of a man accused of taking indecent liberties with a young boy, based on the admission at trial of incompetent and prejudicial

---

359 *City Hall Graft on All Sides, Stedman Says,* CHI. TRIB., March 4, 1916, at 9; *More Split Salary Deals Are Threatened – Trial Ends,* DAY BOOK (Chi.), March 4, 1916, at 30.

360 *Decision for Mrs. Rowe in the "Maizie" Case,* CHI. TRIB., April 21, 1916, at 1.

361 *Hoyne to Drop Petticoat Quiz, Aid* [sic] *Indicates,* CHI. TRIB., April 22, 1916, at 15.

362 *$200,000 Booze Trial Jan. 25, Landis Order,* CHI. TRIB., Dec. 28, 1920, at 7.

363 *Women's Club Page,* CHI. TRIB., Jan. 16, 1921, at 59.

364 United States v. Russell, 255 U.S. 138 (1921). Haywood was later convicted of anti-war activities during the Red Scare and sentenced to 20 years in prison. While free pending appeal, he fled to Russia and spent the rest of his life there.

evidence at trial.[365] In early 1922, Stedman failed to overturn the criminal contempt conviction of two men accused of selling liquor in violation of the National Prohibition Act.[366] Later, he represented the losing side in an intra-Socialist Party dispute involving the Workers' Educational Association of Michigan.[367] And in mid-1923, the Stedman firm failed to win a new trial, on the ground of improper cross-examination, for a man convicted of converting property owned by the United States to his own use.[368]

In October 1922, a news report appeared stating that Stedman's law firm, now Stedman, Kessler & Dingle, had moved its offices to North Wells Street.[369] In November 1925, Stedman won the acquittal of book seller Adolphe Kroch, who was charged with selling obscene pictures. The paintings involved were 13 picture postcard reproductions of famous paintings in European art galleries. The warrant against him had been sworn out by an anti-obscenity activist, Mrs. William Harrison Cade. In dismissing the case, Chief Justice Harry Olson declared that he might as well order the Art Institute of Chicago closed as to place a ban on the pictures in dispute.[370] Stedman had several other reported civil and criminal cases as late as 1935.[371]

---

365 People v. Bouderioyni, 299 Ill. 96 (1921).

366 McGovern v. United States, 280 F. 73 (7th Cir. 1922), *cert. denied*, 259 U.S. 580 (1922).

367 Workers' Educ. Ass'n v. Renner, 218 Mich. 302 (1922).

368 Wild v. United States, 291 F. 334 (8th Cir. 1923).

369 Untitled, CHI. EAGLE, Oct. 21, 1922, at 4.

370 *Dismiss Obscene Picture Charge Against Kroch*, CHI. TRIB., Nov. 25, 1925, at 18.

371 *See, e.g.*, Eichler v. Hoeft, 163 Ill. App. 166 (1911)(losing a fraudulent conveyance case); McMechen v. Chicago, B. & Q. Ry. Co., 166 Ill. App. 150 (1911) (winning a procedural issue in a personal injury case); Collins v. Penn-Wyoming Copper Co., 203 F. 726 (1912) (losing a shareholder suit challenging the company's sale of assets); Tompary v. Giovan, 210 Ill. App. 174 (1918) (losing a building contract claim); Illinois ex rel. Hoyne v. Grant, 283 Ill. 391 (1918) (losing an attempt to oust certain trustees of the American Medical Association); Martin v. Drexel Ice Cream Co., 80 F.2d 768 (7th Cir. 1935) (winning a bankruptcy preferences case).

Chapter 3
Electoral Politics

Only two of our lawyers devoted a significant part of their careers to electoral politics. Socialist Morris Hillquit ran for Congress five times and for New York City mayor twice. He never won. Seymour Stedman first ran for Chicago city attorney in 1885 and lost. He actually won a seat in the Illinois House of Representatives in 1912 but was not reelected in 1914. The following year, he ran unsuccessfully for mayor of Chicago, and in 1920, he ran for vice president with Eugene Debs but lost again. Charles Recht devoted his nonlegal time to literary pursuits.

Morris Hillquit

Hillquit quickly rose in the ranks of the new Socialist Party, serving as the New York representative to the party's national committee from 1901 through 1906, and generally staking out a centrist position on the issues facing that fragile coalition.[1] In 1903, he published the first edition of his *History of Socialism in the United States*, with this optimistic conclusion: "New gains in members and supporters, new acquisitions in the press, and new victories at the polls are being reported steadily, and if all indications do not deceive, Socialism will be a potent factor in this country within a very few years."[2]

Still, socialism had yet to achieve full acceptance within the American political establishment. By 1904, Hillquit was back in court to protect the socialists' access to the ballot. Hillquit represented the Social Democratic Party in an action seeking to overturn the New York secretary of state's validation of the SDP's certificate of nomination for federal and state offices in the election of November 8, 1904.[3] The objection turned on whether the party's name was substantially the same as that of the traditional Democratic Party and calculated to confuse the voting public. The New York Supreme Court upheld the secretary's

---

[1] NORMA FAIN PRATT, MORRIS HILLQUIT: A POLITICAL HISTORY OF AN AMERICAN JEWISH SOCIALIST 56 (1979).

[2] MORRIS HILLQUIT, HISTORY OF SOCIALISM IN THE UNITED STATES 346 (1903) [hereinafter HISTORY 1903].

[3] In re Objections to the Original Certificate of Nomination of the Soc. Democratic Party of Candidates for Presidential Electors & for Governor & Other State Officers to Be Voted for at the Election to Be Held November 8, 91 N.Y.S. 941 (N.Y. Sup. Ct. 1904). The name "Social Democratic Party" was used in New York to preserve automatic ballot status, even though the New York party was now part of the relatively new Socialist Party of America.

determination that the names were not substantially the same and that no rights of the Democratic Party had been infringed.[4]

That decision was appealed, but there was no resolution before the election. The SDP ran a full slate of candidates in New York, all of whom lost in a Republican sweep. The decision was affirmed by Appellate Division in May 1905,[5] but reversed by the Court of Appeals.[6] That court acknowledged that the issue was academic with regard to the 1904 elections but said the issues presented could arise at some time in the future and needed to be addressed. The court based its reversal on both jurisdictional and substantive grounds, holding that the New York SDP must change its name to that of the national Socialist Party.[7] Within days after the ruling came down, the Socialist Labor Party filed a futile protest with the Board of Elections claiming use of the word "Socialist" infringed its own name.[8] The SLP petition was denied by the board, but the SLP vowed to take the matter to court.[9]

With that squabble done for the time being, Hillquit focused on the upcoming municipal elections, particularly attacking William Randolph Hearst, the newspaper magnate running on a "Municipal Ownership" platform. At a rally on October 15, 1905, to ratify its slate of candidates—headed by Algernon Lee for mayor—Hillquit declared: "Of all the frauds in this country, the municipal ownership fraud of Hearst is the worst. Municipal ownership operated by capitalists or run by political gangs would be the heaviest curse the country could have." He predicted that the Hearst campaign would take votes away from the Socialists. "Under normal circumstances," he said, "we would have expected a vote of 35,000 in this city this year .... [W]e do not anticipate the normal increase, if there is to be an increase at all, this year on account of the Hearst campaign."[10] And he was right. Lee polled only 11,817 votes. Hearst ran second to the winning Democratic candidate, incumbent Mayor George B. McClellan Jr.[11]

---

[4] *Id.* at 945.

[5] In re Objections to the Original Certificates of Nomination by the Soc. Democratic Party, 1905 N.Y. App. Div. LEXIS 2048*4 (May 1905).

[6] In re Social Democratic Party, 75 N.E. 415 (N.Y. 1905).

[7] *Id.* at 419.

[8] *Trouble Getting a Name,* N.Y. TIMES, Oct. 7, 1905, at 6.

[9] *De Leon Wing Will Fight,* N.Y. TRIB., Oct. 18, 1905, at 2.

[10] *Will Lose Votes to Hearst,* N.Y. SUN, Oct. 15, 1905, at 6; *Socialists Have Only Hisses for Hearst,* N.Y. TIMES, Oct. 16, 1905, at 2; *Call Other Parties Bad,* N.Y. SUN, Oct. 16, 1905, at 2.

[11] New York Historical Society, THE ENCYCLOPEDIA OF NEW YORK CITY (1995).

In 1906, Hillquit ran for public office for the first time. Hillquit saw running for office as an "inescapable part of the work of the active Socialist propagandist," and he would run twice for mayor of New York City and five times for Congress. In 1906, Hillquit ran for Congress from the Ninth Congressional District on the Lower East Side, which he poetically, if grimly, described in his letter accepting the nomination: "The Ninth Congressional District is the home of the tenements, pushcarts, paupers, and tuberculosis," he wrote. "Geographically it is located in the slums; industrially it belongs to the sweat-shop system; politically it is a dependency of Tammany Hall."[12]

In his autobiography, Hillquit describes the campaign as kindling "an indescribable fire of enthusiasm" in the district, highlighted by the presence of Russian author Maxim Gorky on the stump.[13] The newspapers covered his campaign perfunctorily, noting a dinner in his honor on October 16[14] and a parade through the district on October 27.[15] They also suggested that Hillquit loyalists spread false rumors that the Tammany candidate, Henry M. Goldfogle, would pull out of the race,[16] and touted Republican Charles S. Adler's prediction that Hillquit would carve out a share of Goldfogle's vote, leaving Adler to claim the win. Noting that Adler had been born and raised on the Lower East Side, the always-hostile *Tribune* pointedly reported that Hillquit and Goldfogle lived uptown. [17] In the end, Hillquit outpolled Adler but received less than half of Goldfogle's tally.[18] Hillquit attributed the loss to Goldfogle's appearance on the ballot under both the Democratic and Hearst's Independence League banners.[19]

As the Socialists regrouped to face the 1908 elections, it first appeared that Eugene Debs would "retire" as head of the ticket in favor of William Haywood,[20] but Haywood declined the nomination at the Socialist Party's Chicago convention in May.[21] Debs was nominated for the third time,[22] and Hillquit was philosophical about it. In announcing the premier issue of the socialist newspaper,

---

[12] MORRIS HILLQUIT, LOOSE LEAVES FROM A BUSY LIFE 107-108 (De Capo Press 1971) (1934) [hereinafter LOOSE LEAVES].

[13] *Id.* at 109.

[14] *Dinner to Morris Hillquit,* N.Y. TIMES, Oct. 17, 1906, at 10.

[15] *Fine Parade for Hillquit,* N.Y. SUN, Oct. 28, 1906, at 10.

[16] *Goldfogle Won't Quit,* N.Y. SUN, Oct. 22, 1906, at 2.

[17] *Adler Is Confident,* N.Y. TRIB., Oct. 16, 1906, at 3. At the time, Hillquit was living on 7th Ave. at 118th St. *Socialist Party,* N.Y. TRIB., Nov. 3, 1906, at 14.

[18] *City Vote for Congressmen,* N.Y. TIMES, Nov. 7, 1906, at 2.

[19] LOOSE LEAVES, *supra* note 12, at 114-115.

[20] *Debs To Go for Haywood,* N.Y. SUN, Jan. 23, 1908, at 2.

[21] *Socialists To Defy Police Censorship,* INTER-OCEAN (Chi.), May 13, 1908, at 5.

[22] *Debs Nominated; Charge Gag Rule,* CHI. TRIB., May 15, 1908, at 3.

The Call, and declaring it the chief instrument of the Socialist Party campaign, Hillquit seemed uncharacteristically—at least in public—skeptical of the party's chances at the national level. "Not that we expect to elect anyone," he wrote. "Our presidential candidate, and the candidate for the vice-presidency, are sure to go down to defeat, and yet the only campaign of serious results is the Socialistic campaign."[23]

At the local level, however, Hillquit was quite optimistic as he stood again for election to Congress from the Ninth District against incumbent Goldfogle. He later recalled that the situation and prospects for success appeared even brighter than in 1906. While the Hearst organization was still supporting Goldfogle, he conceded, the Socialist organization in the district had grown stronger over the past two years. "The campaign attracted greater interest than the preceding one among Socialists and sympathizers outside the district," he wrote. "Hordes of young intellectuals came down daily to speak at street corners, distribute campaign literature, canvass voters, and make themselves generally useful to headquarters."[24]

Hillquit expressed that optimism contemporaneously in an interview with the *Times*, predicting "with a great deal of assurance that he would be elected and take his seat as the first representative of the Socialist Party in Congress."[25] Hillquit's analysis was detailed, logical and persuasive, but wrong. He was defeated by 2,000 votes.[26] "Once more my election was confidently predicted," he wrote.

> Once more I failed. In the closing days of the campaign the Democratic camp became thoroughly panicky. A deal was speedily made with the local Republican machine, which openly urged its supporters to vote for Henry M. Goldfogle .... Mr. Goldfogle received all of the votes of the Democratic Party and the Independence League and most of the Republican votes.[27]

There would be a "first representative of the Socialist Party in Congress" six years hence. It would not be Morris Hillquit, but Meyer London, elected to represent the Twelfth District, redrawn to include most of the old Ninth, in 1914. London, like Hillquit, was a young socialist lawyer whom Hillquit described as "an idealist and a dreamer ... endowed with a peculiar unadorned eloquence" and

---

23 *Socialist Daily Tomorrow*, N.Y. SUN, May 29, 1908, at 3.

24 LOOSE LEAVES, *supra* note 12, at 115.

25 *Hillquit, Socialist, May Go To Congress*, N.Y. TIMES, Oct. 19, 1908, at 2.

26 *Socialists Hopeful*, N.Y. TRIB., Nov. 5, 1908, at 3.

27 LOOSE LEAVES, *supra* note 12, at 116.

one of the best-loved men on the East Side.[28] Hillquit would abstain from campaigning for office until 1916, concentrating on his legal practice, labor issues, and socialist activism.

Perhaps the most dramatic aspect of Hillquit's political life during this period was his battle with the Socialist Party's left wing, which supported the goals of the I.W.W. Pratt points out that Hillquit opposed the I.W.W. on at least four major points.

> First, the Wobblies wanted to organize industrywide unions for skilled and unskilled workers and in this way challenge the trade union leadership of the AFL .... Second, the IWW encouraged strikes and discouraged collective bargaining in the garment industry .... Third, the IWW advocated a syndicalist philosophy in which the trade union was to play a centra role in the organization of socialism. Fourth, the IWW's "tone" was militant and its rhetoric included concepts of violence which antagonized Hillquit who hoped to convince Americans that radical ideas were "respectable."[29]

Hillquit's support for a gradual and lawful transition to socialism brought him increasingly into conflict with the left wing of the party and especially with I.W.W. leader Big Bill Haywood. The battle grew in intensity during 1911 and 1912, notwithstanding Hillquit's debilitating tuberculosis, and culminated in Haywood's expulsion from the party in 1913.[30]

In the fall of 1916, Hillquit campaigned for a seat in Congress from the Twentieth District of New York. As he describes it in his autobiography, the Twentieth District was located on the upper East Side, "a comparatively new but typical working-class district ... very similar in ethnic composition and social character to the old Ninth ten years earlier, except that it contained a larger element of Irish, Italian, and German workers, and that the people were somewhat better situated economically."[31]

That constituency, now in the Twelfth District, was represented by Meyer London, who successfully ran for reelection in 1916. Hillquit said the New York Socialists concentrated their efforts on those two districts in the hope of electing both candidates. "It was a lively campaign," Hillquit wrote, "and was conducted largely in the same spirit of enthusiasm and hope as my earlier congressional campaigns." Unfortunately, Hillquit's efforts were not rewarded, and Republican Isaac Siegel won the day with 36.11% of the vote to Hillquit's

---

[28] *Id.*

[29] PRATT, *supra* note 1, at 99-100.

[30] *Id.* at 112.

[31] LOOSE LEAVES, *supra* note 12, at 117.

32.83%, a plurality of about 350 votes. Democrat Bernard Rosenblatt polled 31.06%. In his autobiography, Hillquit blamed his loss on a last-minute under-the-table deal between the old-line parties to snatch his defeat from the jaws of victory. He announced the final figures with tears in his eyes.[32]

On July 8, 1917, Hillquit was nominated to run for mayor of New York City by the Socialist Party in a convention at the Labor Forum in Manhattan. He would run on a platform that discouraged city employees from neglecting their duties by attending military camps, called for a union scale of wages and hours for city employees, and advocated a system of taxation that would "appropriate unearned income and readjust present inequalities in wealth." William Karlin, chairman of the resolutions committee, predicted "a vote of 150,000 for Hillquit because of the dissatisfaction on the part of many people with the war, which they consider unnecessary."[33] Hillquit himself said he accepted the nomination "with no illusions about my chances of election."[34]

That said, Hillquit confessed to being surprised by the way the Socialist campaign had "taken fire," attributable largely to "the all-absorbing issue of war and peace." In his acceptance speech, delivered at a mass meeting on September 23 in Madison Square Garden to ratify the Socialist candidates, Hillquit declared in no uncertain terms: "We are for peace .... Not warfare and terrorism, but Socialism and social justice will make the world safe for democracy."[35]

Hillquit's opponents were the incumbent John Purroy Mitchel, running as an independent after losing the Republican primary to William F. Bennett, and Democrat John F. Hylan, who had the support of the Hearst organization and Tammany Hall. Mitchel was outspoken in his support for the war, while Hillquit describes Hylan's position as "lukewarm" at best. Bennett was never a factor in the race.[36] Hillquit's opposition to the war was, of course, a principal focus of the forces arrayed against him, especially Theodore Roosevelt, a Mitchel supporter. "Morris Hillquit is pandering to treasonable and cowardly Americanism," Roosevelt charged, "to the pacifists, the pro-Germans, and the man who wishes Uncle Sam to negotiate an inconclusive peace. Yellow calls to yellow."[37]

---

[32] *Id.* at 117-18.

[33] *Morris Hillquit Named for Mayor by Socialist Party,* N.Y. TRIB., July 9, 1917, at 12.

[34] LOOSE LEAVES, *supra* note 12, at 182. *See also 10,000 Socialists Ratify Hillquit,* N.Y. SUN, Sept. 24, 1917, at 6.

[35] LOOSE LEAVES, *supra* note 12, at 183.

[36] *Id.* at 185-87.

[37] *Id.* at 193.

Then again, his opposition to the war drew considerable support, with ovations lasting up to 15 minutes, as well as hostility toward his opponents. One mid-October newspaper report spoke of Republican and Democratic speakers harassed by boos and jeering by Hillquit supporters at street gatherings on the East Side and in the Bronx, with one candidate opining that the crowds believed that if Hillquit should win, he would bring about peace. Tammany Hall, in particular, was said to be "gravely apprehensive" over the possible Socialist showing.[38]

In addition to the war, the Socialists opted to make woman suffrage a major issue in the campaign.[39] On October 10, Hillquit addressed an open letter to all his opponents, calling their attention to a referendum on the same ballot that would amend the New York state constitution to grant the franchise to women.

> If each of us will make an appeal, an earnest appeal, to his supporters to vote for woman suffrage, the measure will carry and we will be instrumental in righting the age-old wrong. Knowing the great importance of the direct and indirect issues involved in the city campaign, I assert that the issue of woman suffrage overshadows them all as a permanent measure of social justice and progress.[40]

All of the candidates ultimately backed the proposal, which carried by some 100,000 votes.

Apart from the war and woman suffrage, the campaign was punctuated by a number of smaller controversies that were featured prominently in the press and in Hillquit's autobiography. For example, when Hillquit sought to address the soldiers stationed at Camp Upton on Long Island—where his opponents maintained offices—he was denied on the ground that the Socialist Party was "subversive of military discipline." That led to an exchange of letters with the camp commander, but no opportunity to speak with the 60,000 soldiers there. Hillquit had to settle for an open letter to those soldiers eligible to vote in New York and the claim that he enjoyed widespread support there.[41] Other contretemps involved his accusation that Mayor Mitchel was using city buildings and parks

---

38 *Bronx Socialists Break Up Meetings of Old Parties,* N.Y. TRIB., Oct. 18, 1917, at 14; *Big Socialist Gains in the City Scare Tiger,* N.Y. SUN, Oct. 19, 1917, at 1.

39 *Hearst League Again in Politics,* N.Y. TIMES, Oct. 7, 1917, at 1.

40 LOOSE LEAVES, *supra* note 12, at 208-10.

41 *Id.* at 194-198. *Upton Ban Unfair Declares Hillquit,* N.Y. TRIB., Oct. 20, 1917, at 18; *Bell Tells Why He Barred Hillquit from Camp Upton,* N.Y. TRIB., Oct. 26, 1917, at 12; *Hillquit Claims Camp Upton Votes,* N.Y. TRIB., Oct. 28, 1917, at 13.

for his campaign, but refusing to extend the same courtesy to him,[42] and a brouhaha over his refusal to purchase liberty bonds, prompting one *Tribune* reader to say, "Every word he speaks in advocacy of his candidacy is a bullet in the back of an American soldier."[43]

As election day grew closer, various straw polls and wagering odds were showing Hillquit doing quite well, always coming in second to Mitchel or Hylan and always ahead of Bennett.[44] He picked up the endorsement of Dudley Field Malone, a former Collector of the Port of New York, confidant of President Wilson—with whom he broke over the suffrage issue—and an ardent supporter of the war effort.[45] He also won the support of Amos Pinchot, an activist of many political affiliations, who seemed more eager to vote against Mayor Mitchel than for Hillquit.[46] At the same time, Hillquit was attacked for his war stance by socialist Henry L. Slobodin, who called him a traitor to socialism, [47] as did a number of former members of the Socialist Party.[48] John A. Dyche, former secretary of the ILGWU, alleged that Hillquit received exorbitant fees to defend the labor leaders and engaged hooligans to disrupt political meetings.[49]

Even more vicious was the *Tribune*'s attack on "Morris Hillquit, a Jew, born at Riga, the Milwaukee of Russia," which depicted Hillquit in a German army helmet.[50] The *Tribune* also gave most of three columns to a reader's letter calling the socialist movement a "racial movement threatening Americanism by an alliance of Germans in the West with Russian Jews here."[51] And the last days of October featured another exchange of invective between Hillquit and

---

[42] LOOSE LEAVES, *supra* note 12, at 208-10; *Fight on Bennett in All Boroughs*, N.Y. TIMES, Oct. 6, 1917, at 1.

[43] LOOSE LEAVES, *supra* note 12, at 190-91; *Dealing with Mr. Hillquit*, N.Y. TRIB., Oct. 25, 1917, at 10; *Does Hillquit Want a German Peace?* N.Y. TRIB., Oct. 26, 1917, at 12.

[44] *See, e.g.*, *Mayor Gets 341, Hillquit 217 in Columbia Straw Vote*, N.Y. TRIB., Oct. 23, 1917, at 16; *Quotes Hylan Odds*, N.Y. TIMES, Oct. 23, 1917, at 6; *Mitchell Keeps Lead in Columbia Ballot*, N.Y. SUN, Oct. 24, 1917, at 7; *Hylan or Mitchel To Win Close Race*, N.Y. SUN, Oct. 31, 1917, at 7.

[45] *Dudley Field Malone Out for Hillquit*, N.Y. SUN, Oct. 27, 1917, at 5; *Anti-War Talks Are Featured at Hillquit Rally*, N.Y. TRIB., Oct. 30, 1917, at 14.

[46] *Amos Pinchot Joins Hillquit; Calls Mitchel "Rich Man's Mayor,"* N.Y. TRIB., Oct. 29, 1917, at 12; *Anti-War Talks*, *supra* note 495, at 14.

[47] *Hillquit Branded Socialist Traitor*, N.Y. SUN, Oct. 27, 1917, at 5.

[48] *Accuse Hillquit as Democracy's Foe*, N.Y. TIMES, Oct. 29, 1917, at 4.

[49] *New Attack on Hillquit*, N.Y. TIMES, Oct. 27, 1917, at 6.

[50] Herbert Flint, *Who's Who Against America: Morris Hillquit, of Riga*, N.Y. TRIB., Oct. 28, 1917, at 1.

[51] *Komerads and Comrades*, N.Y. TRIB., Oct. 31, 1917, at 10.

Theodore Roosevelt. Roosevelt referred to Hillquit as an "aid to the Prussianized autocracy of the Hohenzollerns." Roosevelt said he did not like the Hun outside our gates, "but I tell you I like him more than the Hun inside our gates."[52] Hillquit responded that Roosevelt "represents the very essence of the spirit of militarism and Prussianized autocracy in this country.

"The issue of patriotism is just now being furiously and shoutingly emphasized by that one source and fountainhead of all simon pure patriotism—Colonel Roosevelt," Hillquit told a crowd of 2,800 at the Brooklyn Academy of Music.

> Since the Colonel, in his capacity of political stump speaker for Mayor Mitchel, has been good enough to refer to me as an 'aid to Prussianized autocracy and the Hohenzollerns' and 'a Hun inside our gates,' may I invoke the privilege of political campaign repartee to say that I consider the Roosevelt type of politics as the most serious menace to American democracy and the Roosevelt agitation as the true 'enemy within.'[53]

The last week of the campaign featured more of the same kind of rhetoric, with pro-war socialists condemning Hillquit,[54] nonsocialist activists praising him,[55] and all of the candidates publicly predicting victory.[56] Hillquit recalled the moment in his autobiography: "About one week before the election, the feeling gained that I would carry the city," he wrote. "Consternation spread in the camps of my opponents and the New York Stock Exchange experienced a sinking spell avowedly caused by the menace of my candidacy."[57]

Election day finally arrived on November 6, and the preliminary count the next morning showed that Hylan had won with 297,000 votes, greater than the combined tallies of Mitchel at 150,000 and Hillquit at 141,000.[58] Hillquit increased

---

[52] *Roosevelt Calls Hillquit Ally of Hun,* N.Y. TRIB., Oct. 30, 1917, at 1.

[53] *T.R. Preaches War for Rich, Says Hillquit,* N.Y. TRIB., Oct. 31, 1917, at 16; *Hillquit Attacks T.R. and Is Booed,* N.Y. SUN, Oct. 31, 1917, at 7; *Meanness of Near Treason,* WALL ST. J., Nov. 1, 1917, at 1.

[54] *Socialists Applaud Mitchel Speakers,* N.Y. SUN, Nov. 3, 1917, at 4; *Hillquit Stole Socialist Party to Start Kaiser's Peace Drive,* N.Y. TRIB., Nov. 5, 1917, at 1; *Kaiserism, Not Socialism,* N.Y. TRIB., Nov. 2, 1917, at 8.

[55] *14,000 Cheer Hillquit and Early Peace,* N.Y. TRIB., Nov. 1, 1917, at 16; *Drift to Hillquit Seen at Camp Upton,* N.Y. TRIB., Nov. 4, 1917, at 10.

[56] *4 Candidates Predict Victory Next Tuesday,* N.Y. TRIB., Nov. 4, 1917, at 10.

[57] LOOSE LEAVES, *supra* note 12, at 204.

[58] *Hylan Elected with 297,000 Votes; Mitchel Gets 150,000; Hillquit 141,000; All Fusion Men Lose; Suffrage Wins,* N.Y. SUN, Nov. 7, 1917, at 1; *Hylan and Tammany Ticket Win; Suffrage Carries City and State,* N.Y. TRIB., Nov. 7, 1917, at 1. Final results put Hylan at 313,956, Mitchel at 155,497, Hillquit at 145,332, and Bennett at 56,438. LOOSE LEAVES, *supra* note 12, at 206.

the Socialist vote by nearly fivefold, uniformly in all five boroughs, over four years earlier. While Hillquit ran well ahead of his ticket, he would deny that the vote was a "mere personal triumph," calling it a "legitimate victory of the Socialist Party." Indeed, the Socialists did well across the board, seating ten state assemblymen, three aldermen, and a municipal court judge.[59]

In July 1918, Hillquit was again nominated to run for Congress from the Twentieth District. In keeping with the mainstream parties' practice of sponsoring coalition candidates in vulnerable districts, including Hillquit's,[60] in order to ensure a Socialist defeat, the Democrats endorsed the Republican incumbent Isaac Siegel to run against Hillquit again.[61] And once again, Socialist leaders were predicting victory.[62] The campaign was a bitter one, with the Socialists accused of a "colonizing scheme," that is, importing "a horde of foreign-born young men and women, the former long-haired and the latter short-haired" into Hillquit's district, even as he was recuperating at Saranac Lake.[63] Just two days before the election, Fiorello La Guardia, running for reelection to Congress in the Fourteenth District, denounced Hillquit as "the biggest asset the Kaiser ever had." The only reason Hillquit was not in prison, La Guardia said in response to a question, "is that he has been too shrewd." La Guardia accused Hillquit of hypocritically "harping about trusts" while he had a financial interest in Burns Brothers coal and ice dealers.[64]

When the results were tallied, all the Socialist candidates for Congress, including Hillquit, were defeated. Hillquit had been unable to campaign personally in his district because of his tuberculosis, but it seems unlikely that he could have overcome the fusion landslide. Overall, the Socialist vote in the state fell dramatically everywhere, with Siegel outpolling Hillquit 60.9% to 38.8%.[65]

In the spring of 1920, Hillquit's attention turned again to electoral politics. In the spring, Hillquit focused on the forthcoming presidential election, endorsing Debs for the Socialist Party nomination in a March 16 telegram to the party's national committee. "The Socialist party would destroy its moral integrity if it

---

[59] *Heaviest Vote Brings Joy to Socialist Camp,* N.Y. TRIB., Nov. 8, 1917, at 5; LOOSE LEAVES, *supra* note 34, at 208.

[60] *Plan to Keep Congress Free of Socialists,* N.Y. TRIB., May 26, 1917, at 10.

[61] *Republicans Will Join with Tammany to Beat Socialists,* N.Y. TRIB., July 31, 1918, at 6.

[62] *Socialists Hope to Send London and 2 More to Congress,* N.Y. TRIB., Sept. 16, 1918, at 5.

[63] *Socialists Accused of Colonizing,* N.Y. TRIB., Oct. 30, 1918, at 14.

[64] *La Guardia Calls Hillquit Greatest Asset of Kaiser,* N.Y. TRIB., Nov. 4, 1918, at 3.

[65] *All Socialists Defeated Here for Congress,* N.Y. Trib., Nov. 6, 1918, at 2; *Smith Leads in New York by 265,661,* N.Y. TRIB., Nov. 7, 1918, at 4; MICHAEL J. DUBIN, UNITED STATES CONGRESSIONAL ELECTIONS, 1788-1997: THE OFFICIAL RESULTS OF THE ELECTIONS OF THE 1ST THROUGH 105TH CONGRESSES (1998).

failed to nominate Debs at this time," he wrote. "Debs would not be true to himself and his inspiring record if he refused to make the fight at this time." The phrase "at this time," which Hillquit repeats in his message, seems to refer to the fact that Debs was then serving his ten-year sentence for violating the Espionage Act in a speech at Canton, Ohio.[66] Hillquit was also named to a special committee to meet with President Wilson at the White House to plead for the release of Debs and others convicted under the Espionage Act.[67]

The party's national convention was held in New York City in May; Hillquit was named chairman of the platform committee. As a joke, he suggested the convention nominate Assembly Speaker Thaddeus C. Sweet for president and Assemblyman Louis A. Cuvillier for vice president. Both had been instrumental in the ouster of the five Socialists from the New York legislature in 1919.[68] "I think we should nominate the man who had done most for Socialism within the last year," Hillquit quipped, adding that Attorney General A. Mitchell Palmer—infamous for his raids against leftists—might be a good second choice for vice president.[69]

In his keynote address on May 8, however, Hillquit was deadly serious, with a scathing attack on President Wilson:

> Wilson, the pacifist, drew us into the world's most frightful war. Wilson, the anti-militarist, imposed conscription upon a country in war and urged universal military training, a large standing army, and a huge navy in peace. Wilson, the Democrat, arrogated to himself autocratic powers grossly inconsistent with republican forms of government. [70]

As to the likely nominee for president, Hillquit declared,

> We have but one candidate, the man of biggest heart, the finest soul and the most humane spirit in America, the saint in prison garb—Eugene V. Debs. Our candidate is in jail, but millions of citizens know that for the good of the country he should be free. The potential candidates of the old parties are all at large, but millions of citizens feel that for the good of mankind, some of them should be locked up.[71]

---

66 *Hillquit to Support Debs,* N.Y. TRIB., March 17, 1920, at 7. *See* Part II.

67 *Socialists Will Parade in Effort to Free Debs,* N.Y. TRIB., March 21, 1920, at 11.

68 *See* Part II.

69 *Hillquit Suggests Sweet as Nominee of Socialist Party,* N.Y. TRIB., May 7, 1920, at 4.

70 *Socialists Cheer Debs 10 Minutes,* N.Y. TRIB., May 9, 1920, at 1.

71 *5,000 Socialists Hail Name of Their Party Leader, Debs,* N.Y. DAILY NEWS, May 10, 1920, at 2; *6,000 Socialists Cheer for Debs,* N.Y. TIMES, May 10, 1920, at 1.

On May 13, the convention unanimously nominated Debs for president and Seymour Stedman for vice president.[72]

If the candidate enjoyed near universal support, the platform was an altogether different matter. Hillquit thwarted an early effort from the leftists to refer the platform that he had presented to a new, presumably more left-wing committee. According to press accounts, considerable bitterness arose during the debate on the procedures to be followed, though the Hillquit faction claimed to have a clear majority. They said they intended to see to it that no plank was adopted that would suggest that the party advocated the violent overthrow of the government.[73] The following day, the centrists defeated another motion to amend the platform to call for creation of a dictatorship of the proletariat.[74] On May 13, the convention adopted Hillquit's platform.[75]

With the national campaign off to a positive start, at least from Hillquit's perspective, the now perennial candidate for Congress turned to his own electoral prospects. Once again, Republicans and Democrats teamed up to put a Fusion candidate on the Twentieth District ballot to ensure another Socialist defeat.[76] And once again, Hillquit's opponent would be incumbent Isaac Siegel, a Republican who would run on the Democratic ticket as well.[77]

Both Hillquit and Debs were defeated in November, with Hillquit polling 8,454 votes to Siegel's 11,145. Debs's total vote was 918,000, compared with 898,481 in 1912, and 1920 would be his last run for the office.[78] Hillquit, though, had one more campaign, running for mayor again in the special election of 1932, occasioned by the resignation of Mayor James J. Walker. The Socialist Party nominated him on September 15, 1932, in a city convention at the Rand School. The platform called for an appropriation of $75 million for employment relief, for publicly owned and operated utilities, and against any pay cut for city employees receiving $4,000 or less.[79] Democrat John P. O'Brien was elected with

---

[72] *Debs Nominated Amidst Ovation of 25 Minutes,* N.Y. TRIB., May 14, 1920, at 1.

[73] *'Mild' Socialists Win on Platform,* N.Y. TIMES, May 11, 1920, at 3.

[74] *Radical Socialists Element Defeated on Platform Vote,* N.Y. DAILY NEWS, May 12, 1920, at 10; *Socialists Reject Plank of Radicals,* N.Y. TRIB., May 12, 1920, at 1.

[75] *Debs Nominated, supra* note 522, at 1.

[76] *Fusion to Defeat Socialists for Congress Urged,* N.Y. TRIB., July 26, 1920, at 3.

[77] *Fusion Sought to Beat Socialists in Race for Congress,* N.Y. TRIB., Aug. 11, 1920, at 3; *Complete List of Nominees for Congress in New York,* N.Y. EVE. WORLD, Sept. 15, 1920, at 3; *Organizations Win Nearly All in Primaries,* N.Y. TRIB., Sept. 15, 1920, at 3.

[78] *Vote for Congress in New York City,* N.Y. TRIB., Nov. 5, 1920, at 2; *Socialists Tell Why That Party Gained No More,* N.Y. HERALD, Dec. 20, 1920, at 6.

[79] *Socialists Name Hillquit for Mayor,* N.Y. DAILY NEWS, Sept. 16, 1932, at 48.

a popular vote of over one million; Hillquit polled third with nearly a quarter million votes.[80] It was the largest vote ever cast for a Socialist in New York City.[81]

Seymour Stedman

Seymour Stedman began his career as a Democrat, but left that party in 1894 to protest the Cleveland Administration's sending troops to put down the great strike of Eugene Debs's American Railway Union. Stedman briefly joined the People's Party and ran for Chicago city attorney in 1885.[82] The party's platform focused on the devolution of authority from the state legislature to the city to manage public works projects of all sorts, along with a call for public ownership of "[any] general service which the people find to have become a monopoly."[83]

After the People's Party was solidly trounced in the April 2 election,[84] Stedman maintained a busy speaking schedule[85] although the party itself was torn by internal dissention.[86] At the People's Party convention in September 1895, Stedman offered himself as a candidate to fill a judicial vacancy, but withdrew on account of his personal disapproval of the platform.[87] The following year, at the People's Party convention in St. Louis, Stedman declared his support for Debs as the party's presidential candidate, but said he would support William Jennings Bryan if Debs declined the nomination, putting him in the so-called "middle of the road" camp.[88]

There were two contesting Chicago delegations at the convention, which, at one point, led to a fist fight between Stedman and the leader of the opposing delegation. Initially, the national committee offered each member of both

---

80 *O'Brien Elected, but M'Kee Gets 100,000 Votes,* N.Y. DAILY NEWS, Nov. 9, 1932, at 2; *New York City Special Election,* Nov. 8, 1932, Our Campaigns, https://www.ourcampaigns.com/RaceDetail.html?RaceID=79428.

81 *Morris Hillquit, Socialist Party Leader, Is Dead,* BROOKLYN TIMES UNION, Oct. 9, 1933, at 1.

82 *Holmes for Mayor,* CHI. TRIB., Feb. 23, 1895, at 6; *Chicago's Populist Ticket,* N.Y. TIMES, Feb. 23, 1895, at 1. *See also People's Party Ticket Ratified,* CHI. TRIB., March 15, 1895, at 4.

83 *Chicago Populists,* MODERN LIGHT (Columbus, Kan.), March 14, 1885, at 2.

84 *Swift Is A Winner,* CHI. TRIB., April 3, 1895, at 1.

85 *See, e.g., Metal Workers' Outing,* CHI. CHRON., Aug. 26, 1895, at 2; *Feast of Labor Men,* CHI. CHRON., Sept. 1, 1895 (in which Stedman is prematurely identified as "formerly connected with the People's Party").

86 *See, e.g., Debs is Their Idol,* CHI. TRIB., Sept. 8, 1895, at 4; *Populists Have a Row,* CHI. TRIB., Sept. 24, 1895, at 1.

87 *Debs Is Their Idol, supra* note 86, at 4.

88 *Pulling Three Ways,* INTER OCEAN (Chi.), July 20, 1896, at 1.

delegations half a vote, but later voted to seat the pro-Bryan delegation.[89] Stedman had collected more than 400 written pledges for Debs out of the 1,300 delegates, however, and the Bryan campaign offered to nominate Debs for vice president. That offer was refused by the Debs camp, including Stedman and Victor Berger, and in the end, Debs withdrew from the contest.

Even so, Stedman would find himself embroiled in the schism that plagued the People's Party throughout the summer and fall of 1896. In late August, for example, Stedman participated in an effort by the "middle of the road" populists in Illinois to convene the following month to nominate a state ticket and presidential electors. They charged that a convention held in Springfield on August 12 by the so-called "fusion populists" was a betrayal of the party and its principles.[90] In fact, the dispute got so hot that a number of the "middle of the road" populists threatened to reject Bryan altogether.[91] The animosity in local party politics remained virulent until late October,[92] but the fusion faction eventually emerged on top.[93] Stedman had already begun stumping with Debs, or as Debs's surrogate, in support of Bryan's unsuccessful campaign against William McKinley in the November 1896 election.[94]

During the first half of 1897, Stedman continued his active participation in People's Party politics even as he maintained his law practice. In April, for example, Stedman's name appears on a tentative judicial ticket presented by the party's executive committee. He was also appointed to a committee to assess the prospects of uniting all pro-silver forces under the People's Party banner.[95] Within days, however, any effort toward unity had collapsed in

---

89 *Id. See also National Committee Work,* KANSAS CITY STAR, July 22, 1896, at 8; *Both Claim a Majority,* DECATUR (ILL.) HERALD, July 22, 1896, at 1; *Two Conventions,* RUTLAND (VT.) DAILY HERALD, July 22, 1896, at 1; and *Populist National Convention,* GAZETTE (Stevens Point, Wis.), July 29, 1896, at 8.

90 *Populists Call State Convention,* CHI. TRIB., Aug. 29, 1896, at 8. "Fusion" referred to the alliance of Democrats who backed a silver standard and the pro-Bryan populists. *Threaten to Shelve Bryan,* INTER OCEAN (Chi.), Sept. 15, 1896, at 3.

91 *Threaten to Shelve Bryan,* INTER OCEAN (Chi.), Sept. 15, 1896, at 3.

92 *See On the Official Ballot,* CHI. TRIB., Oct. 20, 1896, at 12; *People's Party Faction Fight,* Chi. Chron., Oct. 20, 1896, at 4; *Political Contests are Heard,* CHI. CHRON., Oct. 21, 1896, at 4.

93 *See Factions Come to Terms,* CHI. CHRON., Oct. 23, 1896, at 3; *Cook County Nominees,* CHI. CHRON., Oct. 24, 1896, at 11; *Five Refuse to Resign,* INTER OCEAN (Chi.), Oct. 25, 1896, at 3.

94 *Eugene V. Debs on the Stump,* CHI. CHRON., Oct. 12, 1896, at 2; *Breath of Anarchy,* INDIANAPOLIS J., Nov. 2, 1896, at 8; *Debs Failed to Come,* INDIANAPOLIS NEWS, Nov. 2, 1896, at 5. *See also* William M. Feigenbaum, *Seymour Stedman: Socialist Candidate for Vice-President,* NEW AGE (Buffalo), June 17, 1920 (reprint at 2).

95 *People's Party Caucus,* CHI. CHRON., April 27, 1897, at 7.

factional chaos.[96] Several judicial tickets were put forward; Stedman's appeared on the "Silver Anti-Machine Association" ticket, but none of the others.[97]

By mid-year, however, Stedman's political career began to take a dramatic turn. On June 18, 1897, Debs's American Railway Union convention—actually a membership meeting of remnants of the dying union—changed the organization's name to the Social Democracy of America and merged with the Brotherhood of the Cooperative Commonwealth, an even more radical organization that sought to establish socialist colonies in Colorado. A colonization committee spent the better part of a year trying unsuccessfully to make that happen.

Party work and public speaking occupied the rest of Stedman's year. In early September, for example, he offered a speech on the evolution of what he called "the Debs movement" from and through the labor unions to take a "commanding position as the most potent factor in the social and political economics of today." He took particular aim at the "coal barons," accusing them of converting human beings into beasts of burden and treating them even worse.[98] He also spoke extensively on the value of socialism, especially versus the "single tax" that he had previously endorsed.

At one meeting on September 26, Stedman addressed a local branch of the Social Democracy on "The Aims of Social Democracy."[99] That same night, Stedman advocated for socialism in a formal debate, "Resolved, That the Single Tax Will Solve the Labor Question." Stedman said that equal land apportionment would benefit only those who had enough money to improve their land, leaving those without funds worse than paupers.[100] By contrast, he said, government ownership of railroads and telegraph and the establishment of industrial equity would give employment to everyone, rich or poor.[101]

In November, Stedman presided over a convention of mostly labor union officers and representatives meeting to advocate adoption of the initiative and referendum in state and municipal governance. In addressing the convention, Stedman blamed state legislatures for most of the ills of the day and said the referendum would go further toward solving that problem than any other instrument.[102] The following day, the convention voted to organize permanently

---

96 *Silver Forces in a Row,* CHI. CHRON., April 30, 1897, at 4; *Local News Notes,* CHI. CHRON., May 1, 1897, at 7.

97 *Aspire to be Judges,* CHI TRIB., May 2, 1897, at 14.

98 *Talks of Social Democracy,* CHI. CHRON., Sept. 6, 1897, at 5.

99 *Quiets a Rude Disturber,* CHI. CHRON., Sept. 27, 1897, at 3.

100 *Merits of the Single Tax,* CHI. TRIB., Sept. 27, 1897, at 3.

101 *Debate Single Tax Theory,* CHI. CHRON., Sept. 27, 1897, at 12.

102 *Favor Direct Laws,* CHI. CHRON., Nov. 19, 1897, at 4.

on a nonpartisan basis and adopted a platform calling for an amendment to the Illinois constitution to implement the principles of direct legislation. Stedman was elected one of ten vice presidents to serve on the organization's executive committee.[103]

By 1898, a split had emerged in the Social Democracy of America between those still favoring colonization and those who had become disillusioned with the idea and had turned to direct political action. The divide became increasingly intense, reaching its apotheosis at the convention of June 7, 1898.[104] There were 70 delegates at the convention, with Debs presiding. The colonizers had chosen a number of anarchists, including Emma Goldman and Lucy Parsons—who, the previous year, had been barred from speaking at a labor-organized meeting on the Spanish issue[105]—to capture the meeting. Debate lasted until 2:30 a.m., when the convention voted 53-37 in favor of the colonizers. Most of the 37 who voted against—including Debs, Stedman, and Victor Berger—withdrew from the convention, held their own caucus, and launched the Social Democratic Party of America. Jesse Cox of Illinois was named temporary chairman, and William Mailly of Tennessee was named temporary secretary. Debs, Stedman, Berger, Cox, and Fred Heath of Wisconsin were named to the executive board.[106]

A party platform announced on June 11, 1898, called for vigorous use of the ballot to remedy all labor troubles; public ownership of all monopolies, railroads, telegraph lines, and mines; introduction of the initiative and referendum; abolition of war; women's rights; nationalization of farm mortgages; improvement of farm lands by use of national credit; and uniform rates for the transportation of grain.[107]

On June 16, Stedman and 32 others signed a letter advising all members of the Social Democracy about the breakaway Social Democratic Party of America. The letter revealed that Debs was too ill to attend the formative meetings of the new party, though he supported its aims, and his brother Theodore was chosen temporary national secretary and treasurer. Stedman was identified as secretary of the executive board. The letter admitted that the party was "entirely without funds and require[s] office equipment, printing, supplies, etc.," and urged members to contribute. Otherwise it struck a highly optimistic note: "Never was the outlook more promising," he wrote. "East,

---

103 *Direct Rule Plan Formed*, CHI. CHRON., Nov. 20, 1897, at 10.

104 Feigenbaum, *supra* note 94 (reprint at 3).

105 *Mrs. Parsons Is Muzzled*, CHI. TRIB., June 14, 1897, at 11.

106 *Debs Goes Out: Social Democracy is Split into Two Factions*, CHI. CHRON., June 12, 1898; Feigenbaum, *supra* note 94 (reprint at 3).

107 *The Platform* (ASSOC. PRESS), L.A. TIMES, June 12, 1898, at 12.

West, North, and South, comrades are with us and ringing messages of approval cheer us on the course we have taken." [108]

In August, Debs, Berger, and Stedman incorporated the new party and began to develop a campaign strategy of fielding candidates where it could and otherwise cooperating with middle-of-the-road populists. Ultimately, the party envisioned a national ticket with Debs as candidate for the presidency.[109] To that end, Stedman went on the stump, speaking, for example, at the establishment of a Social Democratic club in Oshkosh, Wisconsin,[110] and at a demonstration at the Bohemian Gymnasium in St. Louis.[111] Along with Victor Berger, Stedman traveled to Kansas City in December to monitor the American Federation of Labor convention and push for more recognition from that organization.[112]

The Social Democratic Party's national convention in Indianapolis on March 6, 1900, had two important objectives: the selection of candidates for president and vice president in the election of November 1900, and consideration of an overture from the Socialist Labor Party to merge. After first declining the presidential nomination on the ground of ill health, Debs had a change of heart and accepted the nomination for president. In an effort to achieve a modicum of unity, Job Harriman of California's SLP was nominated as vice president.[113] The SLP had itself undergone a devastating schism, and the "Kangaroo" faction that had convened in Rochester, New York, in January that year sent a delegation led by Morris Hillquit to the SDP convention in Indianapolis to negotiate the proposed merger. Stedman was appointed to a committee to work on the amalgamation, but, like others in the SDP leadership, was not terribly enthusiastic about the possibility of losing control.[114]

The committees on union met in New York on May 20, 1900, but made little or no progress.[115] During the summer, Stedman campaigned to raise money for the Socialist newspaper *Appeal to Reason* published in Girard, Kansas;[116] spoke on the new social democracy in Michigan in connection of the formation of a

---

[108] Open Letter to Members of the Social Democracy of America, June 16, 1898, APPEAL TO REASON July 2, 1898, at 4.

[109] *Plan a New County Ticket,* CHI. TRIB., Aug. 27, 1898, at 7.

[110] *Social Democrats in Oshkosh,* OSHKOSH NORTHWESTERN, Oct. 22, 1898, at 6.

[111] *Campaign Notes,* ST. LOUIS GLOBE-DEMOCRAT, Oct. 30, 1898, at 13.

[112] *Socialists Not Satisfied,* BOSTON GLOBE, Dec. 14, 1898, at 7.

[113] G.B. Benham, *Unity Achieved,* THE CLASS STRUGGLE, March 17, 1900, at 1, 4. *See also The Social Democrats,* INDIANAPOLIS J., March 6, 1900, at 2; *Eugene Debs Party,* PITTSBURGH POST-GAZETTE, March 7, 1900, at 4; *Debs the Candidate,* BALT. SUN, March 7, 1900, at 2; and *Socialist Parties Unite,* INTER OCEAN (Chi.), March 8, 1900, at 6.

[114] Pratt, *supra* note 1, at 37 (1979).

[115] *Socialists Unite!,* HAVERHILL SOCIAL DEMOCRAT, May 26, 1900, at 1.

[116] *Appeal Army Helpers,* APPEAL TO REASON, June 23, 1900, at 4.

new SDP branch there;[117] and addressed a congressional nominating committee of Fort Wayne, Indiana, socialists.

By August, the SDP found itself with competing campaign committees, one headed by Stedman, the other by Thomas J. Morgan. The split was said to have been caused by a dispute as to who would handle the campaign funds.[118] It hardly mattered. On November 6, Debs finished fourth, with 88,000 popular votes, less than half the votes garnered by the Prohibition Party.[119]

Almost immediately, the fragile alliance between Debs and Harriman for the election fell apart. Debs supporters convened in Chicago on January 15, 1901, ostensibly to unite the two factions; Stedman was chosen to chair the convention and also to serve on its organization and constitution committees. But the Harriman faction sent a letter protesting the convention itself and threatening to leave the party altogether if its actions were not referred to referendum. The letter was widely construed as insulting to Debs, whose supporters accused him of trying to injure the Debs cause during the campaign. Debs said he was tempted to scuttle the amalgamation: "If the 'kangaroos' desire harmony, as they profess to do, why do they insult us in this manner?" Nevertheless, he urged every effort to try to reconcile the split.[120]

That opportunity arrived with the so-called Unity Convention that opened in Indianapolis on July 29, 1901. Of the 125 delegates, 70 came from Hillquit's Springfield faction, as the SLP Kangaroos were renamed, with almost 5,000 votes, while 47 represented the Debs-Berger-Stedman SDP, with 1,300 votes. Notwithstanding the discrepancy, Hillquit called for equal representation on the various committees. The Socialist Party of America was born.[121]

During the summer of 1902, Stedman wrote a lengthy essay for the *International Socialist Review* defending the socialists' practice of making "immediate demands" on the capitalist establishment for reforms against other leftists who saw such demands as abandonment of the long-term goal of replacing the capitalist system with a socialist one.[122] This had been one of the key issues debated in

---

[117] *No Show for Bryan*, NEWS-PALLADIUM (Benton Harbor, Mich.), Aug. 3, 1900, at 2.

[118] *Socialists Are at War*, CHI. AM., Aug. 8, 1900. In July, Stedman had declined renomination to the national executive board in order to dedicate himself as secretary of the Debs campaign committee. *Debs Declines*, SOCIAL DEMOCRATIC HERALD, Aug. 18, 1900, at 4.

[119] David Leip, *1900 Presidential Election Results*, DAVE LEIP'S ATLAS OF U.S. PRESIDENTIAL ELECTIONS, https://uselectionatlas.org/.

[120] *Debs for Harmony*, INTER OCEAN (Chi.), Jan. 16, 1901, at 5. *See also* A.S. Edwards, *The Social Democratic Party of America Stands for Consolidation of Socialists*, SOCIAL DEMOCRATIC HERALD, Jan. 26, 1901, at 1.

[121] PRATT, *supra* note 1, at 40-44.

[122] Seymour Stedman, *Immediate Demands*, Southwestern Advocate, July 24, 1902, at 1.

the 1901 Unity Convention,[123] and here Stedman stood foursquare with Hillquit in supporting "immediate demands." [124]

The following year, Stedman accepted the Socialist nomination for circuit court judge.[125] Like other Socialists, however, he failed to receive the endorsement of the Chicago Bar Association, earning only six of 655 votes cast.[126] He also maintained a steady speaking schedule,[127] including another debate with single taxers toward the end of the year.[128] He also represented the interests of streetcar employees in sweeping litigation involving the Chicago Union Traction Co.[129]

Election year 1904 once again saw Stedman debating against single taxers[130] and in support of municipal ownership.[131] He addressed a mass meeting to support striking Colorado miners[132] and urged a program to free the "farmer proletariat" from the "warehouse, grain elevator and packing-house exploiters."[133]

When the Socialist Party of America convened its nominating convention in May in Louisville, Stedman served on the rules committee; as expected, Debs was again nominated for president, this time with New York's Benjamin Hanford as the vice-presidential candidate.[134] Later that month, Stedman led Cook County Socialists in endorsing the national party platform and opposing an alternative declaration of principles posed by more radical members. The vote was 266-85 in favor of the moderates.[135]

---

123 PRATT, *supra* note 1, at 41-42.

124 Stedman, *supra* note 122.

125 *Socialists' Judicial Ticket*, CHI. TRIB., May 3, 1903, at 7.

126 *Lawyers Choose List of Judges*, CHI. TRIB., May 9, 1903, at 1.

127 *See, e.g., Future Events*, JANESVILLE (Wisc.) DAILY GAZETTE, April 3, 1903, at 5; *Literary Notes*, FALL RIVER (Mass.) DAILY HERALD, Oct. 5, 1903, at 4; *To Advocate Municipal Ownership*, INTER OCEAN (Chi.), Oct. 29, 1903, at 3.

128 *Announcements*, CHI. TRIB., Dec. 20, 1903, at 7.

129 *Order of Court Stirs Traction Men*, INTER OCEAN (Chi.), Dec. 19, 1903, at 3; *City in No Fear of Musty Files*, INTER OCEAN (Chi.), Dec. 26, 1903, at 5.

130 *A War of Ideas*, TIMES (Streator, Ill.), Jan. 5, 1904, at 5; *They are Strong Debaters*, TIMES (Streator, Ill.), Jan. 6, 1904, at 1.

131 *Debate on City Ownership*, CHI. TRIB., Jan. 20, 1904, at 4.

132 *Labor Massmeeting Is Called*, CHI. TRIB., Feb. 14, 1904, at 6; *In the World of Trade and Industry*, INTER OCEAN (Chi.), Feb. 14, 1904, at 30; *Aid for Colorado Miners*, CHI. TRIB., Feb. 15, 1904, at 8.

133 *Should Assist the Farmer Proletariat*, APPEAL TO REASON, April 23, 1904, at 1.

134 *Socialists May Bid for the Negro Vote*, COURIER-JOURNAL (Louisville, Ky.), May 2, 1904, at 4.

135 *Socialists Stand by Party*, CHI. TRIB., May 23, 1904, at 3.

That vote was just the beginning of yet another split in Chicago's socialist ranks. On May 29, the local party expelled its anarchist members at its nominating convention. "The whole trouble came about over the platform adopted at the recent national convention," Stedman, who chaired the convention and was nominated for state's attorney, told the press. "The platform was adopted unanimously, but later several members of the county central committee and some of the national delegates called a meeting and drafted a new platform. They had no authority to do this and their action was ignored."[136]

The next day, Stedman traveled to Davenport, Iowa, to publicly debate local Republican Charles Grilk on whether the "welfare of the human race requires the adoption of the principles of Socialism."[137] When the campaign got underway in the fall, Stedman traveled throughout Illinois, Iowa, and Missouri, on the stump for Debs and other Socialists.[138] Debs ran third in the November 8 election, earning more than 400,000 popular votes, compared with 88,000 in the previous election.[139] The Socialists were elated with the results, nationally and in Illinois.[140] Within a couple of weeks, however, Stedman was back at his law practice[141] and the lecture circuit.[142]

In September 1905, Stedman again became a Socialist Party candidate for the county judiciary. Fewer than 3,000 people voted in the primary, though officials

---

136 *Socialist Party Will Oust "Reds,"* WASH. TIMES, May 29, 1904, at 18; *Select a County Ticket,* CHI. TRIB., May 30, 1904, at 3.

137 *Is Socialism What We Need?*, QUAD-CITY TIMES (Davenport, Iowa), May 31, 1904, at 9. *See also To Debate Socialism,* DAILY TIMES (Davenport, Iowa), May 24, 1904, at 5; *Will Debate on Socialism,* QUAD-CITY TIMES (Davenport, Iowa), May 29, 1904, at 8; *Democrat to Preside,* DAILY TIMES (Davenport, Iowa), May 30, 1904, at 6.

138 *Socialist Candidate for President to Come,* ROCK ISLAND (ILL.) ARGUS, Sept. 30, 1904, at 7; *Candidate Debs Due in Rock Island 14th,* DISPATCH (Moline, Ill.), Oct. 1, 1904, at 5; *Seymour Stedman Speaks Tuesday Night,* DAVENPORT (Iowa) MORNING STAR, Oct. 8, 1904, at 7; *For Socialist Rally,* DAILY TIMES (Davenport, Iowa), Oct. 10, 1904, at 10; *Socialists To Open Campaign,* ST. LOUIS POST-DISPATCH, Oct. 14, 1904, at 6; *Socialist Challenge,* Decatur (Ill.) DAILY REV., Oct. 16, 1904, at 1.

139 David Leip, *1904 Presidential Election Results,* DAVE LEIP'S ATLAS OF U.S. PRESIDENTIAL ELECTIONS, https://uselectionatlas.org/.

140 *The Socialist Vote,* L.A. TIMES, Nov. 9, 1904, at 4; *Debs' Vote Analyzed,* APPEAL TO REASON, Nov. 19, 1904, at 4; *Some Reasons Why the Socialists Increased Their Vote About 500 Per Cent in the Late Election,* MONTANA NEWS (Lewiston, Mont.), Nov. 23, 1904, at 1 (from the CHI. DAILY RECORD).

141 *New Incorporations,* CHI. TRIB., Nov. 26, 1904, at 13 (listing Stedman as an incorporator of the Oriental Coffee Co., Chicago).

142 *Announcements,* CHI. TRIB., Dec. 10, 1904, at 5 (announcing a speech by Stedman that evening).

were expecting closer to 5,000. The reduction in voting put the Socialists' ability to hold a taxpayer-funded primary in jeopardy.[143] At the nominating convention, which he chaired a few days later, Stedman was formally nominated to stand for an open circuit court judgeship.[144]

As usual, the bar association declined to endorse Stedman or any other Socialist for the judiciary in its straw poll. Stedman received only seven votes, three fewer than the Prohibition Party nominee, out of more than 700 votes cast.[145] Of course, neither Stedman nor any other Socialist stood a chance in November's general election, and Stedman was trounced by the Republican candidate.[146]

Stedman's Socialists scored a dramatic victory in April 1906 when the Illinois Supreme Court struck down as unconstitutional the state's new law regulating primary elections. The law had allowed the Cook County election board to deny Socialists the right to hold an aldermanic primary on the ground that they had not cast at least 20% of the total Cook County vote in the last presidential election. So the Socialists filed suit, and Stedman was elated with the outcome. "It was just what we expected," he said. "We knew we were right when we attacked the law."[147]

Later that month, the Socialists held their judicial primary, and Stedman was once again nominated, this time for supreme court justiceship.[148] Once again, he failed to receive the bar association's endorsement,[149] and once again, he failed to win a seat on the bench, polling far below all candidates except that of the Prohibition Party.[150] Undeterred, Stedman again sought the nomination for a municipal judgeship in the fall, once again losing the bar association endorsement.[151] He lost, of course, but gave a "red hot" speech at a Socialist rally on election night, where party loyalists celebrated a record turnout.[152]

---

143 *Forty-Dollar Vote Case,* CHI. TRIB., Sept. 17, 1905, at 4.

144 *Meet, Denounce, and Nominate,* CHI. TRIB., Sept. 21, 1905, at 4.

145 *Bar Association Votes on Judges,* CHI. TRIB., Oct. 14, 1905, at 4.

146 *Republicans are Victors in Fight in Cook County,* INTER OCEAN (Chi.), Nov. 8, 1905, at 1.

147 *Primary Act Void; Chaos in Politics,* INTER OCEAN (Chi.), April 6, 1906, at 1.

148 *Socialists Vote to Hold Primaries Next Saturday,* CHI. TRIB., April 16, 1906, at 4; *Socialists Poll 3,267 Votes at the Primaries,* CHI. TRIB., April 22, 1906, at 8.

149 *Bar Association Prefers Carter,* CHI. TRIB., May 19, 1906, at 7.

150 *Voters to Elect Two Justices Today,* CHI. TRIB., June 4, 1906, at 3; *Carter Elected; Also Carpenter,* CHI. TRIB., June 5, 1906, at 1.

151 *Bar Committee Rakes Tickets,* CHI. TRIB., Oct. 13, 1906, at 4; *Republicans Win at Bar Primary,* CHI. TRIB., Oct. 29, 1906, at 1.

152 *Claim a Socialist Gain,* CHI. TRIB., Nov. 7, 1906, at 3.

In April 1908, Stedman hosted William D. "Big Bill" Haywood of the Industrial Workers of the Worlds (I.W.W.) at a meeting of the Young People's Socialist League supporting Haywood's candidacy for president on the Socialist ticket.[153] Haywood was apparently the first choice of Eugene Debs, who was recovering from throat surgery and did not want the 1908 nomination. Stedman had written Debs asking him to attend the convention in May to dissuade delegates from nominating him.

Debs sent "Steddy" a telegram, declining the invitation on the ground that he was too busy. Stedman read the telegram into the record at the convention as part of his speech nominating Algie M. Simons for the presidency.[154] Largely because of the growing rift within the party, the convention chose Debs as the best person to keep the party together. Benjamin Hanford was again chosen to be his running mate, and the ticket garnered almost half a million votes or nearly 3% of the total popular vote.[155]

Stedman again carried the Socialist Party banner in local elections, running for state's attorney for Cook County.[156] Despite his taking advantage of the synergy between the Socialist and suffragist campaigns,[157] Stedman lost again, this time to Republican John E. W. Wayman, taking only about 16,000 votes, far fewer than even the Prohibition candidate.[158]

Stedman again spent the better part of 1911 and 1912 in public speaking and futilely running to fill judicial vacancies. In September, Stedman became embroiled in a leadership dispute within the Socialist Party, seeking to oust the chief of the local party organization, Thomas J. Morgan. Morgan had attacked a number of Socialist politicians, including Victor Berger, in a self-published pamphlet.[159]

The presidential election of 1912 brought substantial changes in Stedman's career. While Woodrow Wilson was elected president by a large margin, and Democrats took both the House and Senate, the Socialist Party scored significant gains throughout the country. Eugene Debs was once again the party's presidential

---

[153] *Honor Haywood by Student Yells*, CHI. TRIB., April 6, 1908, at 3.

[154] *National Convention of the Socialist Party Held at Chicago, Illinois, May 10 to 17, 1908* (John M. Work, ed. 1908).

[155] David Leip, *1908 Presidential Election Results, Dave Leip's Atlas of U.S. Presidential Elections*, https://uselectionatlas.org/.

[156] *Protests Follow Petitioners' Race*, CHI. TRIB., July 2, 1908, at 4.

[157] *Suffragettes Talk in Air*, CHI. TRIB., July 8, 1908, at 9.

[158] *Wayman Is Elected by 40,000 Plurality*, INTER OCEAN (Chi.), Nov. 4, 1908, at 1; *Election Results in Cook County*, CHI. TRIB., Nov. 5, 1908, at 1.

[159] *Would Oust Socialist Chief*, CHI. TRIB., Sept. 16, 1911, at 3.

nominee, and, in many states, he received double the number of popular votes cast for him in 1908. Significantly, Seymour Stedman finally won public office, his first and only political victory, as a member of the Illinois House of Representatives, on the Socialist ticket.[160] In fact, Stedman himself outpolled all other candidates in the Thirteenth District.[161] Later, he would predict—without any evidence—that Socialists would soon control both the House and Senate in Illinois.[162]

Stedman hadn't even taken his seat before plunging back into the political fray, as both attorney and party functionary. Throughout the election season, Stedman was in the middle of a bitter dispute between two factions of the Woman's Party of Cook County, representing an unincorporated faction headed by the party's existing central committee against a splinter group that had incorporated under the party's name. On the day after the election, a circuit court judge ruled that the name belonged to the incorporated faction, and Stedman began preparing an appeal.[163]

In December, Stedman represented William A. Cunnea, a Socialist candidate who ran third in the race for Cook County state's attorney and was now seeking a recount. Stedman's petition charged that 15,000 votes credited to the other candidates rightly belonged to Cunnea. The 64-page petition also alleged specific irregularities in each precinct.[164] In the weeks that followed, the dispute morphed into a contest over which judicial authority would conduct the recount.[165] Recounts were ordered in four, then six more, wards,[166] with Cunnea gaining votes all along the way.[167]

Also in December, Stedman successfully led an insurgent faction of the Socialist Party in a sometimes-violent intra-party dispute over the reestablishment of the socialist press in Chicago. Stedman's faction supported the immediate establishment of a socialist weekly to be controlled by a stock corporation of

---

160 *New House of Representatives; Socialists Vote Shows Big Gain,* CHI. TRIB., Nov. 7, 1912, at 3.

161 *Revised Vote in Cook County,* CHI. EXAMINER, Nov. 7, 1912, at 5.

162 *Socialists Expect Control of Illinois Legislature,* INTER OCEAN (Chi.), May 19, 1913, at 7.

163 *Woman's Party, Inc., Wins Right to Name,* CHI. EXAMINER, Nov. 7, 1912, at 15.

164 *Cunnea Contests Hoyne Election,* CHI. TRIB., Dec. 1, 1912, at 5.

165 *Like Hoyne Plan, But Bar Owens,* CHI. TRIB., Dec. 22, 1912, at 5; *Hoyne Attacks Judge Tuthill,* CHI. TRIB., Dec. 23, 1912, at 17; *Maclay Hoyne Still Objects to Tuthill in Contest Case,* INTER OCEAN (Chi.), Dec. 23, 1912, at 2.

166 *Judge Orders Six More Wards Recounted,* Day Book (Chi.), Feb. 8, 1913, at 26; *Extends Recount of Hoyne Vote,* CHI. TRIB., Feb. 8, 1913, at 4.

167 *Cunnea Continues Gaining in Recount,* INTER OCEAN (Chi.), May 1, 1913, at 12.

party members. His opposition urged the restoration of a daily newspaper owned by the party organization.[168]

And before the year was out, Stedman announced that all four Socialist members of the new House would vote on every ballot for Barney Berlyn, a Chicago cigarmaker, for U.S. Senator, spoiling the chances of an easy Democratic win. "There is a principle involved here," Stedman said. "We have our own candidate in Mr. Berlyn, who was our candidate in the primary and was indorsed by the party. I'd like to see the color of the Socialist's hair who would dare to come down here and vote for any of the old party candidates." It had become clear that Stedman would be the de facto leader of the Socialists in the Illinois House and would play the roles of spoiler or enabler in the coalition politics of the chamber as it suited them. Stedman asserted that his party's priority was a constitutional amendment that would make further amendments easier to obtain.[169]

Shortly after the New Year, Stedman met with the other three Socialists in the House to decide how they would use their unified votes to exploit the factionalism in the established parties, particularly in the deadlocked race for Speaker of the House.[170] When that vote came, all four Socialists voted for Stedman on each of the 10 ballots taken on the first day, preserving the deadlock.[171] A second day of voting brought about no substantial change, even after 14 more votes were taken, and there was concern that the inauguration of new Governor Edward F. Dunne.[172] When two more votes produced no significant change, the legislature adjourned, and the inauguration was postponed. At one point, Stedman's name was put forward as a compromise candidate who might attract enough Republican and Progressive votes to win,[173] and, in a meeting with Governor-elect Dunne, Stedman reportedly agreed to throw Socialist support behind any nonpartisan candidate who could garner the necessary 77 votes.[174]

---

168 *Socialists Riot; Blows Struck; Bunting Burns,* INTER OCEAN (Chi.), Dec. 9, 1912, at 1.

169 *Socialists Pick Berlyn for Senate,* INTER OCEAN (Chi.), Dec. 28, 1912, at 7; *Berlyn for Cullom's Seat,* CHI. TRIB., Dec. 28, 1912, at 5.

170 *See Deadlock on Speakership at Springfield,* INTER OCEAN (Chi.), Jan. 3, 1913, at 1.

171 *House Deadlock Blocks Election; 10 Ballots Taken,* INTER OCEAN (Chi.), Jan. 9, 1913, at 1.

172 *House Deadlock; Dunne Inaugural May Be Delayed,* CHI. TRIB., Jan. 10, 1913, at 1. Provisions of the state constitution effectively prohibited the governor from taking office until a speaker was chosen. Charles N. Wheeler, *Stead Blocks Plan of Dunne to Take Office,* INTER OCEAN (Chi.), Jan. 18, 1913, at 1.

173 *Assembly Quits; Inaugural Off,* CHI. TRIB., Jan. 11, 1913, at 4.

174 Charles N. Wheeler, *Stead Blocks Plan of Dunne to Take Office,* INTER OCEAN (Chi.), Jan. 18, 1913, at 1.

In the end, William McKinley, a Chicago Democrat and Dunne supporter, emerged as the compromise candidate for speaker, winning on the 76th ballot by a margin of 119 to 4—Stedman's Socialists voting once again for Stedman.[175] The next big battle would be the election of two United States senators, with Stedman and his Socialists initially backing Barney Berlyn.[176] Once again, intra-party factionalism prevented an early decision,[177] and the deadlock lasted 43 days before a compromise sent one Democrat and one Republican to Washington. It would be the first time in Illinois history that two U.S. senators were elected in one day, and the last time the state legislature would elect any senators at all.[178]

The fact that Stedman controlled only four votes in the House did not mean that he was an inactive legislator. Stedman was initially named a member of the important committee on committees,[179] although his name mysteriously disappeared from the list submitted to the governor, replaced by a member of the Bull Moose Party.[180] He was, however, named to the House Elections Committee.[181] Stedman also led a bitter, but ultimately unsuccessful, fight to defeat legislation authorizing the sanitary district of Chicago to build an outer harbor in the Lake Calumet district of South Chicago. Stedman charged that the bill would hand over valuable state land to private interests. "The harbor is a great necessity," he said, "but we pay more than it is worth in adopting this bill. I believe that we can get the harbor without giving away several million dollars' worth of property ...."[182]

Stedman also supported, without success, a resolution to put an "initiative and referendum" proposal on the ballot in Illinois,[183] but he succeeded in leading a fight against legislation to give citizens some choice as to which terms of court they might serve as jurors.[184] He also backed a doomed old-age pension bill, noting that while the nation and state are paying millions annually in pensions to veterans for killing their brothers in war, they are paying not one

---

175 *M'Kinley Wins for Speaker; War on Floor,* CHI. TRIB., Jan. 30, 1913, at 1.

176 Charles N. Wheeler, *Caucus Blocked When Democrats Refuse to Attend,* INTER OCEAN (Chi.), Feb. 11, 1913, at 1.

177 *No Senate Choice; Deadlock Feared,* CHI. TRIB., Feb. 12, 1913, at 1.

178 *Lewis Gets Long Term; Sherman Elected to Short,* INTER OCEAN (Chi.), March 27, 1913, at 1.

179 *Sherman Insists on the Long Term,* INTER OCEAN, Feb. 18, 1913, at 1.

180 *Assembly May Oust M'Cormick from House Seat,* INTER OCEAN (Chi.), March 13, 1913, at 2.

181 *Home Rule Here to Get Hearing,* CHI. TRIB., April 17, 1913, at 2.

182 *Outer Harbor Bill Passed After Fight,* INTER OCEAN (Chi.), April 24, 1913, at 5.

183 *I.-R. Reported by House Body; Trick Charged,* INTER OCEAN (Chi.), April 30, 1913, at 1; *Referendum One Vote Shy on Final Test,* CHI. TRIB., May 14, 1913, at 1.

184 *Juul Amendment Passed by House; Ready for Senate,* INTER OCEAN (Chi.), May 15, 1913, at 2.

cent for pensioning the men and women who have contributed to the industrial prosperity of the country.[185] The comparison was condemned on the editorial page of *The Inter Ocean,* which said it "betrays a moral degeneracy and a mental incapacity that is both pitiable and appalling."[186]

Stedman's position on prohibition was more nuanced. The Socialists voted with the generally successful "drys" on most important issues, but vigorously opposed and helped to defeat an "anti-shipping" measure that would have prohibited shipping liquor from one saloon territory to another. In that debate, Stedman declared that nationalizing the traffic in liquor was the real solution to the entire question and that the methods of the Prohibition Party and the Anti-Saloon League in this regard were unreasonable, unjust, and un-Christian. Stedman said that they were merely postponing the time when the nation would assume direct control of the business and conduct it legitimately. The Socialists also successfully opposed a "county option" provision that would have given counties the option of deciding whether to be "wet" or "dry," but the "drys" won the day by giving that option to "residence territories," essentially neighborhoods meeting certain standards.

Other progressive legislation enacted by the legislature during Stedman's first year included limited suffrage for women, who could now vote for presidential electors and a variety of local offices, but not state or federal constitutional officers; direct election of U.S. senators, applying the Seventeenth Amendment to the U.S. Constitution; workmen's compensation reform to provide for a more definite award to injured employees and establish an independent commission to fix the amount awarded; improvements in railway and mine safety programs; and enhancements in the widows' and teachers' pension funds.[187] Stedman also worked on legislation to enable cities to establish and maintain municipal banks[188] and reform the inheritance tax.[189]

In August 1914, Stedman's campaign for reelection to the Illinois House of Representatives from the Thirteenth District began in earnest.[190] Despite his endorsement by the Chicago Federation of Labor[191] and the Legislative Voters

---

185 *Tax Commission Act Advanced in House,* INTER OCEAN (Chi.), May 30, 1913, at 12.

186 *The Socialist and the Soldier,* INTER OCEAN (Chi.), May 31, 1913, at 6.

187 *Important Bills Passed by Illinois Legislators at Session Just Ended,* CHI. TRIB., June 21, 1913, at 2.

188 *A Municipal Bank,* DAY BOOK (Chi.), July 3, 1914, at 6.

189 *Stedman Would Have People Share in Riches,* DAY BOOK (Chi.), Jan. 15, 1915, at 25.

190 *Last Filing Day Sees Near 1,400 Candidates Out,* CHI. TRIB., Aug. 1, 1914, at 8.

191 *Labor Reports on Members of Illinois Legislature,* DAY BOOK (Chi.), Aug. 4, 1914, at 24.

League of Illinois,[192] however, Stedman lost in November, coming in last in a field of five candidates in a race where the top three were elected, garnering only 8,879 votes, or 13.32% of the total. In his previous campaign, he had come in second to the Progressive Party candidate, Elmer Jacob Schnackenberg, with 13,052 votes, or 15.34% of the total. In 1914, both Schnackenberg and Stedman were defeated by one Democrat and two Republicans.[193]

Stedman closed out the year by all but announcing a run for mayor of Chicago in the election of April 1915. "If I become a candidate," he said, "I will give them all I have in the shop. I am on the point of starting and I am all but ready to begin." Stedman said his health was all that stood in the way of immediate action, but it was considered all but certain that he would be nominated on the Socialist ticket.[194]

Between elections, Stedman lost a significant case in the cause of woman suffrage. The state of Illinois, on behalf of a number of interested voters, had sought a writ of mandamus commanding the Cook County board of election commissioners to provide separate ballots for women voting in Chicago's November 3, 1914, election. The women's ballots would exclude candidates for county commissioners, which the state argued were "constitutional officers," rather than "legislative officers," and therefore beyond the reach of state statutes giving women a limited right to vote. Stedman was part of the team representing the board in opposing the writ, but on December 16, the Illinois Supreme Court agreed with the state and awarded the writ.[195]

Following his official nomination for mayor, Stedman campaigned on creating a municipal telephone system, with one-cent calls. "The automatic phone system belongs to the city of Chicago," he declared, "and the city should seize the system under the forfeiture clause of the franchise granted the Illinois Telephone & Telegraph Co."[196] He also called for municipal stores and icehouses, clean streets, sanitary jails, and less crime.[197]

Despite his support from many in organized labor, Stedman did not fare well with the general public. Of 692,116 votes cast in a *Tribune* straw poll, Stedman got 14,030, trailing Republican and Democratic candidates in all occupational

---

192 *L.V.L. Condemns 72 Legislators,* CHI. TRIB., May 25, 1914, at 4; *L.V.L. Selections for Legislature,* CHI. TRIB., Nov. 3, 1914, at 4.

193 IL State House 013, Our Campaigns, https://www.ourcampaigns.com/RaceDetail.html?RaceID=933417.

194 *Boom Stedman for Mayoralty,* CHI. TRIB., Dec. 4, 1914, at 3.

195 People ex rel. Jurgensen v. Czarnecki, 265 Ill. 489 (Dec. 16, 1914).

196 *Says Seize the Phone System,* DAY BOOK (Chi.), Feb. 1, 1915, at 2.

197 *Telephone Calls 1 Cent if Stedman Wins, He Says,* CHI. TRIB., Feb. 1, 1915, at 9.

categories.[198] That Stedman was the only candidate to respond to questions from the Chicago Political Equality League, a suffragist organization, seemed not to help at all. Among other things, Stedman called for free textbooks and free lunches for all school children, and urged that public schools should be social centers in the evenings for music, dances, sociables, and other entertainments.[199]

Another recurring theme in Stedman's campaign concerned the traction companies, which he accused of paying more for rail cars than other cities. "The city of Chicago lost over $100,000," he said.[200] Stedman noted that San Francisco was running its own streetcar lines and making money. Similarly, Cleveland owned its own lighting plants and charged less than half what the "chumps" in Chicago pay—three cents per kilowatt hour, versus 10 cents—and still makes money.[201]

Though far behind in the polling, Stedman sometimes gave the appearance of optimism.

> We are approaching the season of predictions," he said, perhaps disingenuously. "The greatest reason why I expect to be elected is because the majority of the people are not infants. I should get the votes of the men and women .... As to our majority, we cannot say. There is no way to measure the increase of intelligence among the voters in the last two years."[202]

On other days, though, he was far less sanguine: "[Democrat Robert M.] Sweitzer will probably be elected," he said just a few days later, noting that Sweitzer was supported by most of the trade union leaders and also has the support of the most pronounced opponents of organized labor—the Illinois Manufacturers' Association.[203]

A few days later still, he predicted that a large "silent vote" in Chicago would support him on election day.[204] But the very next day, he labeled "cowards" those Chicago voters who believed as he did but voted otherwise because they

---

198 *Sweitzer Spurt Gives Final Lead in Straw Vote,* CHI. TRIB., April 4, 1915, at 2; *Sweitzer Goes Further Ahead in Straw Vote,* CHI. TRIB., March 26, 1915, at 5; *Sweitzer Gains All Along Line in Straw Vote,* CHI. TRIB., March 18, 1915, 9; *First Returns on Mayoral Straw Vote,* CHI. TRIB., March 12, 1915, at 15.

199 *Only Stedman Answers Quiz,* CHI. TRIB., March 18, 1915, at 9.

200 *Stedman Says the City Is Short on Car Income,* CHI. TRIB., March 25, 1915, at 8.

201 *Chicago Trails 'Wayback,' Socialist Candidate Says,* CHI. TRIB., March 26, 1915, at 5.

202 *Stedman Predicts Rivals Get Kindergarten Vote,* CHI. TRIB., March 27, 1915, at 3.

203 *Stedman Sees Opposing Forces Working for 'Bob,'* CHI. TRIB., March 30, 1915, at 3.

204 *"Silent Vote" for Him, Seymour Stedman Asserts,* CHI. TRIB., April 2, 1915, at 9.

thought he had no chance. "I would prefer to have them give some other reason for not voting for me. Any reason is better than a confession of cowardice."[205] And when the *Tribune* asked the candidates to predict the outcome, Stedman demurred, asserting that "[the] majority of the people believe the same as I do on the vital issues in Chicago. If they vote the way they believe we will elect every candidate on the Socialist ticket."[206]

The election results told a quite different story. Stedman may have expected like-minded voters to support Sweitzer; if they did, there were far fewer than he anticipated. Republican William H. "Big Bill" Thompson trounced Sweitzer, 390,691 votes to 251,202; Stedman wasn't even close with 23,826 votes.[207] Stedman attributed the small Socialist vote to the business depression and large numbers of idle workers in the city. He said the two Socialists elected to the city council would introduce a resolution reducing the rates of the Commonwealth Edison Co. "The rate of 10 cents per kilowatt hour here is two cents higher than in any other large city of the United States."[208]

In June 1916, the Socialist Party nominated Stedman to run for governor of Illinois.[209] Despite vigorous campaigning throughout the summer and fall, Stedman's total vote was 59,588 compared with 706,532 for the victor, Republican Frank O. Lowden.[210] Stedman appeared on the ballot again in April 1917 as the Socialist Party's candidate for state senator.[211] "I'm not exactly claiming my election," he declared in April, "but I will triple the Socialist vote in the Seventh Ward. We will gain all over Chicago and will elect at least three Socialist aldermen .... We may get more."[212] Notwithstanding that enthusiasm and the endorsement of the Legislative Voters' League,[213] Stedman again came in third, polling 6,036 votes, compared with the victor's 9,475.[214]

Stedman again ran for office in the fall of 1917, this time for a seat on the Superior Court bench. When his anti-war record was challenged, Stedman replied, "It was a case of save the people or save Wall Street. The government ran to the rescue, and Wall Street became the synonym of liberty and democracy.

---

205 *Voters' "Yellow Streak" Arouses Stedman Wrath,* CHI. TRIB., April 3, 1915, at 4.

206 *Forecasts of Candidates and Managers,* CHI. TRIB., April 4, 1915, at 2.

207 *The City's Vote for Mayor,* CHI. TRIB., April 7, 1915, at 1.

208 *War Upon Edison Light Rate, Plan of Socialists,* CHI. TRIB., April 8, 1915, at 13.

209 *Socialists Pick Stedman To Run for Governor,* CHI. TRIB., June 18, 1916, at 4.

210 *Rainey Protest Halts Election Proclamation,* CHI. TRIB., Nov. 29, 1916, at 4.

211 *Primary Forces Rest on Arms for Final Drive,* CHI. TRIB., Feb. 25, 1917, at 10.

212 *Talk Gives Way to Action in City Election Today,* CHI. TRIB., April 3, 1917, at 13.

213 *Pre-Election Notes on the Political Campaigns,* CHI. TRIB., March 28, 1917, at 11.

214 *Democrats Win Council, Smash City Hall Ticket,* CHI. TRIB., April 4, 1917, at 5.

Never was there such an imposition upon a peace-loving and industrious people." Morris Hillquit was running for mayor of New York City at the same time, and some of the Chicago Socialists campaigned for both Hillquit and their own slate of judicial candidates. "Tell the comrades in Chicago that the people everywhere are with us this year," Chicago Alderman John C. Kennedy wrote the *Tribune* from New York. "They want peace—and our party is the only one that stands fearlessly for a genuine program of peace and democracy."[215]

In the end, Hillquit was defeated in New York, although Socialists elected ten aldermen and several assemblymen, and Stedman and the other Socialist candidates were likewise defeated in Illinois.[216] Stedman himself led all Socialist candidates with 82,648 votes, but his total was just over half that of his Democrat and Republican opponents.[217]

In May 1920, Stedman, Berger and Hillquit led the National Socialist Party Convention in Madison Square Garden, where Debs—still in prison—would be nominated as the party's candidate for president. At the convention, Stedman outlined the 1920 campaign as conceived by the party's executive committee. Domestically, he advocated "industrial action" to reinforce political action, public ownership of railroads, and release of political prisoners. He also called for an international peace congress; cessation of the "exploitation of Poland" as a means to attack Soviet Russia; and the independence of Ireland, India and Egypt.[218]

On May 13, 1920, the convention formally nominated Debs and, by unanimous vote on the second ballot, selected Stedman as his running mate.[219] One of his first acts was to chair a committee appointed to petition President Wilson and Attorney General A. Mitchell Palmer to release Debs and other "political prisoners."[220] Wilson's private secretary, Joseph Patrick Tumulty, told Stedman he was sure the president would give the petition "conscientious consideration."[221] In June, Stedman traveled to Atlanta to formally notify Debs of his nomination,[222] then opened the campaign in Chicago. A formidable campaigner, Stedman blasted the opposition. "The railroads wanted [Illinois Gov. Frank Oren] Lowden,"

---

[215] *Socialists Hope To Win on Stand Opposing War,* CHI. TRIB., Oct. 30, 1917, at 9.

[216] *Hylan Victor Over Mitchel by 145,000,* CHI. TRIB., Nov. 7, 1917, at 1.

[217] *Ward Totals on Vote for Judges,* CHI. TRIB., Nov. 7, 1917, at 2.

[218] *Socialists To Launch Debs in 1920 Race Today,* CHI. TRIB., May 9, 1920, at 4; *Socialists Hail Debs as Leader; Police on Guard,* CHI. TRIB., May 10, 1920, at 5.

[219] *Socialists Dig Debs Out of 'Pen' for Presidency,* CHI. TRIB., May 14, 1920, at 6.

[220] *Appeal for Debs' Release,* CHI. TRIB., May 15, 1920, at 5.

[221] *Socialists Ask Debs' Release for the Campaign,* CHI. DAILY NEWS, May 16, 1920, at 5.

[222] *Political Gossip,* CHI. EAGLE, June 5, 1920, at 3.

he said. "Wall Street wanted [California Sen. Hiram] Johnson. The Republicans selected as a compromise [Warren G.] Harding, a man without a record or a biography, because they thought it best."[223] He had no great love for Democrats either, having earlier called them "a party that has hardly enough friends left to write its epitaph."[224]

Of course, the Debs-Stedman ticket had no chance of winning. The Republican Harding-[Calvin] Coolidge ticket polled 16 million popular votes, 60% of the total, and 404 electoral votes. The Democratic Cox-[Franklin D.] Roosevelt ticket finished far behind, with nine million popular votes, 34%, and 127 electoral votes. The Socialists barely registered, with fewer than a million popular votes, or 3% of the total, and carried not a single state. Still, the Socialists could take heart in the fact that they polled 50% higher than Allan L. Benson had in the 1915 election.[225]

In 1923, Stedman once again threw his hat into the electoral ring, this time running for Congress from the second district in the April election as part of a concerted effort to put Socialists on the ballot in every district.[226] It may have been thought in some quarters that ongoing strikes by railroad workers and coal miners might influence the Illinois elections, but Stedman was skeptical. "It may influence the Socialists' vote slightly," he told the *Chicago Tribune*, "but those who, as a protest, will vote the Socialist ticket, will come back to the good old Republican or Democratic Party the election following."[227] As expected, Stedman lost the race to the Republican, Morton D. Hull, with nearly 6,000 votes compared with Hull's 56,000.[228]

---

223 *Rain Falls on Silk Shirts of the Socialists*, CHI. TRIB., June 14, 1920, at 10.

224 *Rowdy Radicals Silenced at West Side Party Debate*, CHI. TRIB., Jan.26, 1920, at 19.

225 *1920 Presidential Election Results*, David Leip's Atlas of U.S. Presidential Elections, https://uselectionatlas.org/RESULTS/national.php?year=1920&f=0&off=0&elect=0.

226 *Socialists Plan Giant Drive to Take Congress*, CHI. TRIB., May 22, 1922, at 12.

227 *Hold Radicals Won't Gain from Labor Unrest*, CHI. TRIB., July 29, 1922, at 4.

228 *Hull Triumphs Over O'Hara in Congress Race*, CHI. TRIB., April 4, 1923, at 1.

Chapter 4
Beyond Law and Politics

Morris Hillquit

Morris Hillquit was a prolific interpreter of socialist ideology as both a writer and lecturer. His base for these pursuits was often the Rand School, established with a bequest of $200,000 from the late Mrs. E. D. Rand in the fall of 1905. Hillquit was named one of the trustees of the school, and he would lecture there for many years to come. Announcing the bequest, Hillquit said the school would provide for an "intellectual centre for the Socialist movement in the United States" and a "centre of information concerning international socialism and sociological data."[1]

In March 1906, Hillquit attended a conference that he considered "a talk fest ... of almost historic significance" because of the participation of leading progressive intellectuals of the period. In his autobiography, Hillquit saw this period as a kind of "Golden Age" characterized by just such conferences, by the Rand School, by Upton Sinclair's Intercollegiate Socialist Society, and by the X Club, whose members included not only leading socialists but also journalists, academics, and social reformers.[2]

The following year, Hillquit attended the International Socialist Congress held in Stuttgart, Germany, in August 1907. Nearly 900 delegates from 25 nations attended the Congress, including such luminaries as V. I. Lenin and Maxim Litvinov from Russia; George Bernard Shaw and Ramsay MacDonald from Great Britain; and August Bebel, Karl Kautsky, and Rosa Luxemburg from Germany. Among the Americans attending were Hillquit's running mate in the last election, Algernon Lee, and his arch nemesis, Daniel De Leon. Resolutions adopted at the Congress addressed militarism, colonialism and women's suffrage.

On August 18, opening day, Hillquit delivered a report on "Recent Progress of the Socialist and Labor Movements in the United States." Hillquit began his report by detailing the growth of American capitalism. "The march of capitalist progress degenerated into a mad, frenzied race for wealth in which thousands participated while the millions were trampled underfoot," he declared.

---

[1] MORRIS HILLQUIT, LOOSE LEAVES FROM A BUSY LIFE 55-78 (De Capo Press 1971) (1934) [hereinafter LOOSE LEAVES].

[2] *Id.* at 55-78.

"Capitalism became rampant and reckless, and the inherent viciousness of the system became more apparent and manifest every year."[3] He went on to suggest that reformist movements among political parties and organized labor were having a detrimental impact on the growth of true socialism.

> The powerful reform movements holding out to the impatient masses the phantom hope of instantaneous relief, distracted their attention from the more radical but slower remedies offered by the Socialist Party, and while the socialist vote during the last few years on the whole shows a marked increase, it does not by any means keep pace with the growth of the socialist sentiment in the United States.[4]

That sentiment, Hillquit said, would, sooner rather than later, inevitably lead to a "larger and more commanding movement of socialism which is bound to spring up in the United States within a short time." Predicting that the reform movements would ultimately collapse, Hillquit asserted that, on the day of that collapse, "the socialist movement of America will reap a rich harvest, and that day is not far off."[5]

With respect to the labor movement, Hillquit described the growth of the American Federation of Labor and the Industrial Workers of the World, with a particular focus on the mine workers' struggle in Colorado and the murder trial of William D. Haywood and other union officers a few weeks earlier. Giving more than a little credit for Haywood's acquittal[6] in that case to socialist agitation, Hillquit concluded that the "powerful march of economic development is bound to shake up the working classes, to force them ahead to more harmonious action and to socialistic consciousness."[7]

Hillquit had begun teaching classes in "Socialism and Municipal Government" at the newly endowed Rand School,[8] and had published a new book, *Socialism in Theory and Practice*, that drew a thoughtful and favorable, if skeptical, review in the *Times*. "Socialism does seek to overturn the present order of things," the

---

3 MORRIS HILLQUIT, RECENT PROGRESS OF THE SOCIALIST AND LABOR MOVEMENTS IN THE UNITED STATES 3-4 (1907) [hereinafter RECENT PROGRESS].

4 *Id.* at 9.

5 *Id.* at 12.

6 *See Verdict Sets Haywood Free,* N.Y. SUN, July 29, 1907, at 1. Hillquit is quoted in the story touting Haywood as a Socialist candidate for President in 1908. Hillquit would later break with Haywood.

7 *Id.* at 13-32.

8 *Socialism Via the Drama,* N.Y. SUN, March 7, 1909, at 22.

unsigned review states, "and not even so careful and instructed a Socialist as Mr. Morris Hillquit can present the case in such a manner as to soften the blow to the conservative mind."[9]

Hillquit's ideas about socialism were put to the test in a debate with fellow lawyer Martin W. Littleton at the New Rochelle People's Forum in mid-January 1910. It was the largest, and by all accounts, most vociferous audience ever to attend that venue. In just one of their many exchanges, Littleton asserted that socialism sought to destroy economic liberty, to which Hillquit responded that Littleton must have meant the economic liberty of the master and capitalist, not the worker. The only economic freedom today's worker has is the freedom to choose his master, he said.[10]

A week or so later, Hillquit again took the debate stage, this time against NYU Law School Professor Isaac Franklin Russell at the Labor Lyceum in Brooklyn. Again, Hillquit asserted that socialism advocates only one basic reform: that the business of America's principal industries be conducted by the people and for the people, not by one small class for their individual enrichment. Russell charged socialism with economic error and heresy for its attacks on capitalists, declaring that capital is indispensable to enterprise.[11]

Also in January came word that Funk & Wagnalls was bringing out a fifth revised and enlarged edition of Hillquit's *History of Socialism in the United States.*[12] In his preface to the new edition, Hillquit noted that his book had been printed four times without any change in the text. "I feel that the task of subjecting it to a thorough revision can no longer be delayed," he wrote. The task of bringing the text up to date "has made necessary the addition of an entirely new and somewhat extended chapter to analyze the character of the American socialist movement and to forecast its probable future." [13] It concludes on a positive note:

"Socialism is at last beginning to get a hearing before the people, and the people of the United States move fast once they are set in motion."[14]

---

[9] *Some New Works Upon Socialism,* N.Y. TIMES, March 13, at 21.

[10] *Argue Socialism,* N.Y. TRIB., Jan. 17, 1910, at 3; *Miss Morgan Hears Socialist Debate,* N.Y. TIMES, Jan. 17, 1910, at 7.

[11] *More on Socialism,* N.Y. TRIB., Jan. 24, 1910, at 5.

[12] *Books and Authors,* N.Y. TRIB., Jan. 29, 1910, at 8.

[13] MORRIS HILLQUIT, HISTORY OF SOCIALISM IN THE UNITED STATES 5 (1910).

[14] *Id.* at 364-65.

Hillquit often appeared in public during the first part of 1910,[15] and he was nominated by the party as a candidate for associate judge of the New York Court of Appeals.[16] Once again, Hillquit was asked to attend the International Socialist Congress, this year in Copenhagen in late August and early September. Along with Victor Berger, both named "International Secretaries," Hillquit prepared and delivered the report of the Socialist Party of the United States. Their report noted that the socialist movement in America had suffered a period of hard struggle against adverse political and social conditions since the last international congress. "It has witnessed many setbacks and disappointments for the Socialist Party, but also some victories and triumphs; and on the whole it has marked a distinct step in the direction of progress."[17] Hillquit returned to New York on September 8.[18]

Hillquit closed out the decade of socialist activities with an address to Upton Sinclair's Intercollegiate Socialist Society at the home of portraitist Helen Phelps Stokes—sister-in-law to Rose Pastor Stokes—in Greenwich Village. Hillquit told his audience of largely well-to-do students that socialism makes its appeal most powerfully to those interested in its promises, the workers, and that nothing as fundamental as a revolution could be achieved without the masses behind it. "Don't try to evolve a special brand of your own," he warned, "a more refined, a more spiritual socialism than that of the common laborer. The moment you do, you fail."[19]

The coming of war in Europe raised an existential question for socialists everywhere: Could socialists support the war effort of their respective countries and remain true to their internationalist aspirations? That issue would divide the American socialist movement even more seriously than the left-right split of previous decades. Hillquit's answer was unequivocally negative ... and wrong. Interviewed on July 27—one month after the assassination of Archduke Ferdinand in Sarajevo and one day before Austria-Hungary declared war on Serbia—Hillquit told a *Tribune* reporter that, even if the socialists could not prevent the war, they would be a powerful influence in stopping it.

---

[15] *See, e.g., Church Services Tomorrow,* N.Y. TIMES, Feb. 12, 1910, at 12; *Club and Social Notes,* N.Y. TRIB., Feb. 27, 1910, at 57; *Russell Rouses 'Em,* N.Y. TRIB., March 12, 1910, at 16.

[16] *State Socialists Nominate,* N.Y. TRIB., June 27, 1910, at 3.

[17] MORRIS HILLQUIT, REPORT OF THE SOCIALIST PARTY OF THE UNITED STATES TO THE INTERNATIONAL SOCIALIST CONGRESS AT COPENHAGEN 1 (1910).

[18] Arriving Passengers from Ancestry.com.

[19] *Miss Stokes an Artist,* N.Y. TRIB., Dec. 30, 1910, at 3; *Parlor Socialists Sit on the Floor,* N.Y. TIMES, Dec. 30, 1910, at 7.

On one point, however, Hillquit's assessment was prescient: "The case of Russia is a special one," he said.

> The last war brought about a revolution and the country is in the same condition now. The spirit of revolt among the workers is raising its head, and if Russia takes sides or participates in a general European war it would mean just what it meant in the Japanese war. The army would be disaffected and rebellious, and most likely would suffer defeat. The Socialist party of Russia is much better prepared than it was ten years ago.

But overall, his optimism was misplaced. "I think ... the powers will be slow to go to war, not alone on account of the doubtful outcome of the struggle, but because of their internal conditions." In any event, a meeting of the International Socialist Congress was scheduled for August 23, the *Tribune* noted, "unless by that time the war rumors have not abated." Hillquit, slated to be a delegate, said the Congress would take a very energetic stand and decide on very practical measures for stopping, if not actually preventing, wars.[20]

It took only a few months for Hillquit to realize how wrong he had been. In a November 19 lecture on "Socialism and the War" at Cooper Union under the auspices of the Socialist Party and the Intercollegiate Socialist Society, Hillquit admitted that any notion of an international war strike had been utopian and that a national anti-war policy would have to be established in every country before an international anti-war policy could be practical. Hillquit would neither endorse nor condemn the German socialists "at this distance" and predicted that, when the war was over, socialism would have learned many lessons. Armed with this knowledge, he said, it will keep up the work of bringing about lasting international peace and the socialist order of society.[21]

Many years later, in his autobiography, Hillquit admitted that he still had no answers to the fundamental question. Not only was he dismayed by the "sudden collapse of human reason and the ugly sight of the world denuded of its thin veneer of civilization," but he realized the "failure of the Socialist movement and the desertion of so many of its trusted leaders." Before August 1914, he wrote, the movement seemed "thoroughly harmonious" and "united in common struggle against the capitalist system ... and all capitalist wars." Yet socialists in both hostile camps rallied to their capitalistic governments and engaged in the "ghastly business of mutual slaughter."[22]

---

[20] *Socialists Plan Anti-War Strike,* N.Y. TRIB., July 28, 1914, at 2.

[21] *War Stike Utopian, Says Morris Hillquit,* N.Y. SUN, Nov. 20, 1914, at 4.

[22] LOOSE LEAVES, *supra* note 1, at 145-46.

Notwithstanding his disappointment in the reaction of European socialists to the war, Hillquit was asked to represent the United States at an international peace conference of the socialist parties of neutral nations in Copenhagen on January 1, 1915.[23] He declined the invitation, however, on the ground that even the so-called neutral countries "are somewhat biased in favor of one or the other belligerent countries."[24] Instead, Hillquit ended that tumultuous year with an address to the Sixth Annual Convention of the Intercollegiate Socialist Society.[25]

Hillquit continued to speak on socialism and world affairs, including a public debate with Rep. August P. Gardner (R-Mass.) on whether the United States needed to prepare its military for war. In what the *Sun* called a "perfectly polite debate" in Carnegie Hall on April 2, 1915, Hillquit dismissed the congressman's concern that the country was in danger of war and unprepared for it. Hillquit asserted that the United States would never face another war unless it deliberately sought trouble. "We are economically self-sufficient," he said. "We have no vexatious boundaries. We have no national grudges to settle. We need fear no invasion."[26]

The following month, Hillquit published an article in *The American Socialist* expressing optimism for the future of the international socialist movement, notwithstanding the disruption caused by the war. "The Socialist program must remain international in character," he said, "because it will continue to voice the same general demands all over the world, after the war as before the war .... International Socialism is imperishable."[27]

Hillquit also kept up his speaking engagements, addressing a socialist peace rally at Cooper Union in June,[28] and debating whether socialism should prevail in the United States at the Brooklyn Academy of Music in October.[29] In the latter, Hillquit appeared with Scott Nearing against the Rev. Dr. John Belford, a Catholic priest of well-known anti-socialist leanings, and Professor Frederick Davenport, a former progressive candidate for governor. Hillquit argued that American democracy could never be complete without socialism, despite a

---

23 *Socialists Call War Conference*, N.Y. TRIB., Nov. 29, 1914, at 4.

24 NORMA FAIN PRATT, MORRIS HILLQUIT: A POLITICAL HISTORY OF AN AMERICAN JEWISH SOCIALIST 118 (1979) (citing letters from Morris Hillquit to Walter Landferseik, Nov. 21, 1914, and others, in the Hillquit Papers).

25 *Intercollegiate Socialist Convention*, BARNARD BULLETIN, Jan. 4, 1915, at 3.

26 *Debate on Defence Perfectly Polite*, N.Y. SUN, April 3, 1915, at 5. *See also* MUST WE ARM: HILLQUIT-GARDNER DEBATE (1916) (the Rand School's publication of the transcript of that debate).

27 Morris Hillquit, *The "Collapse" of the International*, AM. SOCIALIST, May 1, 1915, at 3.

28 *Bryan to Speak at Peace Rally*, N.Y. TRIB., June 19, 1915, at 3.

29 *Debate on Socialism*, N.Y. TIMES, Oct. 21, 1915, at 22.

"certain semblance" of political democracy, since an oligarchy controls the industrial side of our existence, "how and whether we shall work and live."[30]

In June 1916, the *Times* devoted nearly a full page to an interview with Hillquit in anticipation of his forthcoming trip to The Hague for the next International Socialist Congress. Hillquit took pains to deny that the movement was moribund, or even sleeping; rather, he insisted that it was "wide awake to all aspects of this world struggle." Hillquit envisioned two consecutive peace conferences, where representatives of first one, then the other, alliance of belligerents would meet with a delegation from neutral countries, to try to hammer out an agreement based on the principles of evacuation, no indemnities, arms reduction, and a court of arbitration.[31]

Unfortunately, the Hague congress was postponed from June 16 to July 31, and Hillquit was unable to attend because of labor unrest in New York. Once he was again free to turn his attention to international socialism, Hillquit gave the *Times* another full-page interview reflecting on the congress he could not attend.

> The conference just closed was [the International Socialist Bureau's] first effort for a general getting together of the neutral delegates since the beginning of the war. There is no doubt that at the first propitious moment, surely as soon as a truce is declared, the socialists of all countries will be brought together to perfect the details of a plan for action in behalf of permanent peace.[32]

In retrospect, Hillquit's predictions seem painfully naïve. His vision of a "permanent peace" with no annexations and no reparations, led by altruistic socialists around the world—and especially those in the United States—might have appeared to be possible in the summer of 1916. But those illusions could never survive the cataclysmic events of 1917 and the repression that was to follow.

It is safe to say that neither Hillquit nor anyone else in his circle could have predicted the life-changing events of 1917, from revolution in Russia to repression in America. America's entry into World War I brought conscription, resistance, reaction, and punishment with a harshness and cruelty not seen since the Civil War. Hillquit's hope of a peaceful ascension of international socialism in a world without territorial annexations or vengeful reparations would be forever shattered.

---

30 SHOULD SOCIALISM PREVAIL: A DEBATE 21 (Rand School 1916).

31 *"International Socialism Not Even Sleeping,"* N.Y. TIMES, June 4, 1916, at 70.

32 *No Indemnity in Socialist Peace Program*, N.Y. TIMES, Aug. 6, 1916, at 13.

For Hillquit, the year began on a hopeful note. In January, the National Executive Committee of the Socialist Party of the United States, on which Hillquit served, tried once again to persuade the International Socialist Bureau to convene an international peace congress. In a letter that was also sent to all European Socialist parties, the NEC wrote:

> Convinced that the time is ripe for a revival of the Socialist International on the basis of a concerted working-class movement for an immediate, just and lasting peace, the Socialist Party of the United States requests that an International Congress be called June 3, 1917, at The Hague. Unless by March 1st, the Bureau takes steps to call such Congress, our party will consider itself justified in taking direct initiative."[33]

In a separate statement to American party members, the committee explained its reasons for demanding an international congress. The statement begins by recounting the horrors of war, asserting that the socialist movement can be the greatest force for peace, and rallying the forces of the working class to ensure that the peace is just and lasting by ending the reactionary "capitalist devices" that are likely to provoke future wars. Foremost among these is militarism, "the greatest menace to all efforts toward industrial freedom," and the Socialist Party stands opposed to military preparedness and any appropriations for war. It specifically listed six demands to safeguard the peace:

1. Repeal of all laws and appropriations to increase the U.S. military.
2. Removal of all war powers from the president, with foreign policy to be determined by Congress, subject to popular referendum.
3. No declaration of war without a referendum vote of the people, except to repel invasion.
4. Abandonment of the Monroe Doctrine.
5. Independence for the Philippines.
6. A call for a congress of all neutral nations to establish a lasting peace.[34]

As relations between the United States and Germany continued to worsen with Germany's announcement of unrestricted submarine warfare on January 31 and the American cutting of diplomatic ties with Germany a few days later,[35] Hillquit intensified his anti-war rhetoric. "Never was war waged between two

---

[33] THE AMERICAN SOCIALISTS AND THE WAR 31 (Alexander Trachtenberg, ed. 1917) (published in June 1917 by the Rand School with an introduction by Morris Hillquit) [hereinafter AM. SOCIALISTS].

[34] *Id.* at 27-29.

[35] DAVID M. KENNEDY, OVER HERE 10 (2004).

or more nations that had less justification or was declared on more frivolous pretext than this threatened war between America and Germany," he told an anti-war rally at Carnegie Hall on February 5.[36]

An Emergency Committee of the Socialist Party called on President Wilson to impose a complete embargo on "all shipments of whatsoever kind" from the United States to any and all of the belligerent countries. It was, the committee said, the only way to preserve this country's neutrality.[37] The proposal was immediately denounced by the *Wall Street Journal* as playing into Germany's hands, which concluded its front-page editorial with a personal dig at Hillquit. "According to Morris Hillquit, 'our national honor and dignity are in no way threatened by Germany.' Just what is the Socialistic idea of honor? Or dignity?"[38]

Hillquit had a chance to explain his position on the war at length in another full-page interview in the *Times*.

> [If] our armies are to be recruited by volunteer enlistments, the Socialists, as a whole, will refuse to enlist if they remain consistent to their present belief that this country's participation in the war is wholly unjustifiable. If the armies are raised by conscription, of course we will have to serve as other citizens. I do not believe that the Socialists will advocate any general industrial strike to handicap the country in its war preparations and I do not believe there will be any such strike. I know of no instance in any country where we have tried a general strike either to prevent or promote a war.[39]

Before the month was out, however, the first Russian Revolution would spark a "decisive change" in the Socialist attitude toward the war. According to Hillquit, it created an entirely new situation for socialists in both belligerent camps. "Those of the Central Powers could no longer justify their support of the war by the specter of a triumphant Russian despotism," he wrote in his autobiography.

> Those of the Allied countries had no excuse for rejecting the peace program of their Russian comrades. To the Socialists of the whole world, peace had become an urgent necessity, not only for its own sake, but also for the preservation of democracy and for the success of the rapidly growing Socialist and labor movement of Russia.[40]

---

36 *4,000 Workers Here Decry War*, N.Y. TRIB., Feb. 6, 1917, at 4.

37 AM. SOCIALISTS, *supra* note 34, at 34.

38 *Review and Outlook*, WALL. ST. J., Feb. 9, 1917, at 1.

39 *Socialists in U.S., Says Morris Hillquit, Opposed to War*, N.Y. TIMES, Feb. 11, 1917, at 2.

40 LOOSE LEAVES, *supra* note 1, at 154-55.

At the time, Hillquit seemed overjoyed by the February revolution for its own sake, rather than for its impact on the war. "Russia is free!" he proclaimed at a rally of some 12,000 people in Madison Square Garden in March. "All the dark powers of tyranny and reaction, of persecution and oppression, under whose baneful rule the Russian people have been suffering for generations, have been conquered and destroyed .... Replaced by the triumphant red flags of the revolution."[41]

By the end of the month, however, the entry of the United States into the war appeared imminent, and the Emergency Committee sent off a message to President Wilson on March 30 urging him to refrain from issuing a declaration of war and demanding a popular referendum on the issue.[42] It was much too late, and on April 6, 1917, the United States declared war on Germany. An Emergency National Convention was hastily convened in St. Louis, and Hillquit was named chairman and gave the keynote address. Hillquit lamented the decline in Socialist Party membership since the last convention, in 1912, and decried the fact that the United States "has been violently, needlessly, criminally drawn" into the war. He correctly predicted the repression that would accompany America's entry, but expressed optimism that the Russian Revolution heralded "the arrival of our movement; the unmistakable signs of the collapse of our inveterate foe, the capitalist system."[43]

But the St. Louis convention was far from harmonious and revealed that the party was divided over the war. A "Majority Report," which Hillquit helped to draft and signed, reaffirmed its allegiance to the principle of internationalism and proclaimed its unalterable opposition to the war just declared by the United States.[44] A "Minority Report" acknowledged the U.S. entry as a fact, reflecting the failure of the Socialist movement to stop it. "Our aim now must be to minimize the suffering and misery which the war will ring to our own people."[45] The language of both reports was rather more centrist than the extremes of party sentiment, and later that month, Hillquit condemned the charge levelled by fellow socialists, Algie Simons and Allen Benson, that the anti-war report was treasonable.[46] The rift would get worse before it got better.

Meanwhile, the dormant International Socialist Bureau had aroused sufficiently to organize a peace conference in Stockholm on May 15. Hillquit was designated by the Socialist Party of America as a delegate and immediately applied for a

---

[41] *Crowd of 12,000 Cheers Mention of "Free Russia,"* N.Y. TRIB., March 21, 1917, at 4.

[42] AM. SOCIALISTS, *supra* note 34, at 37.

[43] *Keynote Address to the 1917 Emergency National Convention of the Socialist Party, St. Louis, Mo. – April 7, 1917,* THE WORLD (Oakland, Calif.), April 20, 1917, at 6.

[44] AM. SOCIALISTS, *supra* note 34, at 39.

[45] *Id.* at 43.

[46] Morris Hillquit, *As to Treason,* N.Y. CALL, April 26, 1917, at 6.

passport. But his passport was denied by the State Department under the Logan Act of 1799, which prohibited Americans from negotiating with any foreign government in relation to any dispute with the United States without government authorization. Secretary of State Robert Lansing called the proposed Stockholm meeting "a cleverly directed German war move," and, although the Bureau offered to postpone the meeting until the Americans could arrive,[47] other Allied governments followed Lansing's lead, and the meeting was never held. Instead, the Bureau served as a clearinghouse for mostly written reports.[48]

Hillquit condemned the State Department action, characterizing it as a blunder. "Our Administration has shown itself to be exceedingly credulous, arbitrary and shortsighted," he said on May 23.

> The basis for the decision was the assumption that the conference was of German origin and that the object was to promote a separate or pro-German peace. This theory was spread by a few persons who were themselves ignorant of the origin and aims of the conference and who succeeded in frightening the Administration and the American public in general into belief in their fairy tales.[49]

In a snide retort, the *New York Sun* mused that "[one] good reason for not letting Mr. Morris Hillquit go abroad is what he has been saying about the war at home. Still, a one-way passport might have been a good bit of diplomacy."[50]

Hillquit continued to attack American socialists who supported the war. In an article for the *Call*, he characterized a pro-war German socialist as a "bungling amateur compared with our own accomplished masters in the art of party treachery."[51] Earlier, in a letter to the *Times*, Hillquit called on American socialists to refrain from interfering with or trying to influence the course of the Russian Revolution. The most prominent of the pro-war socialists, novelist Upton Sinclair, responded to the latter by pointing out that the Germans were sending hundreds of social revolutionists into Russia to undermine their war effort. "May it not be that the reason Comrade Hillquit is willing to sit back so complacently and let events in Russia take their course is because the course which they are taking is the one which he considers desirable ...?" Sinclair wrote.[52]

---

[47] *Socialists' Congress May Await Americans*, N.Y. TIMES, April 28, 1917, at 13.

[48] LOOSE LEAVES, *supra* note 1, at 155-57.

[49] *U.S. Erred in Refusing Passports to Socialist Delegates, Hillquit Says*, N.Y. TRIB., May 24, 1917, at 2.

[50] Untitled, N.Y. SUN, May 25, 1917, at 14.

[51] Morris Hillquit, *Out-Scheidemanning Scheidemann*, N.Y. CALL, May 19, 1917, at 2.

[52] *Sinclair Answers Hillquit*, N.Y. TIMES, May 25, 1917, at 10.

Still suffering from another bout with tuberculosis, Hillquit was well enough by March 1919 to write an introduction to an edition of the transcript of the *Nearing* case published by the American Socialist Society. Citing all the major Socialist cases of the moment, Hillquit said it was largely fortuitous that Scott Nearing had been acquitted, while most of the others were convicted "and sentenced to savagely heavy prison terms." Hillquit predicted that these trials were only the "harbingers of an era of systematic governmental prosecution of all radical opinion and radical movements in the United States .... In the capitalist soviets of America, the dictature of the bourgeoisie reigns supreme."[53]

While convalescing at Saranac Lake, Hillquit undertook a lengthy piece for the *New York Call* on "The Socialist Task and Outlook." In that article, he blamed the socialist movement's "physical disunion, moral ferment, and intellectual confusion" coming out of the war not on right-leaning parliamentarianism, as had been charged, but on the organized labor movement. He characterized the labor movement as the "movement of a class within a class, a movement for the benefit of the better-situated strata of labor—the skilled workers." The accumulated wealth and political power of this semi-privileged class created certain vested interests in the capitalist regimes of their respective countries, while the organization of the labor unions created a "psychology of craft solidarity, rather than class solidarity, and deflects the workers' attention from the ultimate goal to immediate benefits."

Hillquit said the first task of the postwar Socialist International "must, therefore, be to organize and reorganize all grades and strata of labor on broad class lines, not only nationally, but internationally. Not as trade unions, or even as mere industrial unions, but as one working-class union." He called for achieving this goal in the United States through propaganda and organization. He lamented the fact that "the energies of the Socialist Party should at this time be dissipated in acrimonious and fruitless controversies brought on by the self-styled 'Left Wing' movement." Hillquit condemned the leftward drift of the party as "reactionary and non-socialistic" leading nowhere. "To prate about the 'dictatorship of the proletariat' and of 'workers' soviets' in the United States ... is to deflect the socialist propaganda from its realistic basis, and to advocate 'the abolition of *all* social reform planks' in the party platform means to abandon the concrete class struggle..." Significantly, he called on the left to separate itself from the mainstream party, "honestly, freely, and without rancor," each to organize and work it its own way. "The time for action is near. Let us clear the decks."[54]

---

[53] Morris Hillquit, *Introduction* to AM. SOCIALIST SOC., THE TRIAL OF SCOTT NEARING AND THE AMERICAN SOCIALIST SOCIETY 4-5 (1919) [hereinafter Nearing Trial].

[54] Morris Hillquit, *The Socialist Task and Outlook,* N.Y. CALL, May 21, 1919, at 8.

Hillquit's article was taken very seriously by the party, which began expelling leftists almost immediately, and even drew the notice of the mainstream press. The political divorce continued throughout the summer and into the fall of 1919,[55] yet, notwithstanding Hillquit's conviction that a Soviet-style dictatorship of the proletariat was wrong for the United States, he hailed the second anniversary of the Soviet Union in a brief article for *The Call.* Despite every effort to destroy it, he wrote, "the Socialist Republic of Russia lives. The 2nd Anniversary of its birth finds it strong and stable, confident and invincible, dreaded and cursed by the oppressors of all lands, acclaimed and cherished by the forward-looking workers of all nations and races. Hail, Soviet Russia!"[56]

Hillquit spent much of the fall of 1920 writing. In September, he published *Present-Day Socialism,* an update of his 1912 *Socialism Summed Up,* with a new chapter on Soviet Russia and substantial revisions to account for the impact of war and revolution.[57] In October, he wrote an article for the *New York Times*'s "October Current History" on "American versus Russian Socialists,"[58] as well as an article on "Radicalism in America" for *The Socialist World,* disparaging the contributions to socialism of the Farmer-Labor Party on the right and the Communist Party on the left.[59]

The following year, Hillquit published a book entitled *From Marx to Lenin* and designed "to clarify the main issues and problems of the present-day Socialist movement," specifically the relationship between socialism and the Russian Revolution. "The Socialist world was not prepared for a social revolution in Russia," he wrote. It was "utterly out of keeping with the conception of social evolution which dominated the international Socialist movement before the war," and "developed a complex of new social institutions, substantially at variance with those prevailing or anticipated in other countries," and this divergence accounts for "the heated discussions in the ranks of the present-day Socialist movement."[60]

In 1923, as Hillquit was working to fuse the Socialist and Farmer-Labor parties into a single entity comparable to the British Labor Party, he published a brief pamphlet entitled *The Story of the British Labor Party,* which he concluded:

---

55 *See, e.g., The "Left Wing" is Clipped,* N.Y. TRIB., June 8. 1919, at 81; *The Left Wing Bolts, Splitting the Socialist Party,* N.Y. TRIB., June 29, 1919, at 57; *Yipsels' Defection Ignored by Leaders of Socialist Party,* N.Y. TRIB., Oct. 3, 1919, at 11.

56 Morris Hillquit, *Socialist Russia Against the Capitalist World,* N.Y. CALL, Nov. 7, 1919, at 8.

57 Morris Hillquit, *Preface,* in Morris Hillquit, PRESENT-DAY SOCIALISM 5 (1920).

58 *October Current History* (advertisement), N.Y. TIMES, Oct. 3, 1920, at 99.

59 Morris Hillquit, *Radicalism in America,* THE SOCIALIST WORLD, Oct. 15, 1920, at 18-19.

60 MORRIS HILLQUIT, FROM MARX TO LENIN 5, 8 (1921). *See also A Socialist on Lenin* (book review), N.Y. HERALD, July 10, 1921, at 66.

> With the crying need for political relief in this country, and with the example and ready methods of England back of us we can form a powerful Labor Party in this country to-day; we can challenge the supremacy of the old parties in a few years. Let us go and do it.[61]

While the creation of an American labor party gained some momentum, it was strongly opposed by the conservative railroad unions and ultimately superseded by socialist support for the La Follette campaign of 1924.[62]

Hillquit continued writing and publishing in the last years of his life. On the death of Eugene Debs in 1925, Hillquit wrote a brief but poignant essay in *The New Leader*. "The world without Gene Debs," he wrote, "is a poorer and drearier place to live in."[63] And in 1930, he wrote a very favorable review of *The Labor Injunction*, by Felix Frankfurter and Nathan Greene, for the *St. Johns Law Review*, even as he condemned the practice. "The intricate and delicate issues of labor disputes present problems of social and human relationship which may be composed by a patient and painstaking process of sympathetic counsel and mediation, but cannot be justly determined by a summary order or judgment of a court."[64]

Morris Hillquit died on October 8, 1933, of tuberculosis. He had become gravely ill since the 1932 election and never fully recovered. He died at his home on East 63rd Street, with his wife Vera, their two children, his sister and two brothers at his bedside. His body was taken to the Debs Auditorium at The People's House, where it was to lie in state for one full day before a procession to his funeral at Cooper Union and cremation. Thousands of mourners filed past his flower-banked bier.[65] In his will, Hillquit left $1,000 each to the American Socialist Society, the Socialist Society of America, and the Leader Publishing Association, with the rest of his estate, more than $10,000, going to his widow.[66]

---

[61] MORRIS HILLQUIT, THE STORY OF THE BRITISH LABOR PARTY 4 (1923).

[62] PRATT, *supra* note 24, at 191-92. Pratt puts some of the blame for the new party's failure on Hillquit himself. "Perhaps it was one of Hillquit's greatest failings as a political leader that he could not act on mass response even when that response coincided with his own deepest beliefs and ambitions." *Id.*

[63] Morris Hillquit, *A Tribute to Debs*, NEW LEADER, Oct. 23, 1925, at 1.

[64] Morris Hillquit, *The Labor Injunction*, 5 ST. JOHNS L. REV. 164 (1930) (book review).

[65] *Morris Hillquit, Socialist Party Leader, Is Dead*, *supra* note 531, at 1; *Nation Mourns Hillquit, Chief of Socialists*, BROOKLYN DAILY EAGLE, Oct. 9, 1933, at 15; *Obituary*, N.Y. DAILY NEWS, Oct. 9, 1933, at 32.

[66] *Socialist Bodies Get $1,000 Each in Hillquit Will*, N.Y. DAILY NEWS, Oct. 26, 1933, at 1.

Seymour Stedman

During the 1920s, Seymour Stedman became increasingly involved in a business venture that would ultimately prove highly problematic for him. The Co-operative Society of America was established in 1919 in Chicago with the goal of allowing people to "avail themselves of the advantages of co-operation as a welcome escape from the unconscionable profiteering of rapacious tradesmen." Led primarily by Harrison M. Parker, the society was established as a common law trust, enlisting more than 150,000 members and accruing some $28,000,000 in subscription income during its first two-and-a-half years. With these funds, the society bought or established grocery stores, banks and insurance companies, canneries, and factories, all with a view toward reducing consumer prices.[67]

Litigation on a variety of issues, including bankruptcy, prompted a major reorganization in 1921;[68] Seymour Stedman was named a trustee of the organization by the bankruptcy judge.[69] Although the reorganization temporarily ended the litigation, it did not end the society's problems. In 1923, Stedman reported that the number of members fell to fewer than 70,000 through the failure of the mail-order branch of the business and defaults in the payment of subscription balances.[70] Stedman admitted rumors that the society's mail-order business lost $200,000 during 1922 and would be discontinued. In the wake of these disclosures, Parker resigned, although Stedman insisted that his resignation was entirely voluntary.[71]

By 1923, Stedman was considered the leading trustee of the society, but the University of Chicago economist Colston Warne, one of the founders of the Consumers Union, cast serious doubts on the accuracy of Stedman's representations as to the society's assets in that year.

> Mr. Seymour Stedman, the leading trustee of the society, claims assets of $4,500,000 pointing to a $1,500,000 increase in the value of the Peoples Life Building, controlled by the society, and a great expansion in the business of the Peoples Life Insurance Co. and the City State Bank of Chicago. It seems unlikely, however, that the assets total more than $1,000,000, from the facts that are available. No balance sheets [have]

---

[67] Colston E. Warne, *The Co-operative Society of America—A Common Law Trust*, 1 UNIV. J. OF BUS. 373, 373-74 (1923).

[68] *Id.* at 376, 383-84.

[69] *Stedman Slated "Co-op" Trustee in New Regime*, CHI. TRIB., March 10, 1922, at 17.

[70] Warne, *supra* note 67, at 373 n. 1.

[71] *Harrison Parker Resigns from Co-op Society*, CHI. TRIB., Feb. 22, 1923, at 6.

been recently issued, the trustees stating that they fear another law suit.[72]

Those fears were certainly justified. One case, seeking fees for certain legal and promotional services allegedly contracted by Parker, dragged on from 1921 through 1928, when the Appellate Court of Illinois upheld two lower-court rulings that plaintiffs had no contract enforceable against the trust estate.[73]

By the end of 1927, matters seemed to be looking up for the society. Stedman announced that the society was ready to make a disbursement of 50 cents per share, not as a dividend, but as assurance that financial progress was being made. Stedman said the asset value of the stock had brought its book value up from $3 a share to $38 a share, the result of sound management by the trustees, increased value of Loop real estate, and continued payments by a small portion of the original investors. He declared the present membership to be 29,000 members who had paid in full, and another 11,000 who would ultimately pay for their stock. In three years, he predicted, the society would be able to pay a substantial dividend at regular periods.[74]

In fact, Stedman's worst problems were just beginning. The society had purchased the majority stock of the City State Bank of Chicago in May 1921 for about $185,000.[75] Stedman was identified throughout the 1920s in the bank's advertising as a director and vice president,[76] and elsewhere as trust officer[77] and, incorrectly, as president in one article.[78] Then, in October 1929, the stock market crashed, and a few days later, on November 2, 1929, State Auditor Oscar Nelson ordered the bank to close for examination. Nelson said he took that step because of the bank's low cash reserve and the "frozen" condition of a portion of its assets. Stedman said that "depositors need not worry, they will be paid 100 cents on the dollar." Stedman blamed the bank's condition on a depression in the real estate market and withdrawals amounting to a "run" on the bank during the recent stock market plunges. [79]

Within a few days, Nelson announced that plans were underway to reorganize the bank—a reorganization that would never happen—and a week later,[80] Gen.

---

[72] Warne, *supra* note 67, at 384 n. 6.

[73] Sykes v. Parker, 250 Ill. App. 299 (1928).

[74] *Co-op Society to Pay 50 Cent Disbursements,* CHI. TRIB., Nov. 26, 1927, at 21.

[75] Warne, *supra* note 67, at 381.

[76] Advertisement for City State Bank, CHI. TRIB., July 6, 1926, at 26.

[77] Advertisement for Sleepy Hollow Mausoleum and Abbey, CHI. TRIB., Sept. 12, 1927, at 20.

[78] *Plan 23 Story Building on North Wells St.,* CHI. TRIB., Feb. 5, 1927, at 21.

[79] *City State Bank of Chicago Is Shut by Nelson,* CHI. TRIB., Nov. 3, 1929, at 1.

[80] *Move to Reorganize Bank in Loop Closed by State,* CHI. TRIB., Nov. 5, 1929, at 2.

Abel Davis, vice president of the Chicago Title and Trust Co., was appointed receiver.[81] Matters only got worse from there, as the Co-operative Society of America, now declared bankrupt, and its affiliated companies came under even closer scrutiny.[82] In December 1929, Davis estimated that bank depositors might get 50–75 cents on the dollar,[83] but when nothing was forthcoming by March 1930, State's Attorney John A. Swanson ordered a new investigation into the bank under pressure from depositors.[84] By May, it appeared that depositors might only get 10% of their deposits, if that.[85] On July 8, however, Circuit Judge William V. Brothers authorized Davis to pay out 20% of deposits before the end of the month, but with no expectation of any future payments.[86]

For Stedman, however, the losses were far more than financial. By April 1931, the investigations by the State's Attorney's office led to his indictment, along with seven other bank officers, for receiving deposits while the bank was insolvent.[87] Soon, more indictments were handed up, involving four more bank officers. The State's Attorney's office created a special bank bureau under Assistant State's Attorney Henry E. Ayers to investigate as many as 14 banks closed in Cook County. By early July, indictments were returned in seven of those banks, with more anticipated.[88]

Bringing these cases to trial proved extremely difficult and time-consuming. Ayers pointed out that his staff had been ready for trial in several of the bank cases, but the judges had granted continuances for one reason or another. In Stedman's case, for example, Judge Walter Stanton had agreed to delay the proceedings on nine occasions in 1931 and another nine occasions in the first half of 1932.[89] During that period, Stedman continued his law practice, failing to persuade the Illinois Supreme Court to reverse the conviction of Lon Fox, charged with embezzling funds from a United Mine Workers of America local.[90] And, in August 1932, Harrison Parker, the leading force behind the Co-operative Society of America, which owned the City State Bank, was convicted of

---

81 *Abel Davis Is Named Receiver of Closed Bank,* CHI. TRIB., Nov. 12, 1929, at 5.

82 *Suit Demands Accounting of Risk Company,* CHI. TRIB., Dec. 6, 1929, at 21.

83 *City State Bank Depositors May Get 50-75c on Dollar,* CHI. TRIB., Dec. 19, 1929, at 29.

84 *Swanson Again Urged to Investigate Bank Affairs,* CHI. TRIB., March 9, 1930, at 2. *See also Waiting for His Money,* CHI. TRIB., May 10, 1930, at 10.

85 *Closed Bank May Pay 10 Per Cent Deposits Soon,* CHI. TRIB., May 11, 1930, at 3.

86 *To Ask Court for City State Bank Decision,* CHI. TRIB., July 4, 1930, at 17; *City State Bank Depositors Get 20% Dividend,* CHI. TRIB., July 9, 1930, at 12.

87 *Indict Stedman, 7 More Officers of Closed Bank,* CHI. TRIB., April 28, 1931, at 11.

88 *14 Closed Banks Under Scrutiny of Prosecutors,* CHI. TRIB., July 6, 1931, at 8.

89 *Swanson Orders One More Plea for Bank Trials,* CHI. TRIB., May 16, 1932, at 18.

90 People v. Fox, 346 Ill. 374 (1931).

embezzling at least $100,000 and as much as $350,000 from the North American Trust Co. Parker was sentenced to one to ten years in prison.[91]

And still the Stedman case languished, postponed again and again in early 1933.[92] When the trial was finally called, on March 22, the *Tribune* carried a photograph of Stedman that seemed to show every one of his 62 years ... and then some. His unruly shock of dark hair looked thin and white as he followed the jury selection process.[93] Jury selection took three days,[94] and when testimony opened on March 27, Judge Francis B. Allegretti's courtroom was packed with depositors who had lost most of their savings. In his opening statement, Assistant State's Attorney John O'Hora declared that the evidence would show that juggling of funds between the bank and the Co-operative Society of America had been going on for years before the bank was closed. "These defendants, Seymour Stedman, Morrison H. Castle and the rest, sanctioned loans of $1,100,000 from the bank to the Co-operative Society while they knew that the society and its affiliated companies were making no income," he said.[95]

The prosecution case lasted almost three weeks. Two former defendants testified for the prosecution against the five remaining defendants, and although the testimony exposed bank officers' and directors' self-dealing, there was no evidence that Stedman was involved in such conduct. The most damaging testimony against Stedman involved his approval of loans to the Co-operative Society of America.[96] At the close of the government's case, Stedman's lawyer, A. C. Lewis, asked for a directed verdict of not guilty, asserting that there

---

[91] *Harrison Parker Guilty of Fraud; Gets 1-10 Years,* CHI. TRIB., Aug. 28, 1932, at 9.

[92] *See, e.g., Judge Grants New Delay in City State Bank Case,* CHI. TRIB., Feb. 1, 1933, at 18; *43d Hearing Is Held on City State Bank Case,* CHI. TRIB., March 4, 1933, at 4; *Orders Stedman and 7 Others to Trial Today,* CHI. TRIB., March 14, 1933, at 17; *City State Bank Case Trial Put Off 49th Time,* CHI. TRIB., March 19, 1933, at 10.

[93] *Officials of Closed Bank on Trial,* CHI. TRIB., March 23, 1933, at 28.

[94] *3 Chosen Tentatively for Jury in Bank Trial,* CHI. TRIB., March 23, 1933, at 4; *Four Selected for Jury in City State Bank Trial,* CHI. TRIB., March 24, 1933, at 14; *City State Bank Officers' Trial Jury Completed,* CHI. TRIB., March 26, 1933, at 15.

[95] *City State Bank Loans Attacked as Trial Opens,* CHI. TRIB., March 28, 1933, at 3.

[96] *See Auditor Will Testify Today in Bank Trial,* CHI. TRIB., March 29, 1933, at 15; *City State Bank Ex-Chief Takes Stand for State,* CHI. TRIB., April 1, 1933, at 9; *Bank Official's Loans for Own Projects Bared,* CHI. TRIB., April 2, 1933, at 22; *Ex-Banker Cries "Liar" at Trial; Gets Reprimand,* CHI. TRIB., April 4, 1933, at 20; *City State Bank Hides Business Bared in Trial,* CHI. TRIB., April 5, 1933, at 15; *Ex-Banker Aids Prosecution in City State Case,* CHI. TRIB., April 6, 1933, at 11; *State's Case in City State Bank Trial Near End,* CHI. TRIB., April 8, 1933; *More Records Introduced in City State Bank Trial,* CHI. TRIB., April 9, 1933, at 3.

was "no larceny or embezzlement in the bank, only bad judgment based on predictions of the return of prosperity."[97]

After deliberating for nine hours and taking 25 ballots, the jury returned verdicts of guilty as to all five defendants on April 26, 1933. Stedman and one other defendant were sentenced to one to three years in the penitentiary and a fine of $210, based on a law prescribing fines of double the loss of the injured depositor identified in the indictment. Three defendants were sentenced to fines only.[98] On May 13, Judge Allegretti heard four hours of argument on a new trial for Stedman; he denied the motion, but said he would hear a petition to stay Stedman's incarceration pending appeal.[99]

Two years later, the Illinois Court of Appeals reversed four of the convictions, including Stedman's, holding that the evidence did not support a finding that the defendants knew the bank was insolvent at the time the deposits in question were received. The fifth defendant had paid his fine and did not join the appeal. In its opinion, the court noted that Stedman had made a substantial deposit the day before the bank closed, that he had a balance of $621 in a commercial account and $580 in a savings account, and that he held bonds and mortgages he bought from the bank.[100]

Stedman resumed the practice of law after his conviction was reversed. In December 1935, he successfully defended his client, Drexel Ice Cream Co., from an action to recover $16,500 allegedly owed to the bankrupt firm of Korbakes Brothers.[101] In 1939, he lost one appeal by his client, A. H. Patek, in a complex trust case,[102] and another appeal on Drexel's behalf to recover on a judgment note.[103] There were no further reported cases.

In 1942, Stedman again appeared in public, this time to eulogize Dr. Ben Reitman, whom the *Tribune* called an "eccentric apostle of many isms" and who was once the lover of anarchist Emma Goldman. "I first met Dr. Reitman in 1920 when I defended him on charges of rioting and disorderly conduct in leading a parade of unemployed through the loop," Stedman said. "I always regarded him as a philosophical anarchist. He was in the class with Ralph Waldo Emerson, Eugene V. Debs [whom Stedman had also eulogized on his death in

---

97 *Judge to Rule Today on Plea to Acquit Bankers*, CHI. TRIB., April 13, 1933, at 8.

98 *Five City State Bank Officials Found Guilty*, CHI. TRIB., April 27, 1933, at 8.

99 *Stedman and 4 Aids Lose Plea for New Trial*, CHI. TRIB., May 14, 1933, at 3.

100 People v. Stedman, 279 Ill. App. 630 (1935); *Banker Stedman Wins Retrial on Appeal; 2 Freed*, CHI. TRIB., March 12, 1935, at 17.

101 Martin v. Drexel Ice Cream Co., 80 F.2d 768 (7th Cir. 1935).

102 Collins v. Baim, 299 Ill. App. 405 (1939).

103 Drexel Ice Cream Co. v. Armenali, 302 Ill. App. 430 (1939).

1926[104]], and Henry Thoreau. I liked him and he liked me." At that point, Stedman burst into tears and fled from the room.[105]

Seymour Stedman died on July 9, 1948, at age 78. He was survived by his widow, Irene; a sister, Myrtle Moulton; and a brother, Howard. He was buried in Oak Woods cemetery.[106]

Charles Recht

When Charles Recht died in 1965, the few obituaries published at the time were terse and without encomium. Typical was the paragraph in New York's *Daily News*:

> Charles Recht, 78, an attorney in this country for the Soviet government since 1919, died yesterday in University Hospital after a heart attack. Recht, who lived at 77 Park Ave., was also a novelist, poet and translator. Services will be held at 1:30 P.M. tomorrow in the Universal Funeral Chapel, Lexington Ave. and 52nd St.[107]

That the clipping emphasized Recht's literary output nearly as much as his legal accomplishment is, perhaps, understandable. Early in his career, Recht co-wrote, with Leigh Danen, *The Newest Freedom*, which his publisher, Irving Kaye Davis & Co., advertised as "A great book on the wreck of the Constitution."[108]

Later, Recht wrote two novels, *Rue with a Difference* in 1924 and Babylon on Hudson in 1932. The murder novel *Rue with a Difference* was favorably reviewed in *The New Republic* by critic R. M. L., who drew parallels with the Leopold and Loeb case that Clarence Darrow was trying in Chicago at the same time. Like Darrow, the critic wrote, Recht "tells us that it is crime with a difference," using the "device of emptying his hero's mind of all the miscellaneous stuff which it contains and finding motivation enough for a dozen murders.

> Again, he joins Mr. Darrow in protest against the threadbare externality of our judicial procedure. 'What did all the circumlocutions mean, and why were trivial incidents being marshalled forth in the finery of matters of import, when the things which actually counted ... were not considered?'
>
> Lest it be thought that Mr. Recht's story lacks interest by reason of seriousness and social criticism, we hasten to add that it is unusually

---

104 *Body of Debs at Terre Haute for Rites Tomorrow*, CHI. TRIB., Oct. 22, 1926, at 9.

105 *Friends Eulogize Dr. Ben Reitman in Chapel Rites*, CHI. TRIB., Nov. 20, 1942, at 16.

106 *S. Stedman, 78, Dies; Banker and Socialist*, CHI. TRIB., July 10, 1948, at 9.

107 *Charles Recht*, N.Y. DAILY NEWS, July 17, 1965, at 20.

108 Advertisement, THE NEW REPUBLIC, July 16, 1919, at 36.

> rich in fictional values. Its action would supply material for a moving picture drama and [the protagonist] Herbert Satterlee's mind would show up well on the screen.[109]

In between the novels, he published a book of poetry, *Manhattan Made*, in 1930, which literary critic Ludwig Lewisohn called "profoundly interesting." This poetry "cuts deep," he said, "it stirs the mind; it is of us and our age."[110] Recht also translated poetry, such as *At the Chasm*, by Jaroslav Vrchlicky, in 1913, and a number of plays, including *The Clouds*, by Jaroslav Kvapil, in 1910; *Countess Julie*, by August Strindberg, in 1912; *Morals*, by Ludwig Thoma, in 1925; and *Heckuba-Hackuba*, by Lajos N. Egri, in 1927 (adaptation). Recht published an article entitled "The Modern Theatre" in *The Reflex* in August 1928[111] and another called "'Movied' to Reflection" in the September issue.[112] Recht's poetry and essays were widely published in *Soviet Russia Pictorial* in the 1920s[113] and such left-wing publications as *Liberator* in the 1910s and 1920s, and *The Fight* and *The New Masses* in the 1930s.

The New Republic received letters from Recht throughout his career. In 1919, writing as attorney for striking cigar makers, Recht told the magazine's readers that "[v]ictory for the striking cigar-makers means better working conditions" and "[b]etter working conditions means better cigars." And he reminded readers that a "union-made cigar ... bears a blue label."[114] In 1936, he critiqued Stuart Chase's book *Rich Land, Poor Land: A Study of Waste in the Natural Resources of America* as the "truth but not the whole truth." Recht said there was "plenty of evidence to point that populations do not necessarily drift away because the land has lost fertility; but that where nations become weakened by wars, pestilence and undisciplined regimes of national economy ... irrigation, drainage and land culture cease and the desert creeps up and swallows the soil."[115] The next year, the magazine cited, but did not republish, a letter from Recht—as the American representative of the International Bureau for Asylum and Aid to Political Refugees—seeking funds to assist Spanish civil war refugees inside the French border.[116]

---

109 *Rue with a Difference* (book review), THE NEW REPUBLIC, Sept. 10, 1924, at 54.

110 Advertisement, THE NEW REPUBLIC, March 26, 1930, at 5.

111 Advertisement, THE NEW REPUBLIC, Sept. 19, 1928, at 28.

112 Advertisement, THE NEW REPUBLIC, Oct. 17, 1928, at 29.

113 *See, e.g., The March "Pictorial,"* THE DAILY WORKER, March 17, 1923, at 4.

114 *Smoke Blue Label Cigars?*, THE NEW REPUBLIC, Oct. 1, 1919, at 25.

115 *"Rich Land, Poor Land,"* THE NEW REPUBLIC, Oct. 21, 1936, at 23.

116 *From The New Republic Mail Bag*, THE NEW REPUBLIC, Feb. 17, 1937, at 23.

By the 1960s, new and different causes—civil rights, Vietnam—had captured the attention of the American left. Recht's early work with the Bureau of Legal Advice, his participation in such important cases as *Masses* and *Gitlow*, and his representation of soapbox orators, draft resisters, embattled teachers, Wobblies and other deportees was long forgotten in the United States. But when Elizabeth Gurley Flynn visited Moscow in 1960, she found old comrades who remembered him fondly. "They ... inquired about attorney Charles Recht who handled many of their cases in the 20s and would be delighted to hear from him," she wrote.[117]

[117] Elizabeth Gurley Flynn, *I Meet Old Friends in Moscow*, THE WORKER, July 1, 1960, at 7.

Part II

Chapter 5
The Major Cases

Johann Most (1901)

Morris Hillquit

In 1901, Morris Hillquit represented his first high-profile political client, the anarchist firebrand Johann Most. Most was born in Augsburg, Germany, in 1846 and worked as a traveling bookbinder throughout Central Europe. In 1868, he joined the Swiss section of the First Socialist International in Zurich and quickly rose to a leadership position. The following year, he led a revolutionary demonstration before the Austrian Parliament, which resulted in the first of his many incarcerations. Expelled from Austria, Most returned to Germany, where he became editor of a socialist newspaper. In 1874, he was elected to the Reichstag, only to be prosecuted for seditious speech and imprisoned once again.

With the enactment of anti-socialist laws in Germany, Most was expelled, and he settled in England, where he established a new socialist newspaper, *Freiheit*. There, Most's impatience with socialist leaders resulted in his expulsion from the Social Democratic Party, and he turned instead to a violent, aggressive form of anarchism. When he extolled the assassination of Czar Alexander II by nihilists in 1881, he was imprisoned in London. After his release the following year, he sailed to New York, where he assumed the leadership of the anarchist movement in the United States. He managed to stay out of jail for five years, but when he made an incendiary speech in New York on the conviction of the eight Haymarket anarchists in Chicago in 1886, he was arrested, tried, convicted and sentenced to one year at Blackwell's Island.

He resumed his publishing activities upon his release and on September 5, 1901, carried a front-page article written around 1850 by another German anarchist, Karl Heinzen, which he had reprinted several times before. The article, *Murder Against Murder*, was a fiery defense of the use of violence and murder to overthrow the despotic rulers of 1848 Europe, who, the article suggested, had achieved their power through violence and murder. Unfortunately for Most, President William McKinley was shot the very next day by another anarchist in Buffalo. Most was arrested and charged with violating a provision of the New York penal code that made it a misdemeanor "to commit an act which seriously disturbs or endangers the public peace or openly outrages public decency."

Most had represented himself in Police Court, where he was bound over for trial before a three-judge panel of the City Court of New York, Special Sessions, First Division. That court directed Most to obtain counsel, and Most, who was free on a $500 bond, called on Morris Hillquit. It was an odd choice, since there was little love lost between anarchists and socialists, and Hillquit recalled that Most did his best to get Hillquit to refuse representation. Most acquiesced when Hillquit offered to take on the defense without charge.

At trial, Hillquit argued that the Heinzen article was 50 years old and aimed at the crowned heads of Europe, not democratically elected officials like McKinley. Heinzen himself was long dead, and the article had been reprinted several times without any problem. Hillquit contended that the statute was vague and, in any event, the speech was protected by the First Amendment.[1] He also asserted that, as soon as Most heard about the assassination, he tried to recall all copies of the paper, though a few were already delivered, and one copy was purchased by the New York City police.[2] The court would have none of it.

> We hold that the teachings of the doctrine of anarchy "seriously disturb or endanger the public peace" and also "openly outrage public decency." To give this construction to the law in no way abridges the liberty of conscience in matters of religion, nor the freedom of speech on all questions of government or of social life, or does it in any way trespass upon the proper freedom of the press.[3]

Most was given the maximum sentence of one year's imprisonment on Blackwell's Island, but Hillquit sought and received a "certificate of reasonable doubt" that allowed Most to remain free pending appeal. Granting the certificate, Supreme Court Justice Charles F. Maclean expressed his belief that Most's publication was constitutionally protected speech. "It is not shown that the defendant's expression of borrowed sentiments has worked injury to any individual by falsifying any fact, or to the public by disturbing or endangering the public peace," he said.[4]

Maclean's confidence was misplaced. Affirming Most's conviction, the New York Supreme Court, Appellate Division, was just as adamant as the lower court had been:

---

1 MORRIS HILLQUIT, LOOSE LEAVES FROM A BUSY LIFE 120-27 (De Capo Press 1971) (1934) [hereinafter LOOSE LEAVES].

2 New York v. Most, 73 N.Y.S. 220, 223 (N.Y. City Ct., Spec. Sess. 1901).

3 *Id.* at 222.

4 LOOSE LEAVES, *supra* note 1, at 128.

> [W]hoever openly or secretly advocates the resort to force, in opposition to the law of the State, for the accomplishment of any purpose, or the righting of any wrong, either real or imaginary, seriously endangers the public peace .... [N]o one has the right to use [freedom of the press] in such a way as to injure his fellow citizens, and one who imagines that he has labors under a serious misconception.[5]

Finally, Hillquit took an appeal to the New York Court of Appeals, the highest court in the state. The results were the same:

> The Constitution... places no restraint upon the power of the legislature to punish the publication of matter which is injurious to society .... It does not deprive the state of the primary right of self-preservation. It does not sanction unbridled license, nor authorize the publication of articles prompting the commission of murder or the overthrow of government by force .... We think that no constitutional right of the defendant was violated by his conviction and that the judgment pronounced against him was rendered in accordance with law.[6]

By the time Most emerged from prison, Hillquit wrote, he was "a broken man, sluggish, cynical, and indifferent. During the remaining four years of his life he went through the accustomed motions of the anarchist writer and propagandist, but he was no longer the former spirited and impetuous Johann Most." The law was changed, too, with the legislature making criminal anarchy—advocating forcible overthrow of government or assassination of any government official—a felony.[7]

Masses I (1917)

Morris Hillquit

In June 1917, Congress enacted the Espionage Act, which would open a new area of Hillquit's practice: defending socialist publications from crippling, often fatal postal sanctions, and defending their editors and contributors from prison. Among the many early victims of the new law were the weekly *American Socialist* newspaper and the monthly socialist magazine *The Masses.* Issues of both were declared unmailable by the Postmaster under the Espionage Act in early July because of articles, poems, and cartoons that criticized the war. The National Executive Committee of the Socialist Party, of which Hillquit was a

---

[5] People v. Most, 75 N.Y.S. 591, 592-93 (N.Y. App. Div. 1902).

[6] People v. Most, 64 N.E. 175, 178 (N.Y. 1902).

[7] LOOSE LEAVES, *supra* note 1, at 128.

member, met in Chicago on July 6 and 7 to plan a strategy. It was decided to send a delegation to Washington to try to resolve the issue facing the socialist press. Hillquit would be on the committee, as well as famed attorney Clarence Darrow, Chicago Socialist Party leader Seymour Stedman, and Frank Walsh of the U.S. Commission on Industrial Relations.[8]

Joined by Amos Pinchot and Roger Baldwin, representing the Civil Liberties Bureau of the American Union Against Militarism; Fannie May Witherspoon of the Woman's Peace Party; Julian Pierce, a socialist national committeeman from the District of Columbia; and Thomas A. Hickey, editor of *The Rebel*, the delegation met with William C. Herron, special assistant to the attorney general for enforcement of the Espionage Act. After three hours, Herron ended the meeting with a promise to issue a statement giving a more concrete interpretation and application of the law. The delegation moved on to the Post Office Department, where Postmaster General Albert S. Burleson repeatedly denied any prejudice against the socialist press and vowed that he would decapitate any local postmaster who used his power for personal spite. Burleson was asked to join Herron in issuing a clear, concise, and definite statement of the law.[9]

The meetings proved futile. Three consecutive issues of *American Socialist* were barred from the mails, then the paper received a notice from the Post Office Department to the effect that the interruption in service violated the regulations governing second-class postage. The letter invited representatives of the paper to attend a hearing on July 20 to show cause why the paper's second-class privilege should not be revoked.[10] While the letter was signed by A. M. Dockery, Third Assistant Postmaster General, Burleson himself conducted the hearing. Stedman had submitted a written argument; Hillquit attended in person.

Hillquit told Burleson that the government bore the burden to show cause why the paper should be barred from the mail, rather than the reverse. If there was a response, Hillquit did not record it. Instead, Burleson pointed to one of Hillquit's own articles, a preface to his pamphlet on *American Socialists and the War*. "It is no more than a restatement of an economic theory and historical doctrine," Hillquit said. "It may be," Burleson replied, "but the article nevertheless conveys the impression that the war is not fought for the high idealistic purposes which the President has announced, but for sordid business advantages. It

---

[8] *Socialist Party Sends Committee to Washington to Confer with Postal Officials on Press Problem*, AM. SOCIALIST, July 14, 1917, at 1.

[9] J.L. Engdahl, *Press Has Right to Oppose Draft Law, Postmaster General Tells Socialists*, AM. SOCIALIST, July 21, 1917, at 1.

[10] *Nation's Press Recognizes American Socialist as Champion of Constitutional Liberties*, AM. SOCIALIST, July 28, 1917, at 1.

tends to impair the spirit of enthusiasm for the war." Hillquit recalled, "I realized the futility of any further attempt to argue the point."[11]

Hillquit got no further with the other issues before them, and the newspaper's mailing privileges were revoked. Twice, the publishers unsuccessfully appealed that ruling,[12] and by September, the newspaper ceased publication. Hillquit wrote that mailing privileges were withdrawn in rapid succession from the *Milwaukee Leader*, the *Jewish Daily Forward*, and from several socialist daily newspapers printed in German, Russian, and Hungarian.[13] When mailing privileges for *The Masses* were also suspended, it challenged the ruling in federal court. Led by an experienced lawyer, Gilbert E. Roe, a close colleague of progressive Sen. Robert La Follette (R-Wis.) and advocate for left-wing activists, *The Masses* won a landmark opinion by U.S. District Judge Learned Hand. Hand overruled the Postmaster's order, but his decision was promptly reversed by the U.S. Court of Appeals for the Second Circuit.[14]

While Hillquit would play no direct role in this civil action against the magazine, he would have a vital role in *Masses*' criminal litigation beginning in late 1917. On November 19, a federal grand jury of the Southern District of New York handed up an indictment for conspiracy to violate §3 and §4 of Title I of the Espionage Act. Named in the indictment were Masses Publishing Co. editor in chief Max Eastman, editor and writer Floyd Dell, reporter John Reed, poet Josephine Bell, cartoonists Henry J. Glintenkamp and Arthur Young, and business manager C. Merrill Rogers Jr. The first count of the indictment accused all the defendants of

> unlawfully, wilfully, knowingly and feloniously [conspiring] together and [agreeing] among themselves, and with divers other persons whose names are to the Grand Jurors unknown, to ... cause, and attempt to cause, insubordination, disloyalty, mutiny and refusal of duty in the military and naval forces of the United States ... through and by means of the publication ... of a certain monthly magazine called *The Masses* and the circulation and distribution of the same.[15]

That count also set out the basis for the charge against each individual defendant: Eastman, for an article entitled "A Question," which extolled the courage of those who resisted the draft on moral grounds; Dell, for an article entitled "Conscientious Objectors," which reprinted letters from imprisoned

---

[11] LOOSE LEAVES, *supra* note 1, at 212-13.

[12] *Americans! Your Country Needs You!* AM. SOCIALIST, Sept. 8, 1917, at 1.

[13] LOOSE LEAVES, *supra* note 1, at 214.

[14] *See* ERIC B. EASTON, DEFENDING THE MASSES 131-48 (2018).

[15] Indictment, United States v. Masses Pub. Co., et al., C10-327 (S.D.N.Y. Nov. 19, 1917), at 1-2.

British C.O.'s and commended their example to American men; Reed, for an article entitled "Knit a Strait-Jacket for Your Soldier Boy," a report on a study of mental illness in the military by the National Mental Hygiene Center, reprinted from the *New York Tribune*, and implying that the frequency of mental disease among soldiers had been unexpectedly high during the war; Bell, for a poem entitled "A Tribute," an homage to Emma Goldman and Alexander Berkman, recently convicted of violating the Conscription Act; Glintenkamp, for a cartoon "representing a skeleton symbolizing 'Death' taking the measurements of a drafted soldier for his coffin"; and Young, for a cartoon entitled "Having Their Fling," featuring characters representing the press, business, government, and the church, all dancing under a shower of money. Rogers was indicted simply for managing the business of co-defendant Masses Publishing Co.[16]

Count two cited the same content, but focused on the aim of the conspiracy to "obstruct the recruiting and enlistment service of the United States military by publishing articles, poems, and pictures calculated and intended to induce persons ... to refuse to submit to registration and draft or enlistment for services."[17] The indictment was signed by United States Attorney Francis G. Caffey, who then moved successfully to impound the company's books and records.[18]

There is nothing in the record to show whether Gilbert Roe—who had handled the *Masses* civil case against the postal authorities—was asked to take on the criminal defense. When the indictment was handed up, however, Roe had already moved on to another, far more lucrative civil case. Hillquit was a logical choice to lead the criminal defense team; less obvious was the decision to make Dudley Field Malone his second chair. Neither a socialist nor a pacifist, Malone had supported Hillquit in his just-concluded mayoral race. Perhaps it was thought that Malone, a confidant of Woodrow Wilson, might bring some political credibility along with his prodigious oratorical skills.

In any case, the defendants were arraigned and released on bail in the days following the indictment. Eastman's bail was set at $5,000 and Rogers's at $3,000. Bell and Young each put up $1,000 bonds, and Floyd Dell $500.[19] John Reed was still in Russia, reportedly waiting to be appointed Soviet Consul General in New York,[20] and Henry Glintenkamp was nowhere to be found.[21]

---

16 *Id.* at 3-4.

17 *Id.* at 6.

18 Order, United States v. Masses Pub. Co., et al., C10-327 (S.D.N.Y. Nov. 19, 1917).

19 Indictment, *supra* note 15 (handwritten notes on cover).

20 *Bolsheviki Call Francis Hostage for 'Consul' Reed*, N.Y. TRIB., Feb. 18, 1918, at 4.

21 LOOSE LEAVES, *supra* note 1, at 226.

Long before the trial began, however, the magazine had ceased publication forever.[22]

The *Masses* trial began on April 15, 1918, in U.S. District Court before Judge Augustus Hand. Hillquit and Malone stood against Assistant U.S. Attorneys Earl Barnes and Vincent A. Rothwell, along with Candler Cobb. The entire day was spent examining prospective jurors, a tedious process prompting Hand to admonish both sides to speed it up. Both Hillquit and Malone participated in the questioning, and, by the end of the day, eight had been selected.[23] The second day was much like the first, with many of the prospects conceding, in Hillquit's words, that they were "prejudiced against pacifists and Socialists, against writers and artists, against anything that tended to disturb the dead level of drab conformity and uniformity, and they gloried in their prejudices." When Hillquit asked Hand to excuse men in that frame of mind, the judge remarked, "You cannot get a jury anywhere in the United States not prejudiced against pacificism."[24]

Finally, a jury was selected, and Hand admonished them that the defendants were not on trial for their views on America's entry into the war or for expressing those views. He reminded them that the defendants should be regarded as innocent until the government proved they were guilty of a violation of the law. The prosecution opened its case the same day. "The government does not propose to prove that these defendants actually accomplished their purpose," Barnes told the jury. "It is necessary only to show they conspired to accomplish it .... No question of the constitutional right of free speech or free press is involved. Neither this government nor this court wishes to deny free speech or free press to any one, and if the government does not prove its case it asks that you acquit them."[25]

Barnes's first witness testified about the incorporation of Masses Publishing Co.; his second testified to printing the August 1917 issue—after enactment of the Espionage Act. Barnes read or showed the jury the excerpts from that issue on which the indictments were based. The next day, Barnes read from an issue that praised the Socialist Party's anti-war platform adopted at the 1916 St. Louis

---

[22] EASTON, *supra* note 14, at 147.

[23] *Five Put on Trial in "Masses" Case; John Reed Missing,* N.Y. TRIB., April 16, 1918, at 7.

[24] LOOSE LEAVES, *supra* note 1, at 230.

[25] *U.S. Opens Case Against Editors of "The Masses,"* N.Y. TRIB., April 17, 1918, at 18. *See, generally,* LOOSE LEAVES, *supra* note 1, at 230; John Sayer, *Art and Politics, Dissent and Repression: The Masses Magazine Versus the Government,* 1917-1918, 32 AM. J. LEGAL HIST. 42, 58 (1988).

convention. Hillquit and Malone objected that the article had been published before the Espionage Act became law and was thus irrelevant as evidence.

The second day also brought more testimony on the magazine's distribution processes, with one addressing-machine vendor telling the jury that Rogers had expressed anti-war and anti-conscription views when the vendor called on the magazine's business office. On cross-examination, Hillquit asked rhetorically, "Was your object in coming here to testify for the government to get newspaper notoriety?" A former publishing assistant testified that both Dell and Rogers had urged conscientious objectors to register and obey the conscription law up to the point of performing military duty, then claim exemption.[26]

At the conclusion of the government's case, Judge Hand dismissed the charges against poet Josephine Bell, holding that the evidence against her—a poem to Emma Goldman and Alexander Berkman—was insufficient to sustain a conviction. In his autobiography, Hillquit recounts Art Young's description of the action:

> Mr. Hillquit was sure that there was no line in the poem that could be construed as illegal, so he appealed to the judge to quash the indictment against Josephine Bell. Mr. Hillquit handed the poem to the Judge to read. His Honor adjusted his glasses, read it slowly, then handed it back to Mr. Hillquit, saying: "Do you call that a poem?"
>
> Mr. Hillquit replied, "Your Honor, it is so called in the indictment."
>
> The Judge said, "Indictment quashed."

Vivid as that description may be, Hillquit felt "impelled to confess that it represents a somewhat colored artistic interpretation of a prosaic legal procedure," and clarified that the dismissal was not based on the poem's artistic merits or lack thereof.[27]

Opening the case for the defense, Hillquit and Malone made "valiant efforts to divorce the jurors from their admitted prejudices against the defendants and their views on war," Hillquit recalls in his autobiography. Each of them, from their different perspectives, discussed the constitutional freedom of thought and expression. "How trite and common place these elementary principles seem in normal times," Hillquit wrote, "and how bold and defiant they sounded on April 18, 1918, in the war-laden atmosphere of the courtroom!"

---

26 *Anti-War Article Read at Trial of "Masses" Editors,* N.Y. TRIB., April 18, 1918, at 5.

27 LOOSE LEAVES, *supra* note 1, at 227. Yet another version of the dismissal appears in William L. O'Neill's biography of Eastman, which attributes the dismissal to Hand's learning that Bell did not know any of her alleged co-conspirators. WILLIAM L. O'NEILL, THE LAST ROMANTIC 75 (1991).

Hillquit went on to explain the mindset of the defendants, the purity of their motives in opposing the war and the draft.

> I argued that true patriotism ... is at least as consistent with a desire to protect [the people] from mass slaughter as with honest war enthusiasm, and I concluded these then were our honest views. Were we wrong? Were we right about it? Gentlemen, you are not called upon to pass on this question. History will be our Jury. No human being today can assume to render final judgment on the great problems which the world catastrophe has put before us. You are called upon to pass on only one thing: Are these men criminals? Did they conspire to injure their country? Did they conspire with the Imperial German Government in this war?[28]

Max Eastman was the first witness for the defense, and Hillquit offered a letter to him from President Wilson to show there was no conspiracy to discourage enlistment and recruiting. The letter confirmed, Hillquit said, that Eastman "went to Washington to consult with the chief of our army and navy" seeking tolerance for conscientious objectors. Under direct examination, Eastman denied having ever tried to circulate *The Masses* among men liable for military duty. "The object of *The Masses* was to combat the ritual of persecution imposed by the newspapers upon those who would not violate their consciences," Eastman said, "and we believe the American people would not withhold from them the admiration they gave to Nathan Hale, Abraham Lincoln and Jesus Christ."

Eastman also denied receiving financial aid for the magazine from any foreign government; denied that he was a pacifist, though he claimed not to be prejudiced against them; and denied that he approved of the anarchy of Goldman and Berkman, though he had urged that they receive a fair trial. At one point, Malone read a poem the magazine had published that was intensely supportive of the French war effort. "That doesn't look pro-German," he quipped.[29]

Under cross-examination the following day, Eastman conceded that students and other draft-eligible men had appealed to him for advice, but said he never advised anyone to evade the law or to take any steps other than to demand the law's repeal. Barnes read one such letter from a Wisconsin student who asked Eastman what he should do to advance the revolutionary movement in the face of conscription and war. Eastman said he sent the student a copy of *The Masses* and wrote a reply that read, "If you get in touch with the organizations which are at work you will find appropriate things suggested to you, I am sure." Barnes

---

[28] LOOSE LEAVES, *supra* note 1, at 231.

[29] *Eastman Denies He Is Pro-German or Violated Spy Law*, N.Y. TRIB., April 19, 1918, at 14.

introduced another letter asking what stand organized pacifists in New York would take in the event of conscription. Eastman replied, "No position in advance has been taken by any existing organization. But I feel sure that a riotous resistance would follow an attempt to conscript for service in Europe."

On redirect, Hillquit elicited the fact that all of this correspondence had been written before the conscription law went into effect. Asked what he meant by "riotous resistance," Eastman said he had been "wrought up" over the issue at that time. "It was not uncommon for people then to hold opposite opinions about conscription."[30] In all, Eastman testified for nine hours, most dramatically when he told Barnes on cross-examination that he had changed his personal position on the war. "I believe now that this war is a war for liberty and freedom," he said, adding that he did not believe that when some of his *Masses* articles were written.[31] Hillquit later attributed Eastman's change of heart to the onerous terms of the Brest-Litovsk treaty that seemed to endanger the Russian Revolution and Wilson's letter to the Pope outlining his famous "Fourteen Points," which Eastman endorsed.[32] Dell and Rogers had also converted by the time of the trial; only Young of the four defendants retained his anti-war convictions.[33]

When Merrill Rogers took the stand, Hillquit elicited from Rogers repeated assertions that the magazine's opposition to conscription was published before the law was enacted and that no attempt was ever made to circulate the publication with a view to inducing men not to enlist or to evade the draft. Hillquit noted one anti-war advertisement that appeared in the June 1917 issue. The full-page ad urged people to sign a pledge saying, "I will not kill nor help kill my fellow men." Rogers testified that the ad had been cleared by George Creel, who headed the wartime Committee on Public Information, the government's propaganda and censorship agency.[34]

That explanation prompted Barnes to ask Creel himself to journey from Washington to testify in rebuttal about the ad; dispatches from Creel's office denied that he had "approved" the ad. In a statement issued before his testimony, Creel said he thought the ad was "infamous" and told Rogers so. "The whole spirit of the magazine, so far as it opposed the war and selective conscription, was objectionable," Creel said, "and I think I made my attitude

---

30 *"Masses" Editors Were Consulted on Fighting Draft Bill,* N.Y. TRIB., April 20, 1918, at 18.

31 *Eastman's Views Change Since U.S. Entered the War,* N.Y. EVE. WORLD, April 22, 1918, at 3; *Creel Passed 'I Will Not Kill' 'Ad.' In 'Masses,'* N.Y. TRIB., April 23, 1918, at 1.

32 LOOSE LEAVES, *supra* note 1, at 228. *See also* O'NEILL, *supra* note 27, at 65, 76.

33 O'NEILL, *supra* note 27, at 76.

34 *Creel Passed 'I Will Not Kill' 'Ad.' in 'Masses,'* N.Y. TRIB., April 23, 1918, at 1.

plain to Mr. Rogers at the time." Creel acknowledged that he had told Rogers that he had no power to prevent him from publishing the ad because the Espionage Act had not yet been enacted.[35]

While the court awaited Creel's testimony, Art Young took the stand to explain his cartoon showing big business drawing up war plans and shooing Congress aside. "Did you intend the cartoon to induce men to refuse to enlist or to evade the draft?" Hillquit asked. "I did not," Young replied. "I tried to present a serious situation, humorously but forcefully, for the public good." Young reportedly found it difficult to explain his thought processes as he penned his cartoons. Even Judge Hand took part in the questioning, finally concluding, "I think it is asking too much to ask an artist to describe his emotions." Floyd Dell, who was the last defendant to testify, said he was in the draft and expected to serve. He, too, testified that anti-conscription articles he had written were published before the law was enacted. Like Eastman, Dell said he was influenced by Wilson's letter to the Pope.[36]

When Creel took the stand in rebuttal, he reiterated his previous statements. "[Rogers] asked me what I thought of the ad. I said I thought it epitomized treason .... I then told him that there was no law then in existence that gave any official authority to forbid the publication of any magazine for seditious utterances." On cross-examination by Hillquit, Creel said he had a keen recollection of the interview with Rogers and agreed that Rogers had said he was anxious to comply with the law. Creel also said he had a high regard for Eastman and other *Masses* staffers and had even written an article for the magazine before the war.[37]

The last day of the trial, April 25, was limited to closing arguments for both sides and Judge Hand's charge to the jury. Malone spoke first, asserting that the defendants did not intend to persuade any man to disobey the law, but rather express their honest and sincere opposition to compulsory military service.

> Whatever a pacifist is, I know there were a great many of them in this country before we went to war. Even at the time these defendants are charged with violating the law, the people of this country were divided. Why, President Wilson was elected by 2,000,000 votes on the ground that

---

[35] *'Masses' Approval Is Denied by Creel,* N.Y. SUN, April 24, 1918, at 7.

[36] *Will Ask Creel to Testify on 'Ad' in 'Masses,'* N.Y. TRIB., April 24, 1918, at 9; *Creel May Testify in the Masses Trial,* N.Y. TIMES, April 24, 1918, at 9; *'Masses' Approval is Denied by Creel,* N.Y. SUN, April 24, 1918, at 7.

[37] *Creel, On Stand, Denies He O'K'D "Ad." In Masses,* N.Y. EVE. WORLD, April 24, 1918, at 5; *Creel Says He Could Not Bar Pacifist "Ad,"* N.Y. TRIB., April 25, 1918, at 9; *Cram 'Ad' Called Treason by Creel,* N.Y. SUN, April 25, 1918, at 16.

> he had kept us out of war. Even *The New York World*, which is considered the organ of the Administration, favored a volunteer army. If these defendants are guilty of conspiracy to obstruct recruiting, then ... all the other contributors are guilty.

Malone described himself as a militarist who favored preparedness, but said he would not refuse to give a pacifist the right to hold the opposite view.

Hillquit devoted most of his speech to analyzing the evidence, but noted that the defendants now believe the war was being fought for democracy.

> [At] the time these articles ... were written, President Wilson had not made known the worthy aims of our entry into the war, which he has worthily done since that time. We accept this war as a fact, but we will not surrender our constitutional rights of opinion and the freedom to express that opinion. Not for one day, not for one hour, will we surrender these constitutional rights. No, not even in time of war, for the government is founded upon the very principle of freedom of speech.[38]

Barnes spoke for three hours, in what was described as a "dispassionate, orderly analysis" of his case, except for two shots at Eastman and John Reed. He reportedly called Eastman "a man without a country," and took Reed to task for mocking the pervasiveness of what was then called "shell shock." Barnes told the jury the defendants were men of education and intelligence and should therefore be held responsible for their actions.[39]

Before charging the jury, Hand dismissed the first count of the indictment on the ground that it did not allege any intended action which would have affected insubordination or disloyalty within the military. As to the second count, obstructing recruitment, Hand reminded the jury that every man has a right to whatever opinions "as seem to him best" and warned them to "divorce yourselves from any prejudice you may have against any defendant by reason of proof of any such opinions on his part." In an unusually defendant-friendly charge, Hand said each defendant had a constitutional right to express those opinions, unless that expression violates the law.

Hand carefully outlined the law regarding conspiracy and the definition of "wilful." He also explained that anti-war and anti-draft articles published before enactment of the Espionage Act were introduced in evidence "for the purpose of allowing the Government to show, if it could, that these defendants ... pursued a course of conduct ... which, if continued and not changed, would tend to show their intention to violate the law afterwards." And he pointed out

---

[38] *Fate of Eastman in the Jury's Hands*, N.Y. TIMES, April 26, 1918, at 20.

[39] *Id.*; *'Masses' Jury Out; Retires for Night*, N.Y. SUN, April 26, 1918, at 7.

that where, as here, the conspiracy charged was sought to be proven by circumstantial evidence, the jury's duty lay in trying to reconcile the conduct of the defendants with a reasonable theory of evidence. If that could be done, he said, the jury must acquit.[40]

After deliberating for ten hours, the jury reported that it was unable to reach a verdict and asked Hand to discharge them. Hand refused, instructing them to return to the Hotel Knickerbocker and go over the evidence once again. They returned to court after 30 hours of deliberation to say they were hopelessly deadlocked, although a majority of the jury had reached a conclusion. In response to Hand's question, six jurors said they thought it might be possible to reach an agreement if they had more time. Hillquit moved to have the jury discharged, but Hand denied the motion and sent them back to the hotel for the night.[41] The following day, more than 40 hours after they had begun, the jury returned to the courtroom and again reported they could not agree. At least two jurors had held out for acquittal, and Hand finally discharged the jury. Barnes moved for a retrial date of May 6, to which Hillquit and Malone objected, urging Hand to postpone any retrial until fall. Hand ordered the retrial to be set for June.[42]

At a victory dinner, Hillquit expressed his view that

> [the] trial had gone wonderfully, especially when Eastman was on the stand, and when quietly, honestly and courageously, at the same time with compelling force he drove home every argument he had made in the *Masses* or in public speeches during those troublous days after we entered the war, when he advocated his right, our right, to think and to speak—and when finally he became so convincing that even half of those jurors, hostile as they were, were won over, and the crowd in the courtroom that had come to scoff remained, as it were, to pray, then I could see that trials of this kind, if continued long enough, if they forced their way into the papers, will be about the only medium of education for the American public.[43]

---

40 WALTER NELLES, ESPIONAGE ACT CASES WITH CERTAIN OTHERS ON RELATED POINTS 28-30 (1918).

41 *Jury in Masses Cases Unable to Reach Verdict,* N.Y. EVE. WORLD, April 26, 1918, at 1; *"Masses" Jurors, Unable to Agree, Must Try Again,* N.Y. TRIB., April 27, 1918, at 18.

42 *Jury in 'Masses' Trial Disagrees,* N.Y. SUN, April 28, 1918, at 7. There are some minor discrepancies in the sources as to how long the jury deliberated (42–48 hours) and how many jurors held out for acquittal (2–3), but the *Sun's* account is as reliable as any.

43 O'NEILL, *supra* note 27, at 77 (citing *Speeches of Max Eastman and Morris Hillquit at the Masses Dinner, May 9,* LIBERATOR, June 1918, at 21.

Coincidentally, John Reed had returned from Europe the day after the jury was discharged and was met at the dock by federal agents who searched his person and property. Barnes had agreed to allow Reed to leave the ship in return for Hillquit's promise to produce Reed at the courthouse the next morning, where he would be asked to plead to the indictment. As he left the dock, Reed denied that he was affiliated with the Bolshevik government in any way. At his arraignment the following day, Reed pleaded not guilty to the indictment and was released on $2,000 bail. Hillquit effectively argued that Reed's bail should be reduced from the $5,000 recommended by the government because he had returned to the United States voluntarily to face the charges. Walter Nelles of the Civil Liberties Bureau, who would become one of the defense lawyers in the second trial, posted the bail.[44] On Malone's advice, Reed declined to give reporters more than perfunctory remarks, though he later gave *The Call* a longer statement discounting rumors that the Germans would ultimately restore the Russian monarchy. "Russia is revolutionary and class conscious to the core," he said, "and no monarchy made and maintained by German bayonets can hope for any permanent life."[45]

Masses II (1918)

Seymour Stedman

Charles Recht

On May 24, 1918, the government filed a new indictment against Max Eastman and his colleagues that differed from the previous indictment in that it alleged several substantive offenses in addition to the conspiracy count.[46] Specifically, the second, third and fourth counts involved elements of the August issue of *The Masses* allegedly intended to obstruct the enlistment service, while the third and fourth counts referred to elements of the September and October issues for the same offense. The last three counts alleged that elements of the August, September and October issues constituted attempts to cause insubordination in the military.[47]

---

[44] Order for Return of Cash Bail, United States v. John Reed, C20-327 (S.D.N.Y. Jan. 20, 1919).

[45] *Government Awaits Writer on "Masses,"* N.Y. SUN, April 28, 1918, at 7; *U.S. Inquiry Into "Masses" Trial Likely,* N.Y. TRIB., April 29, 1918, at 1; *John Reed Freed on Bail, Pending Trial in June,* N.Y. TRIB., April 30, 1918, at 11.

[46] United States v. Eastman, 252 F. 232 (S.D.N.Y. 1918), *nolle prosequi filed* Jan. 9, 1919 (No. C 13-245).

[47] United States v. Eastman, 252 F. 232, 232-33 (S.D.N.Y. 1918).

On June 1, Morris Hillquit filed a demurrer claiming that the new indictment was insufficient because each and every count failed to charge a crime, but rather stated an alleged offense by way of inference, recital, and conclusion, without any distinct and adequate specification of any overt act required by law. He went on to challenge each allegation in the indictment, demanding a judgment dismissing the indictment.[48]

The demurrer was heard by Judge Learned Hand on June 8. Hand had ruled favorably in the civil case, but his decision of August 2, 1918, overruled the demurrer, even though he questioned some counts of the indictment. He noted that his cousin, Augustus Hand, had dismissed the first count of the previous indictment, but said that decision was based on the form of the pleading, not a substantive difference between the two violations, obstruction of enlistment and incitement to insubordination. He also held that "anyone in his senses" would realize that, in distributing the magazine throughout the country, it would probably reach some soldiers. As to Hillquit's demand for more specific allegations in the indictment, Hand said the defense was entitled to a bill of particulars, but that the allegations as written would support a prosecution.[49]

The second *Masses* trial would not begin until October, but by then Hillquit would be out of the picture. Hillquit, who had long suffered from tuberculosis, had a major attack in the summer of 1918 and retreated to Saranac Lake, New York. He was forced to miss the August Conference of State Secretaries and Socialist Officials in Chicago, for which Adolph Germer, executive secretary of the Socialist Party of America, sent his regrets and words of encouragement.[50] From then on, Seymour Stedman would take over the *Masses* case, assisted by Charles Recht and Walter Nelles.

The trial would begin in October before Judge Martin Manton; Barnes again handled the prosecution. This time, defendant John Reed was present in the courtroom; Reed had been in the Soviet Union during the first trial. Indeed, Reed's colorful and moving description of the war in France proved to be one of the highlights of the second trial, along with Max Eastman's address to the jury.

Eastman explained that the intent of *The Masses* was not to obstruct the military:

---

[48] Demurrer, United States v. Eastman, 252 F. 232 (S.D.N.Y. 1918) (No. C 13-245) . *See also Demurrer Is Argued in "The Masses" Case,* N.Y. TRIB., June 9, 1918, at 16.

[49] United States v. Eastman, 252 F. 232, 232-33 (S.D.N.Y. 1918).

[50] Letter from Adolph Germer to Morris Hillquit, Aug. 3, 1918, in Morris Hillquit Papers, Wisconsin Historical Society.

> [Our] intention was to issue into the general current of public opinion our satirical and argumentative and poetic and pictorial comments upon the general policy of the government from a socialist point of view. I am not afraid to spend the better part of my life in a penitentiary, if my principles have brought me to it. I have decided, after experimenting a little in the inside of my own mind and heart, that I am more afraid to betray my principles.[51]

The jury deliberated two days, then reported themselves deadlocked. There would be no third trial.

Rose Pastor Stokes (1918)

Seymour Stedman

In May 1918, Seymour Stedman represented New York activist Rose Pastor Stokes at her Espionage Act trial in Kansas City. In a letter to the *Kansas City Star*, Stokes had declared, "I am for the people, while the government is for the profiteers." The federal government had charged Stokes with violating the act by variously asserting that the Red Cross and the federal food and fuel administrations were "war camouflage," that American soldiers in France were there to "fight for capital, not for democracy," and that they had been "lured there by the slogan 'make the world safe for democracy.'" U.S. District Attorney Francis H. Wilson also alleged that Stokes said she wanted Germany to win the war "if conditions in the United States could be improved by a German victory." And he quoted Stokes as declaring that the Bolshevik government in Russia was "the only true democracy."[52]

In his opening statement for the defense, Stedman did not deny that Stokes had written the letter criticizing the government but denied only that she violated the law in doing so. "She is for the liberation of the peoples and the creation of a world democracy ...," Stedman said. "She claims the right of any free American to criticize the government. Without this right, America would be no democracy."[53]

With few, if any, facts in dispute, the trial lasted only three days. Wilson closed with an extended diatribe that attacked not only Mrs. Stokes but also her husband and Stedman. At the end, he asked rhetorically, "Do you, gentlemen of the jury, stand with President Woodrow Wilson or with Rose Pastor Stokes?" Stedman's closing argument insisted that "The Constitution of the United

---

[51] Sayer, *supra* note 25.

[52] *Open Testimony Taking in Trial of Rose Stokes,* CHI. TRIB., May 21, 1918, at 5.

[53] *Stokes Defense A Word,* Kan. CITY TIMES, May 21, 1918, at 1.

States is not changed in war time. Those who wrote it knew that in times of stress and excitement such as at present it is important that persons have the right to express their opinions." Before submitting the case to the jury, however, Judge Arba S. Van Valkenburgh delivered "instructions" that all but guaranteed a conviction, calling the president in time of war almost a dictator who must be supported. "It is ridiculous to think that the President could stop in the face of the enemy to clean house. We don't stop in the face of a coming thunder storm to hang out our bedding."[54]

Stokes was found guilty on three counts of the indictment, and the court imposed a sentence of ten years on each, to run concurrently. The court also continued her $10,000 bond, allowing her to remain free pending appeal, which would not conclude until 1920. In pronouncing the sentence, Van Valkenburgh said he believed that Stokes was "part of a systematic program to create discontent with the causes and justice of the war and loss of confidence in the good faith and sincerity underlying the conduct of the war and its ultimate aims." Some elements of the program, he said, were undoubtedly inspired by German sources and the lamentable situation in Russia.[55] "If the statement made in this letter ... should meet with credence and acceptance by any appreciable number of its readers, could they fail to produce the temper and spirit that would interfere and tend naturally and logically to interfere with the operation and success of the military ...?"[56]

On March 9, 1920, Stedman won an impressive victory in the Eighth Circuit when a three-judge panel unanimously reversed the conviction. Writing for himself and Judge Kimbrough Stone, Judge Walter H. Sanborn focused on Stokes's use of the word "government" in her problematic letter to the *Kansas City Star*. Pointing out that the word could mean either the body of persons ruling the country or the system established by the Constitution, Sanborn said there was no evidence in the record that Stokes had disparaged the constitutional form of government, which the law prohibited, and that it was prejudicial error to submit that question to the jury.[57] The third judge, John E. Carland, found no prejudice there, but rather in the trial judge's characterization of Stokes as an "Internationalist."[58] Either way, the judgment was reversed, and the government declined to prosecute further.

---

[54] *Bad for Stokes Defense,* Kan. CITY STAR, May 23, 1918, at 1.

[55] *Mrs. Stokes Given 10 Years as Foe of War,* CHI. TRIB., June 2, 1918, at 8.

[56] David L. Sterling, *In Defense of Debs: The Lawyers and the Espionage Act Case,* 83 IND. MAG. OF HIST. 17, 19 (1987).

[57] Stokes v. United States, 264 F. 18, 21-23 (8th Cir. 1920).

[58] *Id.* at 27 (Carland, J., dissenting in part).

Eugene Debs (1918)

Seymour Stedman

Perhaps the most important speech of Seymour Stedman's career was not delivered by him at all, but rather by labor leader Eugene Debs on June 16 in Canton, Ohio. Referring specifically to the Stokes conviction, Debs asked, "What has she said?" and then answered, "Nothing more than I have said here this afternoon. [If] Rose Pastor Stokes is guilty, so am I. If she should be sent to the penitentiary for ten years, so ought I .... Rose Pastor Stokes never said a word she did not have a right to utter." In less than two weeks, a 139-page indictment was handed up by a grand jury in Cleveland, charging Debs with ten counts of violating the Espionage Act.[59]

Born in 1855, Debs began his union career as a railroad worker, advancing to become secretary-treasurer of the Brotherhood of Locomotive Firemen in the early 1880s.[60] In the beginning, Debs was relatively conservative in orientation, tending to favor the traditional craft union concept of the American Federation of Labor over the burgeoning industrial union movement. Several failed strikes in the late 1880s prompted him to move to the left in his thinking, and in 1893, he became president of a new American Railway Union, which was both more inclusive and more confrontational than the brotherhoods had been.

Debs rose to national prominence in the aftermath of the ARU's strike and boycott against the Pullman Palace Car Co., for which Debs was ultimately convicted of contempt for violating a federal court order.[61] In prison, Debs completed his conversion to socialism.[62] Indeed, Max Eastman would later call him the "spiritual chief and hero" of American socialism.[63] Debs was one of the founding members of the Industrial Workers of the World in 1905, but later split with the I.W.W. and Big Bill Haywood over its more anarchistic tendencies and cast his lot with the so-called parliamentary socialists like Morris Hillquit and Victor Berger.[64]

Debs delivered his 1918 Canton speech to the Ohio Socialist Convention, and he opened with a warning about speaking freely that, in retrospect, rings prophetic:

---

[59] Sterling, *supra* note 56, at 19-22. Grand Jury Indictment, S.S.4057, Eugene V. Debs File (Federal Record Center and Archives Branch, Chicago, Ill.).

[60] DAVID RAY PAPKE, THE PULLMAN CASE 8-10 (1999).

[61] *Id.* at 86. *See also* In re Debs, 158 U.S. 564 (1895).

[62] PAPKE, *supra* note 60, at 87.

[63] MAX EASTMAN, THE TRIAL OF EUGENE DEBS 3 (1918).

[64] PETER CARLSON, ROUGHNECK: THE LIFE AND TIMES OF BIG BILL HAYWOOD 156-59 (1983).

> [It] is extremely dangerous to exercise the constitutional right of free speech in a country fighting to make democracy safe for the world. I realize in speaking to you this afternoon that there are certain limitations placed on the right of free speech. I must be extremely careful, prudent, as to what I say, and even more careful and prudent as to how I say it.[65]

However cautious Debs might have been, he was not cautious enough. Among other things, he spoke admiringly of "loyal comrades" Charles E. Ruthenberg, Alfred Wagenknecht, and Charles Baker, who were serving time for violations of the Selective Draft Law;[66] of Kate Richards O'Hare, convicted of violating the Espionage Act by obstructing the enlistment service;[67] and of the aforementioned Rose Pastor Stokes.

Stedman was named Debs's chief counsel, assisted by Chicago attorney William Cunnea, and several others—including Morris Hillquit—at one time or another. Stedman filed a motion to quash the indictment on August 6 and a demurrer to the indictment, with a memorandum of authorities, on August 15. His 35-page brief supporting the motion to quash was filed on August 31. U.S. District Judge David C. Westenhaver made short work of both, noting that "Any contention that the Espionage Act is unconstitutional is, in my opinion, frivolous and entirely devoid of merit."[68]

The trial opened on September 9, but the previous evening, Stedman declared:

> No attempt will be made to excuse or apologize for any statement made by Debs in his Canton speech. Debs and those associated with him recognized this case as an attack on socialism and the freedom of discussion. Debs has instructed his counsel that they must not, under any circumstances, consider him in this case; that the socialist movement, the Socialist Party, and preservation of fundamental American rights must be of paramount consideration.[69]

Following the selection of the jury, after a rigorous *voir dire*, Assistant District Attorney Francis B. Kavanagh read an alleged stenographic report of the Canton speech, declaring that the government would rely on the contents of the speech to prove the charges in the indictment, now trimmed down to focus on the counts involving interference with the military and opposition to the

---

65 SCOTT NEARING, THE DEBS DECISION 6 (1919).

66 *Id. See also* Ruthenberg v. United States, 245 U.S. 480 (1918).

67 NEARING, *supra* note 65, at 8-9. *See also* Debs v. United States, 249 U.S. 211, 213 (1919).

68 Sterling, *supra* note 56, at 22-25.

69 J. Louis Engdahl, *Debs Trial Opens Monday; Defendant Makes Speeches as Lawyers Prepare Case,* MILWAUKEE LEADER, Sept. 9, 1917, at 1-3.

war. Kavanagh charged that Debs was the "very head and palpitating pulse" of a seditious crusade that had been launched in the United States. "By his words he shall be judged," Kavanagh declared, paraphrasing Matthew, "and by his words he shall be condemned."

Stedman accepted the challenge, urging the jury to "Judge him by his words; judge him by his life and by his life's work and we will abide by your verdict." Stedman told the jury that

> [not] one word will be or can be introduced to show that Eugene Victor Debs in his speech had held up the army, the navy, or the constitution to ridicule or disgrace, neither the uniform; that he had made attacks on the form of government, not one word in opposition to the ideal or historic meaning of the American flag or that he had willfully or knowingly opposed the cause of the United States in the war.

At the conclusion of Stedman's speech, applause broke out among the socialists in attendance, and seven of them—including Stokes—were charged with riotous conduct and fined $10 to $25 each.[70]

The prosecution called several witnesses who did little more than testify as to Debs's speech and other socialist pronouncements, completing its case on September 11. A few minutes later, Stedman rested the defense case without calling a single witness. But Debs was allowed to address the jury in closing arguments.[71] He took that opportunity to deliver a far-ranging defense of his speeches, of socialism, of the Russian Revolution, of the "rising of the toiling masses," and of freedom of speech. "I am not guilty of the charges in the indictment," he declared. "What I have said I felt that I was justified in saying under the law of the land."[72]

District Attorney Edward S. Wertz did not mince words in his closing. Wertz called Debs a self-righteous liar, a self-proclaimed Christ who believed that he held a monopoly over virtue and principle, a theorist with a "smattering of knowledge," a champion of the "half-baked" and the "non compos mentis." Wertz told the jury that, based on his own statements, "Debs would bring the Bolsheviki to the United States."[73]

---

[70] J. Louis Engdahl, *Seven Socialists at Debs Trial Held for Applause After Stedman's Speech,* MILWAUKEE LEADER, Sept. 10, 1918, at 1-3.

[71] J. Louis Engdahl, *C.E. Ruthenberg Hurried from Canton Workhouse to Testify in Debs' Free Speech Trial,* MILWAUKEE LEADER, Sept. 11, 1918, at 1-2.

[72] J. Louis Engdahl, *Jury in Eugene Debs' Trial on Free Speech Gets Its Instructions,* MILWAUKEE LEADER, Sept. 12, 1918, at 1, 3.

[73] Sterling, *supra* note 56, at 32.

In his instructions to the jury, Judge Westenhaver defined the four counts on which Debs was tried: attempting to incite insubordination, disloyalty, and mutiny; attempting to obstruct recruitments and enlistments; attempting to encourage resistance to the government; and opposing the cause of the United States at war. Each count carried a possible sentence of 20 years in prison and a $10,000 fine.[74] Westenhaver told the jury that if Debs could reasonably have foreseen that his speech would result in the conduct specified in the charges, then it should find him guilty.[75]

The jury retired for deliberations at about 11 a.m. on September 13 and returned to the courtroom at 6 p.m. that same day. Jurors found Debs guilty on the first three counts of the indictment, and not guilty on the fourth, opposing the cause of the United States at war. The following day, Westenhaver denied Stedman's motions for a new trial and for arrest of judgment, and he sentenced Debs to ten years in the federal penitentiary at Moundsville, West Virginia. Stedman took the first steps toward an appeal, filing a Writ of Error the same day and, on October 8, an Amended Assignment of Errors.[76]

Max Eastman, former editor of *The Masses*, covered the trial for the successor publication he created with his sister Crystal, *The Liberator*. His lengthy article concluded:

> It may be expedient for the government at war to imprison Eugene Debs. From their point of view it may seem prudent and necessary. But I wonder if there are not some among them who have qualms when it comes to such an act—in a war for liberty. I wonder if they ever sense the danger that when the war is done, they may find left only the name of what they were fighting for. Across the face of the County Court House, as the train pulls out of Cleveland, you read in great marble letters this motto: 'Obedience To Law Is Liberty.' And by means of just such fatuous sophisms as that, the powers that want industrial feudalism and bureaucracy perpetuated after this war ends, will get it if they can.[77]

On March 10, the Supreme Court ruled on Stedman's appeal in the *Debs* case. Stedman had raised three main defenses: a First Amendment freedom of speech issue, an insufficient indictment, and the admission into evidence of

---

[74] Engdahl, *Jury, supra* note 72.

[75] Sterling, *supra* note 56, at 35.

[76] *Id.* at 36. *See also* J. Louis Engdahl, *Debs Held Guilty on Three Counts; Will File Appeal,* MILWAUKEE LEADER, Sept. 13, 1918, at 1-2, and *Debs Sentenced to 10 Years in Jail on Three Counts,* MILWAUKEE LEADER, Sept. 14, 1918, at 1.

[77] EASTMAN, *supra* note 63, at 5-12.

the record in other Espionage Act convictions.[78] On the First Amendment issue, Stedman wrote:

> The millions in many countries who respond to the idealism of Eugene V. Debs ... will bluntly speak of the ... case as a free speech fight. They will ask: 'What degree of tolerance of minority sentiments is to be read out of or into the American Bill of Rights ...?'[79]

Justice Oliver Wendell Holmes's opinion for the Court was dismissive, indicating that the Court had already dealt with and disposed of the First Amendment issue. Just a week earlier, the Court had issued its first rulings on the constitutionality of the act. In *Schenck v. United States*,[80] decided March 3, 1919, the Court undercut the First Amendment argument that was the left's last best hope. In his opinion for the Court, Holmes had articulated the "clear and present danger" test that would remain in the law, in one form or another, until 1969.[81] Under that test, the government was empowered to punish any speech that posed a clear and present danger that it would bring about the substantive evils that Congress had a right to prevent.

Holmes was similarly perfunctory in his rejection of Stedman's attack on the indictment. "It is sufficient in form," he wrote. Holmes spent a little more ink on the inadmissibility of the evidence but rejected that argument as well, indicating that the jury instructions would have negated any error. Debs's conviction was affirmed.[82] Historian David Sterling has written that the failure of Stedman and his team to keep Debs out of prison "should not detract from their skilled and spirited defense. Their legal skills have too long been slighted by historians."[83]

Abraham Sugarman (1919)

Seymour Stedman

On the same day that *Schenck* was decided, the Supreme Court also handed down its decision in Seymour Stedman's appeal of the *Sugarman* case. On

---

[78] Debs v. United States, 249 U.S. 211, 215 (1919).

[79] Brief for Plaintiff in Error, quoted in Sterling, *supra* note 56.

[80] 249 U.S. 47 (1919).

[81] Reinterpreted several times, the clear and present danger test was effectively replaced by the incitement standard of *Brandenburg v. Ohio*, 395 U.S. 444 (1969), rejecting the punishment of mere advocacy and requiring that the speaker intended to incite imminent lawless action which was likely to occur. *Id.* at 447.

[82] *Debs*, 249 U.S. 215-17.

[83] Sterling, *supra* note 56, at 42.

October 24, 1917, Abraham L. Sugarman, secretary of the Minnesota Socialist Party was indicted under the new Espionage Act for willfully attempting to "cause insubordination, disloyalty, mutiny, and refusal of duty in the military forces of the United States" by urging young men to refuse conscription. The case was set for immediate trial, and the following day, Sugarman's attorney, Louis L. Schwartz moved for a directed verdict. U.S. District Judge Wilbur F. Booth denied the motion,[84] and the trial proceeded on October 26. It took the jury just 40 minutes to return a guilty verdict, and Booth sentenced Sugarman to three years at Fort Leavenworth. Booth stayed the sentence until December 1, when he would hear arguments for a new trial. Sugarman remained free on $7,500 bail.[85]

Stedman was not Sugarman's trial attorney, but would later take the case to the U.S. Supreme Court.[86] Stedman chose to bypass the Eighth Circuit Court of Appeals and apply directly to the Supreme Court for a writ of error. His application contained 31 exceptions to the rulings of the trial court, but only two referenced the Constitution sufficiently to give the Court jurisdiction. Both involved the trial judge's failure to give the jury certain instructions regarding the First Amendment, but the Court held that the judge's charge fully embodied those instructions even if different language had been used. Without a substantial constitutional question then, the Court found it lacked jurisdiction and dismissed Stedman's application.[87]

Victor Berger (1919)

Seymour Stedman

No sooner had the Debs trial ended than Seymour Stedman was forced to turn his attention to his third Espionage Act trial of 1918, that of Victor Berger and four other prominent socialists. Berger was a founding member of the Socialist Party and editor of the *Milwaukee Leader*, among other socialist newspapers, and he represented Wisconsin's Fifth Congressional District in 1911–12, becoming the first Socialist elected to Congress. Berger was indicted in February 1918 for the same violations that Debs was convicted of committing with respect to the military and the war.[88] Even under indictment, Berger was

---

84 United States v. Sugarman, 245 F. 604 (D. Minn. 1917).

85 *Sugarman Convicted of Sedition; Is Given 3-Year Prison Term,* STAR TRIB. (Minneapolis), Oct. 27, 1917, at 6.

86 Sugarman v. United States, 249 U.S. 182 (1919).

87 *Id.* at 185.

88 Berger would also be indicted on Nov. 30, 1918, by a grand jury of the Western District of Wisconsin for anti-war articles he published in the *Leader*. *Berger Indicted Under*

elected to the House again in November 1918, although he was not allowed to take his seat. Also indicted were Adolph Germer; William F. Kruse, director of the Socialist Youth League; Irwin St. John Tucker, former director of the party's literature department; and J. Louis Engdahl, journalist and editor.[89] Stedman was chief defense counsel and promptly petitioned the court for a change of venue. His petition accused the trial judge, once again Kenesaw Mountain Landis, of violent prejudice against Germans and German-Americans. Landis denied the motion, calling the petition a "mere vehicle of slander."[90]

Following the selection of a jury, which began on December 9 and was completed two days later, Joseph P. Fleming, first assistant U.S. district attorney, presented the government's opening case, alleging in a three-hour speech that the defendants conducted their anti-war conspiracy through speeches, editorials, pamphlets, "flairing" billboards, and the Young People's Socialist League. Fleming said Kruse had met with an enemy alien, Herman Basler, in Chicago to concoct a plan to help draft evaders escape into Mexico through an underground railway. He charged that they had already picked out places of refuge and said he would produce letters to prove it.

Fleming said the socialists were instructed to resist conscription, that resisters who received prison sentences were praised, and that the socialists organized to obtain exemptions as conscientious objectors for party members. He described the *Leader* and the *American Socialist* as avenues of publicity for the defendants and that the *Leader*, in particular, had "decidedly pro-German tendencies." Berger, he said, had ordered editors of the *Leader* to "play up" dispatches from Berlin and run editorials showing "very violent Germanic tendencies."

The next day, December 12, Stedman opened for the defense with a far-ranging address that discussed his clients' opposition to the war, current economic and industrial conditions, the nature of socialism and its differences from anarchism, and even the Bolshevik Revolution. Stedman went through each count of the indictment and declared that he would prove the innocence of the defendants on every one of them. "We will show that the defendants did not meet and conspire, as charged, to violate the law," he declared.

Stedman took particular aim at one of the articles cited by Fleming. "The first overt act [of the alleged conspiracy] is said to be the publication of the poem by Cary E. Norris entitled 'Cheer Up!'" Stedman said. The article calls on American soldiers to "wave your caps and shout for joy" because the government had

---

Espionage Act in This City, LA CROSSE TRIB., Dec. 3, 1918, at 1; United Press, Untitled, KENOSHA NEWS, Dec. 3, 1918, at 1.

[89] *Start Berger Trial Monday*, WIS. ST. J., Dec. 8, 1918, at 5.

[90] *Berger Petition to Change Venue Denied by Landis*, CHI. TRIB., Nov. 17, 1918, at 16.

purchased 200,000 coffins for them. "We will show that this was written and set up in print before June 15, 1917, when the espionage law was put into effect," Stedman declared. "Anything done by the defendants prior to that date ... is not an offense against the espionage law, and must be disregarded." [91]

The first witness called by the government was one Private Arnold Schiller, who had worked for months in Socialist Party headquarters in Chicago. Schiller testified as to plans to instill the anti-war spirit in soldiers, of an underground railroad to Mexico for deserters, and an organized conspiracy to oppose conscription.[92] Schiller's testimony was then reinforced by the government's introduction of documents and articles seized from headquarters, followed by other witnesses authenticating the seized materials and recounting anti-war speeches and other activities by the defendants. During the proceedings, death threats were received by Judge Landis and the prosecutors, prompting officers to search every spectator for explosives before allowing them into the courtroom.[93]

The government completed its case on December 18, after which Stedman offered and Landis denied a pro forma motion for a directed verdict of acquittal. Germer took the stand the following day, testifying that the Socialists' defense fund was never meant for deserters or draft evaders, but rather to secure a fair trial for socialists arrested for distributing literature or making speeches.[94] Germer said that socialists hoped to compel the United States to take the lead in a movement to end the war and enforce disarmament of the world.[95] Under cross-examination, which concluded on December 20, Germer denied that the socialist position was pro-German.[96]

The defense called several more witnesses on December 21, including socialist politicians, journalists, and other defendants.[97] Defense witnesses continued to take the stand through Christmas Eve and resumed the day after the holiday.[98] Berger himself took the stand on December 31 to discuss socialism in America, deny any pro-German sentiment, and assert even-

---

[91] United Press, *Berger Trial Is Now On*, SHEBOYGAN (Wis.) PRESS, Dec. 12, 1918, at 1; Associated Press, *Socialism Is Described by Counsel in the Berger Trial*, OSHKOSH (Wis.) NORTHWESTERN, Dec. 12, 1918, at 1.

[92] *Soldier Is Witness in Berger Trial*, CAPITAL TIMES (Madison, Wis.), Dec. 13, 1918, at 1.

[93] *Death Letter Is Mailed to Judge Landis*, Green Bay (Wis.) PRESS-GAZETTE, Dec. 14, 1918, at 2; *Insults to U.S. Women Shown at "Reds" Trial*, CHI. TRIB., Dec. 15, 1918, at 18.

[94] *Socialists' Case to Jury on Friday*, POST-CRESCENT (Appleton, Wis.), Dec. 19, 1918, at 4.

[95] *First Witness for Defense*, Wausau (Wis.) DAILY HERALD, Dec. 19, 1918, at 1.

[96] *Germer Says Platform Not Pro-German*, CAPITAL TIMES (Madison, Wis.), Dec. 20, 1918, at 11.

[97] *Politicians on Witness Stand for Socialists*, GREEN BAY (Wis.) PRESS-GAZETTE, Dec. 21, 1918, at 1.

[98] *Defense Subpoenas Government Witness*, JOURNAL TIMES (Racine, Wis.), Dec. 26, 1918, at 1.

handedness in his newspaper's war coverage.[99] Following a break for New Year's Day, Berger resumed the stand to distinguish his socialist philosophy from that of the Industrial Workers of the World.[100] Under cross-examination, Berger testified that, although the sinking of the *Lusitania* was a "beastly thing to do," he did not believe it justified entering the war."[101]

Berger was the last defense witness. Closing arguments ran through January 7, with prosecutor Fleming speaking for nearly four hours. "These men were shouting for peace when they knew the only peace possible was a German peace," he declared. "They were doing everything they could do to give aid and comfort to the enemy." Stedman closed for the defense with an appeal for the protection of the rights of free speech, a free press, and free assemblage."[102]

On the morning of January 8, Landis instructed the jury that the defendants had the right to entertain, publish, speak and write their views on the war from economic, political or religious standpoints. But "[if] the defendants acted with a common purpose or cooperation in hindering the war, and the conspiracy is proven by an open action, they must be found guilty." He submitted the case to the jury at 11 a.m.[103] The jury deliberated for nearly six hours before returning guilty verdicts against all five defendants. Stedman immediately moved for a new trial, and Landis set January 23 for arguments on the motion. Stedman said the case would be appealed to the U.S. Supreme Court if necessary to keep his clients out of prison.[104] The defendants remained free on a $10,000 bond.[105]

Following a postponement requested by Stedman,[106] arguments on his motion for a new trial opened January 25, with allegations that a deputy marshal had expressed his view that the defendants were guilty in the presence of jurors before the trial had ended.[107] When arguments resumed on February 3, the jury tampering case was made by Berger's personal attorney, Henry Cochems, while

---

99 *La Follette May Be Called as Witness in Berger Defense*, LA CROSSE (Wis.) TRIB., Dec. 31, 1918, at 6.

100 *Berger Claims He Is Foe of I.W.W.*, WAUSAU (Wis.) DAILY HERALD, Jan. 2, 1919, at 1.

101 *Sinking of* Lusitania *a Beastly Thing to Do Declares Victor Berger*, SANTA ANA (Calif.) REGISTER, Jan. 3, 1919, at 1.

102 *Fleming Flays Victor Berger*, SPOKESMAN-REVIEW (Spokane, Wash.), Jan. 8, 1919, at 3.

103 *The Charge of Judge Landis Is Favorable to the Defendants*, SHEBOYGAN (Wis.) PRESS, Jan. 8, 1919, at 1.

104 *Victor Berger Is Found Guilty*, CARBONDALE (Pa.) DAILY NEWS, Jan. 9, 1919, at 1.

105 United Press, *Berger et al. Face Sentence of from One to Twenty Years*, OSHKOSH (Wis.) NORTHWESTERN, Jan. 9, 1919, at 1.

106 *Berger Wins New Delay*, WIS. ST. J., Jan. 23, 1919, at 6.

107 Associated Press, *Argue for a New Trial in Berger Case*, SHEBOYGAN (Wis.) PRESS, Jan. 25, 1919, at 1.

Stedman focused on more technical grounds.[108] It was all to no avail. On February 20, Landis denied the motions for a new trial and stay of sentence and sentenced each of the defendants to 20 years' imprisonment at Fort Leavenworth.[109]

Stedman appealed to the Seventh Circuit Court of Appeals, charging Landis with prejudice and improper conduct in the trial of his client. Stedman attacked the indictments, court procedure during the trial, and many of Judge Landis's rulings.[110] In one instance, Landis was quoted as declaring that German-Americans' "hearts are reeking with disloyalty." In a relatively unusual move, the Seventh Circuit did not respond directly to Stedman's petition for writ of error, but rather, certified a number of legal questions, "upon which the court is in doubt," to the U.S. Supreme Court.[111]

The Seventh Circuit sought answers to three questions of law raised by the affidavit attesting to Landis's prejudice filed by Stedman before the trial court and rejected by Landis. All of the questions turned on the Court's interpretation of Section 21 of the Judicial Code[112] requiring a judge to recuse himself whenever a party submits such an affidavit: Were Landis's statements sufficiently egregious to support the filing of the affidavit? Did Landis have the lawful right to pass on the sufficiency of the affidavit? And did Landis have the lawful right to preside over the trial after the affidavit was filed?

Writing for the 6-3 majority in January 1921, Justice Joseph McKenna found that Stedman's petition was sufficient, and even though Judge Landis had a right to rule on its sufficiency, he had "no lawful right or power to preside as judge on the trial of defendants upon the indictment."[113] The dissenters—William R. Day, Mahlon R. Pitney and James Clark McReynolds—would have held that Landis's right to pass on the affidavit's sufficiency, subject to appeal, also gave him the right to try the case upon rejecting the affidavit.[114] Nevertheless, the order was sent back to the Seventh Circuit, which reversed Berger's conviction.[115] There was no new trial.

---

[108] *Landis Will Give Decision on Feb. 11*, SHEBOYGAN (Wis.) PRESS, Feb. 5, 1919, at 8.

[109] Associated Press, *Berger Gets Twenty Years*, KENOSHA (Wis.) NEWS, Feb. 20, 1919, at 1.

[110] *Berger Counsel Attacks Landis in Appeal Plea*, CHI. TRIB., March 30, 1920, at 17.

[111] Berger v. United States, 255 U.S. 22, 28 (1921).

[112] Comp. St. § 988.

[113] 255 U.S. at 36.

[114] *Id.* at 37-43.

[115] Berger v. United States, 275 F. 1021, 1022 (7th Cir. 1921).

Scott Nearing (1919)

Seymour Stedman

Scott Nearing, a professor at the Rand School of Social Science and an anti-war activist, was charged with writing a pamphlet attacking the war entitled "The Great Madness: A Victory for the American Plutocracy." Also on trial was the American Socialist Society, which printed and circulated the pamphlet. Both were formally indicted on March 21, 1918, with violating the Espionage Act.[116]

Nearing appeared before Judge Julius M. Mayer the same day for a preliminary pleading to the indictment. He was represented by an attorney from Morris Hillquit's office, who requested the case be put over for two days because Hillquit had just lost a near relative and could not appear. Mayer told Nearing to be ready to furnish a bail bond of $5,000 when court resumed and released him to the custody of his attorney.[117] Nearing subsequently entered a plea of not guilty, and was freed when Roger Baldwin presented the clerk with a $5,000 check.[118] Mayer would later sentence Baldwin, as director of the National Civil Liberties Bureau, to a year in prison for refusing to submit to the draft.[119]

Nearing's trial would not take place until early February 1919; as late as January 23, Hillquit was listed as counsel.[120] In fact, Hillquit had suffered an attack of tuberculosis in the summer of 1918 and retreated to Saranac Lake in New York's Adirondack Mountains to convalesce. He remained largely withdrawn from public life until 1921.[121] So, when Nearing's trial opened on February 5, Seymour Stedman was on his way to New York from Chicago to take over the defense.[122]

Opening statements were hardly surprising, with both Stedman and Assistant U.S. Attorney Earl B. Barnes focusing on the issue of intent. Barnes emphasized the "ordinary rule that a man is presumed to intend natural and ordinary consequences of what he says and does." He acknowledged the truth of

---

116 *Scott Nearing Indicted Under Espionage Act,* N.Y. EVENING WORLD, March 21, 1918, at 3; *Nearing Acquitted, But Socialist Concern Guilty,* N.Y. HERALD, Feb. 20, 1919, at 16. The indictment was subsequently amended to cure some typographical errors. *Amends Nearing Charge,* N.Y. TRIB., May 14, 1918, at 6.

117 *Scott Nearing Is Indicted as Disloyal,* N.Y. TRIB., March 22, 1918, at 1.

118 *Nearing Pleads Not Guilty; Freed on Bail of $5,000,* N.Y. TRIB., March 24, 1918, at 8.

119 *Sent to Prison and Wins Praise of Scott Nearing,* N.Y. EVE. WORLD, Oct. 30, 1918, at 8.

120 *Begin Scott Nearing Trial on Feb. 3,* N.Y. TIMES, Jan. 23, 1919, at 24.

121 NORMA FAIN PRATT, MORRIS HILLQUIT: A POLITICAL HISTORY OF AN AMERICAN JEWISH SOCIALIST 140-41, 224 (1979). Despite his illness, Hillquit ran for Congress from Manhattan in 1918, as did Nearing. Both lost, Nearing to Fiorello La Guardia. *The City's Vote for Congress,* N.Y. TRIB., Nov. 7, 1918, at 4.

122 Associated Press, *Scott Nearing on Trial,* IDAHO STATESMAN, Feb. 6, 1919, at 2.

Stedman's reminder to the jurors that just because a man is opposed to a tariff, that does not make him a smuggler, and because a man is opposed to national prohibition, you do not brand him as running a blind pig [patronizing a speakeasy].

> But gentlemen if you find a man who says he is opposed to any protective tariff, and will never pay a penny of duty, and then you catch him walking through the Customs House with his pockets full of diamonds, you are entitled then to look back at his activities to give you light as to whether or not he intended to smuggle, or whether he denied he had diamonds in his pocket.[123]

At the close of the prosecution's case, Judge Mayer threw out the first two counts of the indictment, holding that there had not been sufficient evidence to prove a conspiracy between the defendants.[124] The highlight of the defense case was Nearing's own testimony. Stedman took Nearing methodically through "Madness" and other writings, defining terms along the way. Barnes's cross examination drew numerous objections and interruptions from Stedman, who admonished his client to answer more slowly. "Mr. Nearing, you answer too quickly. I don't have a chance to object." To Judge Mayer: "I ask your Honor, that the witness's last answer be stricken out, as I want a ruling of this line of questions, and I either get caught by the inability to tell when the prosecution has finished a question or by the football rush of the witness to answer."[125]

Both Nearing and Stedman addressed the jury directly at the close of the defense case. Nearing pointed out that the government could not show a single instance in which recruiting was obstructed or in which insubordination, disloyalty, and refusal of duty were caused. Noting that it had been more than a year since "Madness" was published, Nearing said "the prosecution was unable to bring before you a single instance where these things have actually occurred." Stedman admonished the jury: "You cannot stake the liberty of a nation, which is the liberty of the press and the right to speak on possibilities and the chance that someone being led astray by the publication of a pamphlet or leaflet or speech."[126]

After deliberating for 28 hours on the remaining counts of the indictment, the jury found the American Socialist Society guilty, and Mayer fined it $3,000. Scott Nearing was acquitted of all charges.[127]

---

123 MORRIS HILLQUIT, INTRODUCTION TO AM. SOCIALIST SOC., THE TRIAL OF SCOTT NEARING AND THE AMERICAN SOCIALIST SOCIETY 20-22 (1919) [hereinafter NEARING TRIAL].

124 *Id.* at 249.

125 *Id.* at 39-100, 125.

126 *Id.* at 183, 248.

127 *Id.* at 249. *See also Nearing Acquitted, but Socialist Concern Guilty,* N.Y. HERALD, Feb. 20, 1919, at 16.

Ludwig C. A. K. Martens (1919)

Charles Recht

The earliest public recognition of Charles Recht's formal relationship with the still-evolving Soviet Union came in early June 1919, when the *Tribune* identified Recht as "one of the lawyers of the Russian Soviet Bureau" in New York City. The others included Dudley Field Malone, Morris Hillquit, Gilbert Roe, and George Gordon Battle, a partner in the law firm of Malone's father-in-law, O'Gorman, Battle & Vandiver. Another member of that firm, Edward Stanton, also participated.

The story concerned a document allegedly found by a woman in Grand Central Station, signed "Nikolai Lenine," purporting to commission one Harold C. Keyes for a "secret mission" in the United States on behalf of the "Government of Russian Soviets." Keyes, said to be a member of the Brotherhood of Railroad Trainmen, was reportedly "thrown out" of "The Young Democracy," identified as an organization of conscientious objectors, because he was suspected of being a government agent. Deriding the so-called Lenine commission, Recht was quoted as saying, "People ought to be very careful these days about alleged agents from Soviet Russia. It is really surprising that the federal authorities still fall for that time-honored game of dropping alleged important papers in a conspicuous public place."[128]

The Russian Soviet Government Bureau was real enough, however, although its status as an informal embassy went unrecognized by American authorities. The Bureau was founded in March 1919 and headed by its founder, Ludwig Christian Alexander Karl Martens, until he was deported in 1921. Martens had emigrated to the United States from Russia in 1916, working as a vice president of the engineering firm Weinberg & Posner in New York City. Following the February 1917 revolution, Martens returned to Russia along with nearly 300 revolutionaries, including Leon Trotsky. He returned to the United States in March 1919 to set up the Bureau, seek recognition for the new regime, and oversee Russian commercial interests. With the formation of the New York State Legislature's Joint Legislative Committee to Investigate Seditious Activities, or [Sen. Clayton R.] Lusk Committee, in March, and its raid on the Bureau's West 40th Street offices in June, however, legal issues would dominate his life for the next two years. And Charles Recht would be with him every step of the way.[129]

---

128 *Lenine Letter Hints at U.S. Secret Mission*, N.Y. TRIB., June 3, 1919, at 2.

129 At the height of his representation of the Bureau, in August 1920, Recht was reportedly paid $300 per month. *Ex-U.S. Employee on Soviet Payroll*, BROOKLYN DAILY EAGLE, Aug. 15, 1920, at 47.

On June 13, 1919, virtually every newspaper in New York City carried headlines announcing the raid by 10 agents of the Department of Justice and 10 members of the New York State police. Martens and four others were served with subpoenas *duces tecum* to appear before the committee. Two loads of papers, including many publications characterized as "propaganda," were also taken. The Russians appeared later that afternoon at City Hall, where the Lusk Committee was sitting in secret session. Recht had demanded to represent them before the committee, but was denied access to the proceedings.

That evening, Martens gave a lengthy statement that began:

> The unwarranted and brutal raid on the office of the representative in the United States of the Russian Socialist Federal Soviet Republic I brand as an outrage and as an uncalled-for insult to the people of Russia. The activities of my office have avoided interference in American affairs and the publicity work conducted by my office has had as its only object the bringing about of friendly relations between my Government and the United States.

Martens went on to say he had notified his government of "this outrage" and had filed a protest with the U.S. Department of State.[130]

Malone was also outraged by the raid and, perhaps for the first time, publicly assailed President Wilson at a rally of more than 3,000 men and women in the ballroom of the Hotel Pennsylvania sponsored by two women's peace organizations. Comparing Martens to Benjamin Franklin pleading for his country's revolution in a foreign land, Malone demanded that Martens be accorded the same right that was given to Franklin. "The raid upon the Soviet Bureau shows what America has come to." Malone denounced the Lusk Committee for ordering the raid and concluded his address with an appeal to the women of America and the world to rise and take a hand in the reorganization of the world.[131]

A few days later, Malone addressed a group of some 3,000 Socialist Party members at Madison Square Garden, further denouncing the Lusk Committee, the members of which he called "self-appointed super patriots." Malone derided the committee members' intelligence, saying he doubted "if any one of them has ever cast even an accidental glance inside the covers of a book on an elementary political economy. The people of the State of New York will not

---

130 *Five Russians, Caught in Raid, Must Testify*, N.Y. HERALD, June 13, 1919, at 1. *See also Bolshevik Embassy Here Is Raided*, N.Y. TRIB., June 13, 1919, at 1; *Alleged Bolshevik Agent Says Raid Is "An Outrage"; Dudley Field Malone to Defend Him*, THE BUFFALO COMMERCIAL, June 13, 1919, at 2; *Papers of Reds Seized*, POUGHKEEPSIE (N.Y.) EAGLE-NEWS, June 13, 1919, at 1.

131 *Wilson Jeered by Speakers at Rally of 3,000*, N.Y. TRIB., June 13, 1919, at 1.

permit their policies to be dictated by a legislature of the intelligence we now possess."[132]

Malone denied that the Soviets were attempting to foment rebellion in the U.S., and condemned the raid on the Soviet Bureau as unwarranted and indecent. "Acts of anarchy and violence have not been propelled by organized workers," he said, "but ... by paid agents of capital. We want no anarchy in America, and we shall have none if we control the arrogance of capital and the reactionary politicians."[133]

The *Tribune* attacked him editorially: "Dudley Field Malone, who has taken the oath incident to membership in the legal profession, appears as counsel to a champion of rule by force. If there was a thought dictagraph it would probably report Martens saying to himself: 'These Americans, what fools!'"[134] Criticism of Malone's involvement with the Soviets even reached the U.S. Senate, where Sen. William H. King (D-Utah) remarked that Malone "once masqueraded as a Democrat."[135]

Recht was more circumspect in dealing with the press. Asked whether he believed the raid was an "overt act ... against the Soviet Republic," he responded: "I do not wish to go into that phase of the matter until later. [We] deeply resent the action of the committee, on the ground that it was entirely unwarranted. I shall make a formal statement after I have had an opportunity to converse with my client."[136]

Notwithstanding all the furor over the raid, Martens and staff were back on the job by the following day. Recht told reporters that the raid had been undertaken illegally in some respects. He said that he was considering legal action for the return of the Bureau's papers, but that a search for the original papers upon which the search warrant was issued had proved fruitless.[137] Recht said the Bureau would have no difficulty convincing any court that it was entitled to the return of its papers seized under the circumstances.[138]

The search warrant had been issued by City Magistrate Alexander Brough, and, on June 16, Recht issued a call for Brough's arrest. He also sought an arrest warrant for Archibald E. Stevenson, secretary of the Union League Club and an attorney for the Lusk Committee, whom Recht accused of responsibility for the

---

132 *Raid on Bolshevik Bureau Protested by 3,000 Radicals,* N.Y. TRIB., June 18, 1919, at 15.

133 *Socialists Fail to Mass at Garden,* N.Y. HERALD, June 18, 1919, at 8.

134 *The Man Martens,* N.Y. TRIB., June 18, 1919, at 12.

135 *Malone Is Attacked in Senate as Bolshevik,* N.Y. TRIB., Oct. 11, 1919, at 3.

136 *Bolshevik Embassy Here Is Raided,* N.Y. TRIB., June 13, 1919, at 1.

137 *Raid on Their Bureau Illegal, Say Bolsheviki,* N.Y. TRIB., June 14, 1919, at 3.

138 *Raided Bolsheviki Willing to Go Back,* N.Y. HERALD, June 15, 1919, at 15.

seizure of important papers during the raid.[139] The following day, Recht and several other lawyers appeared before Brough, representing the Bureau or the individuals involved, in an attempt to recover the seized papers, although arguments were put off until the next day. That same evening, a group of about 3,000 rallied at Madison Square Garden to protest both the raid and the recognition of the "White Russian" Kolchak government at Omsk. According to the *Herald*, the crowd was far smaller than had been expected.[140]

On June 18, Brough denied Recht's request to vacate the search warrant, but called on both sides to submit briefs on the issue of whether the entire proceeding should be vacated on the ground that the search warrant was improperly used and that too much violence attended the raid and seizures.[141] Brough put the decision on that issue off until June 24, then again until June 30,[142] when Brough denied the Bureau's request, declaring there was no authority under the law for him to withdraw the warrant, which had been legally executed by police officers of the state. George Gordon Battle, who now represented the Bureau in this matter, said he would appeal to the Court of General Sessions, and had the seized papers transferred to that court.[143]

At a Lusk Committee hearing, also on June 18, Stevenson read a May 29 letter taken from the Bureau's files in the raid. It had been written by Recht in the form of a report, detailing the trial of four I.W.W. members arrested in connection with May Day demonstrations at Chester, Pennsylvania. Recht had been retained to represent several I.W.W. members who had been indicted for riot, aggravated riot, inciting to riot, and destruction of property.[144]

In his report, Recht spoke of a conversation he had with a local attorney, whose collaboration was required for Recht's admission to the Pennsylvania court. "I was amazed at the temper with which he told me about the case," Recht wrote about his conversation with Albert Geary. "He boasted ... that there was no lawyer in Chester who would dare to defend these wretches. He said it was a good thing that those fellows did not get the protection of the law." When the topic of socialist labor leader Eugene V. Debs came up, Recht reported that Geary called Debs a "stinking, flea-bitten, rotten skunk." Recht said the Geary informed him that 64 of the men arrested had been fined $30 each and that all

---

139 *Reds Want Warrant for Magistrate Brough*, N.Y. EVE. WORLD, June 16, 1919, at 13.

140 *Battle Asks Court to Vacate Soviet Warrant*, N.Y. TRIB., June 18, 1919, at 15; *Socialists Fail to Mass at Garden*, N.Y. HERALD, June 18, 1919, at 8.

141 *Says Martens Aided Revolt Plotters Here*, N.Y. HERALD, June 19, 1919, at 1.

142 *Sees Propaganda in Settlement Houses*, N.Y. TIMES, June 25, at 12.

143 *Holds Entire Police Force on Duty Over 4th*, N.Y. TRIB., July 1, 1919, at 22.

144 *Find Soviet Envoy Aided Socialists and I.W.W. Here*, N.Y. TIMES, June 19, 1919, at 1.

but 20 had paid. Four others had been held on $5,000 bail. When Recht asked if the bail was not too high, the lawyer said "the [expletives] Poles and Russians had money to burn and that they were lying in jail merely to spite the government." Geary also said any local lawyer who took the case should be paid $1,000 for the disgrace he would bear.

Recht did find a willing local lawyer to sue out writs of habeas corpus for the four men. A Delaware County judge heard arguments on the writs, which Recht summarized in another letter to Martens. "The result of the proceedings discloses the typical frame of mind of officials of today and the deep-rooted prejudice today against Russians," Recht wrote, noting that the judge went all the way back to 1787 for a precedent under which the defendants could be held on the charges against them. "There is nothing to be done but to work for the record, that is to say, to raise as many legal points as the stupidity of the Judge and his passion will allow," Recht wrote. "And I dare say that probably he will deliver a great many patriotic speeches during the trial. I am quite pessimistic about the result. There is no doubt the Grand Jury will indict these defendants for any offense the District Attorney might choose, even treason."

The writs were dismissed, and, in due course, the four men were indicted. Recht's report bears a penciled annotation in Martens's handwriting: "Ask Comrade Recht to proceed with this case."[145] Lusk took the Recht reports and others like it to mean that the Soviet government was maintaining a bureau for the defense of men arrested and charged with crimes against the United States.[146] "Mr. Martens said he was here solely as a commercial agent for facilitating purchases and shipping of machinery and supplies to Russia. ... In view of these sworn statements, evidence produced today from the correspondence files of Mr. Martens's office is illuminating. It speaks for itself."[147]

Much of Martens's work in the United States was indeed commercial in nature. In June, for example, Malone met with Bureau officials in an effort to facilitate introductions to industrialists who may have wanted to do business with the Soviets.[148] In September, Malone was paid $1,000 to assist in the shipment of $9.6 million worth of goods to Petrograd, but that shipment was ultimately thwarted by the blockade Russian ports. This revelation surfaced during the questioning of Martens by New York Attorney General Charles D.

---

145 *Id.*

146 *Soviets' Bureau Active in Politics, Document Shows,* N.Y. EVE. WORLD, June 18, 1919, at 2; *Berlin Played Up Agitations Here,* STANDARD UNION (Brooklyn), June 18, 1919, at 1.

147 *Martens's Papers Produced at Probe,* N.Y. TRIB., June 19, 1919, at 1, 3.

148 *Russian Reds Urged Ford to Help Projects,* N.Y. HERALD, June 27, 1919, at 7; *Letters Link Henry Ford with Soviet Bureau Here,* N.Y. TRIB., June 27, 1919, at 1.

Newton at a November hearing that implied that Malone had been paid to urge recognition of the Soviet Union in public meetings. Earlier that month, Malone had presided over a mass meeting at Madison Square Garden to protest the blockade and demand the withdrawal of U.S. troops from Russia.[149] But when Martens testified before the Lusk Committee on November 17, 1919, he told the committee that the money paid to Malone was for the shipment of goods and that the issue of recognition never came up.[150]

But Martens's testimony focused on his childhood, education, and early radicalization in Russia. Testifying that he knew Vladimir Lenin in Petrograd, Martens said he was initially deported in 1899, but returned to Russia during the 1905 revolution.[151] He also testified that he had tried, unsuccessfully, to secure $153 million left in the custody of the Russian Embassy when the Kerensky government fell. In addition, Martens told the committee he had taken certain letters and documents sought by the committee to another state.[152]

Malone himself generated some excitement during that hearing, demanding that he be sworn in as a witness. His demand was granted, and upon taking the witness stand, he started to read from a prepared statement: "I have come here to denounce the immoral and cowardly as well as un-American conduct of this investigation." At that point, Newton jumped from his chair and demanded that Malone stop. "I beg your pardon, Mr. Newton. You have no right to stop me," Malone shouted. "I won't take 'stop' from you. Senator Lusk is the only one here that can stop me." After a few minutes' argument, Assemblyman Louis Martin, acting chairman of the committee, ruled that Malone's language was improper, and Malone left the stand but later told the press:

> I have gladly given legal advice to Mr. Martens, the representative of the Russian people, as have other prominent members of the New York Bar .... Does the chief law officer of the State not know that the Constitution

---

149 *11,000 Protest Allied Blockade of Russia*, N.Y. TRIB., Nov. 10, 1919, at 3; *Protest Blockade of Soviet Russia*, N.Y. HERALD, Nov. 10, 1919, at 2; *Lift Blockade of Russia Demand of 8,000 at Madison Square Meeting*, N.Y. DAILY NEWS, Nov. 10, 1919, at 2.

150 *Martens Burns Papers to Keep Soviet Secrets*, N.Y. HERALD, Nov. 26, 1919, at 1. *See also Berkman Must Go Back to Russia; Lusk Committee Quiz Mr. Martens*, N.Y. DAILY NEWS, Nov. 26, 1919, at 2.

151 *Gitlow and Larkin Again Seek Release; Martens is Grilled*, BROOKLYN DAILY EAGLE, Nov. 17, 1919, at 1.

152 *Martens Takes Sudden Trip as Writ Appears*, N.Y. TRIB., Dec. 19, 1919, at 1.

> of our country safeguards the rights of everyone—alien and citizen—to counsel and legal advice?[153]

On December 3, Malone filed a motion in the New York Supreme Court to grant Martens temporary immunity from testifying before the committee, but that was denied by Justice Samuel Greenbaum. Malone then sought a permanent injunction to stop the committee from obtaining Martens's papers based on diplomatic privilege,[154] but that too was decisively rejected on December 9 by Greenbaum, who held that the committee's actions with regard to Martens were in full accord with the authority granted by the state legislature.[155] In one of his last acts for Martens and the Bureau, Malone finally advised Martens to defy the committee and refuse to turn over the documents they demanded,[156] to which the committee responded by seeking contempt charges against Martens in the Supreme Court.[157]

The committee also secured a writ from Greenbaum commanding Martens's appearance. The Committee had asked the court to commit Martens and two colleagues to jail until they agreed to answer the Committee's questions. On December 18, just before the writs could be served, Martens boarded a train for Washington, D.C., telling Recht he had urgent business there. Arguments on the writs had been scheduled for the following day, but Recht pointed out that there could be no arguments because there was no service. Meanwhile, Recht filed an appeal from Justice Greenbaum's order. Asked whether Martens would be back in time for the show cause hearing on the contempt order, Recht said he did not think so,[158] although it might mean the forfeiture of a $1,000 bond.[159]

Then, a few days after Christmas, Recht said Martens would testify before the committee with 48 hours' notice, provided he was not called to appear before any congressional committees in Washington. Lusk agreed, saying the information

---

[153] *Lusk Committee Finds Collector for Red Doughbag,* N.Y. EVE. WORLD, Nov. 26, 1919, at 2; *Dudley Malone Visits Lusk's Committeemen,* N.Y. DAILY NEWS, Nov. 27, 1919, at 2; *Bomb Squad Seeks Reds Indicted Here,* N.Y. HERALD, Nov. 27, 1919, at 5.

[154] *Court Refuses Soviet "Envoy" Immunity Plea,* N.Y. DAILY NEWS, Dec. 4, 1919, at 6.

[155] *Martens Ordered to Produce Papers,* N.Y. HERALD, Dec. 10, 1919, at 20; *Martens Must Reveal Lenine's Secret Letters,* N.Y. TRIB., Dec. 10, 1919, at 7.

[156] *Red Chiefs Here Tried to Get Kerensky Funds,* N.Y. DAILY NEWS, Dec. 12, 1919, at 6; *Martens Defies Lusk Committee,* N.Y. TRIB., Dec. 12, 1919, at 3.

[157] *Martens Faces Contempt Law in Lusk Probe,* N.Y. DAILY NEWS, Dec. 13, 1919, at 4.

[158] *Id.*

[159] *Police Must Tell Why They Put Stop To 'Freedom Walk,'* N.Y. TRIB., Dec. 28, 1919, at 3. In August 1920, Recht sought the return of the $1,000 Liberty Bond that Martens had put up, but his demand was rejected by the State of New York. *State Refuses to Return $1,000 Bond of Martens,* BROOKLYN DAILY EAGLE, Aug. 17, 1920, at 3.

sought from Martens was far more desirable than the $1,000 forfeiture.[160] With that, the committee voted not to return until January 5, 1920, when it would reconvene "until its business was completed," rather than go out of business with the legislature that created it on the first of the year.[161]

On New Year's Day, 1920, Martens returned to New York City to spend the day with his wife and two daughters "hiding" from state troopers seeking to enforce Justice Greenbaum's show cause order. Recht told the press the family wished to spend the holiday together, without being disturbed, and that Martens would return to Washington the following day to prepare to testify before the Senate Foreign Relations Committee, beginning January 5. As for Martens's ducking the would-be process servers, Recht claimed that the Lusk Committee ceased to exist at midnight on December 31 and no longer had authority to question Martens. He added that the federal subpoena to attend the Senate committee hearing took precedence over everything else. Representatives of the Lusk Committee denied that it had expired with the New Year.[162]

Then, on January 2, the government launched yet another raid of communist offices around the country, netting around 4,000 suspects in 33 cities.[163] On the same day, the Department of Labor issued a warrant for Martens's arrest as an alien in the United States in violation of the Immigration Act because he was "a member of or affiliated with an organization that entertains a belief in the overthrow by force or violence of the Government of the United States."[164]

In New York City, Recht and two other attorneys were retained to apply for habeas corpus writs for 201 aliens caught up in the raids and awaiting deportation at Ellis Island. Funds for that project were raised by groups of radicals unaffected by the raids, led by the I.W.W.'s Elizabeth Gurley Flynn, as head of the Workers' Defense Union. On January 4, Recht issued a statement calling on the government to permit the aliens to leave the country of their own accord, rather than sending them to the overcrowded Ellis Island.[165]

---

160 *Police, supra* note 159; *Martens Ready to Testify*, DAILY SENTINEL (Rome, N.Y.), Dec. 27, 1919, at 1; *Soviet "Envoy" To Appear When Committee Asks*, BUFFALO TIMES, Dec. 28, 1919, at 25.

161 *Soviet "Envoy," supra* note 160, at 25.

162 *Martens Here for a Day, But Evades Contempt Order*, N.Y. DAILY HERALD, Jan. 2, 2910, at 11; *Martens Returns Home, But Will Stay in Hiding*, N.Y. TRIB., Jan. 2, 1920, at 1; *Red Mourners Will Picket White House*, N.Y. HERALD, Jan. 2, 1920, at 6.

163 DAVID M. KENNEDY, OVER HERE 290 (2004).

164 In the Matter of L.C.A.K. Martens, An Alleged Alien (Dep't of Labor, Bureau of Immigration 1920) (Brief of Charles Recht on behalf of Mr. Martens) [hereinafter "Martens Brief"], at 1.

165 *"Reds" to Ask Freedom on Habeas Corpus*, N.Y. TRIB., Jan. 5, 1920, at 1.

In a telegram to Attorney General A. Mitchell Palmer, Labor Secretary William B. Wilson, and Immigration Commissioner Anthony J. Caminetti, Recht claimed to represent all of those arrested in the raids from New York and adjacent states, many of whom had expressed a willingness to be deported.[166] "My office is acting as attorney for New York, New Jersey, Connecticut, and Pennsylvania men arrested in the raids" Recht wrote.

> I believe I speak with authority for the majority of Russians, who do not want to contest deportation proceedings. If you will please wire collect, the following information, I may be able to obtain signed consents from many of the men, thus saving the Government expenses, delay and work. The information sought is: How soon you intend to deport these men and women to Soviet Russia? Will you take along wives and children, or dependent parents having no support, and give opportunity to furnish persons with necessaries, such as clothing?[167]

On January 5, Gregory Weinstein, chief clerk of the Bureau and a close aide to Martens, was arrested and, upon his refusal to answer any questions, was also sent to Ellis Island for deportation. Dubbed "the chancellor" by the press, Weinstein was a Russian Jew who had escaped from exile in Siberia. He was described as "a most violent and dangerous Bolshevist," by the Justice Department's George F. Lamb:

> Weinstein is the most influential man in the Communist Party next to Martens. He came to this country with Trotsky and was associated with him for some time in the publication of the *Novy Mir*, a radical Russian newspaper. After [Trotsky] went back to Russia and seized control of the government with Lenine, Weinstein became editor of *Novy Mir* and directed revolutionary activities here. As Martens' 'chief of staff' he is said to know more about radical activities in this country than any one except the so-called 'ambassador' himself.[168]

According to Recht, Weinstein was denied bail, despite his offer of $10,000 in Liberty Bonds—the amount set by the Department of Labor[169]—because he refused to answer questions unless he was furnished with a lawyer. He named

---

[166] *Deportation of Others Awaits the Outcome*, BUFFALO ENQUIRER, Jan. 6, 1920, at 1.

[167] *Begin Procedure to Deport Reds*, N.Y. TIMES, Jan. 6, 1920, at 1.

[168] *Martens' Chief Aid* [sic] *Seized as 'Red' Net is Drawn Again; 46,000 on Palmer's Plot List*, N.Y. DAILY HERALD, Jan. 6, 1920, at 13, 16 (Part II, p. 1, 4).

[169] *Refuse $10,000 Bail for [Weinstein] and Other Red Leaders*, ITHACA (N.Y.) J., Jan. 9, 1920, at 1; *Refuse Bail on Weinstein*, ELMIRA STAR-GAZETTE, Jan. 9, 1920, at 5; *Martens' Chief Aide Held Without Bail, His Counsel Avers*, BROOKLYN DAILY EAGLE, Jan. 9, 1920, at 3; *Weinstein is Mum So Bail is Denied Him*, BUFFALO COMMERCIAL, Jan. 9, 1920, at 12.

Recht as his attorney, but Recht was refused admission to Ellis Island by immigration inspectors claiming to be acting on the order of the Secretary of Labor and the Department of Justice. Recht went to Washington to discuss the matter, but received only excuses.[170]

Recht considered the Weinstein case a "test case" for the habeas petitions he filed on behalf of the many deportees for whom he was acting. He sued out a writ of habeas corpus for Weinstein before U.S. District Judge John C. Knox, who scheduled a hearing for January 13.[171] Publicly, Recht charged the authorities with cruelty in the handling of the political prisoners. "It would seem that we are not only fighting the most deliberate propaganda of falsification that has ever [been] developed," he said, "but officiousness and cruelty of every kind. [Every] protection the law and Constitution affords to individuals has been deliberately violated." Alleging that deportees were being denied bail, even when they had the cash, Recht asserted that

> No one but a person observing closely these outrages can realize the tragedy of it all—the violent despotism and cruelty on the one hand and the helpless innocence of most of the victims ... merely because some of the gentlemen in public life want to satisfy their political ambitions.[172]

Recht also denounced the Labor Department's decision automatically slating for deportation any member of the Communist and Communist Labor parties. "I am informed," Recht wrote Labor Secretary Wilson, "that there was no formal hearing—that this matter was decided by you and the Attorney-General, ex parte. You have practically placed out of the pale of the law some 65,000 or 70,000 people without giving such people an opportunity to be heard." Recht asked Wilson to reopen the matter and release the prisoners on bail pending resolution.[173]

At the January 13 hearing before Judge Knox, Recht pointed out that on December 31, 1919, the immigration rules were changed back to a wartime standard, which enabled inspectors to detain aliens indefinitely until they had answered questions to the inspectors' satisfaction. Judge Knox then sustained the writ, stating that Weinstein was entitled to bail as a matter of right. Knox ordered the release of all other prisoners who applied for the writ, as well as

---

170 *Charges of Illegal Practices of the Department of Justice: Hearings Before a Subcomm.*, S. Comm. on the Judiciary, 66th Cong. 371 (1921) (testimony of Charles Recht) [hereinafter "*Illegal Practices*"]. *See also Martens Ready to Surrender to Congress*, N.Y. TRIB., Jan. 9, 1920, at 13.

171 *Id.*

172 *Red Envoy Martens Is Still at Liberty*, N.Y. HERALD, Jan. 8, 1920, at 24.

173 *Recht Protests Nation's Stand on Communists*, N.Y. DAILY NEWS, Jan. 9, 1920, at 2.

others on whose behalf the writ was taken out, unless the Labor Department was willing to accept bail in the amounts fixed, $10,000 for Weinstein and $1,000 for most others.[174]

Recht shuttled between New York and Washington, presumably to counsel Martens on his appearance before the Senate committee. Two of his associates, Rose Weiss and Irving Klein, assisted with the Ellis Island cases, while Recht focused on Martens. A number of lawyers from various organizations were also representing Ellis Island detainees, among them: Harry Weinberger, best known for his representation of Emma Goldman,[175] and Swinburne Hale and Isaac Shorr,[176] both well-known civil liberties lawyers of the firm Hale, Nelles, and Shorr. Isaac A. Hourwich, who had previously been a lawyer for the federal government, had been appointed acting director of the Bureau's legal department in April 1919.[177]

In Washington, Martens was now scheduled to begin his testimony before a subcommittee of the U.S. Senate Committee on Foreign Relations on January 19; two days earlier, he issued a statement expressing hope that the subcommittee hearings would refute the "wild and unfounded charges" made against him and would "clearly bring out before the American public the whole uncolored truth about Russia."[178]

Martens's testimony before the subcommittee continued intermittently over the next 10 weeks, ending on March 29. Martens asserted that the primary purpose of his mission was to restore trade between the U.S. and Soviet Russia and that he had not supported any organization that advocated a Soviet America. He denied that his mission was to destroy the United States government, going so far as to file a libel suit seeking $1 million in damages from the *Review of Reviews* for an article entitled "The Reds in America." The article called Martens "the self-styled ambassador" whose mission was to "spread all kinds of propaganda looking to the destruction of the Government of the United States."[179] Nevertheless, the subcommittee concluded that Martens had no status as a diplomat and recommended his immediate deportation as an

---

[174] *Illegal Practices, supra* note 170, at 371-75. At the hearing, Recht also represented a detainee named Eugene Neuwald. *Only 14 Reds Now on Silence Strike*, N.Y. EVE. WORLD, Jan. 12, 1920, at 2.

[175] *Refuse $10,000 Bail for [Weinstein] and Other Red Leaders*, ITHACA JOURNAL, Jan. 9, 1920, at 1.

[176] *Martens Ready to Surrender to Congress*, N.Y. TRIB., Jan. 9, 1920, at 13.

[177] *Russian Soviet Government Bureau*, MARXIST HISTORY, http://www.marxhistory.org/subject/usa/eam/rsgb.html. Morris Hillquit was officially the staff lawyer for the Bureau, but was unable to participate because of his health.

[178] Frederick C. Giffin, *The Martens Mission*, 73 INT'L SOC. SCI. REV. 91, 98 (1998).

[179] *'Review of Reviews' Sued by Martens*, N.Y. HERALD, Mar. 25, 1920, at 20.

undesirable alien. At the close of the hearings, Martens surrendered to the Department of Labor to face the charge that he was in the country in violation of the Immigration Act of 1918 by virtue of his communist affiliation.[180]

Recht's brief on behalf of Martens made five points. First, that Martens was an accredited official of a foreign government, albeit unrecognized, and, thus, was explicitly exempted from Immigration Act coverage. Second, that the evidence produced against Martens was mostly irrelevant newspaper clippings and the like, and that Martens's testimony before the Senate subcommittee and the Lusk Committee was privileged and inadmissible in this proceeding. Third, that much of the evidence concerned an alleged conspiracy to smuggle diamonds into the United States and, thus, beyond the jurisdiction of the Labor Department. Fourth, the evidence failed to prove that Martens believed in, advocated, or belonged to any group that advocated the violent overthrow of the U.S. government. And fifth, any evidence pertaining to the legal system of the Soviet government.[181]

More than a dozen separate hearings were held in both Washington and New York between March 31 and December 7 before August P. Shell, the immigration inspector at Ellis Island.[182] At some of those hearings in Washington, Governor-elect Thomas W. Hardwick of Georgia served as lead counsel for Martens, with Recht and Hourwich assisting; Recht conducted the defense at sessions held at Ellis Island.[183] In the end, Recht's vigorous defense was unavailing, and Martens was ordered deported on December 15. Labor Secretary Wilson said Martens's status as an official of the Soviet regime, "taken in conjunction with his expressed belief in and approval of the Third International," established beyond doubt that he favored the forcible overthrow of the American government.[184] Martens issued a response two days later, asserting that Wilson had made a "political decision, dictated by the policy of the present Administration toward the Soviet Government." Martens expressed confidence that "the American people will demand a sensible consideration of the whole question of Russian-American relations."[185]

The following day, Recht told reporters that Moscow would decide whether to contest Wilson's order. "It is possible that the Soviet Government will decide to take no steps to resist the decision," Recht said. "We will do nothing until I

---

180 *Id.*

181 Martens Brief, *supra* note 164, at 3-6.

182 Giffin, *supra* note 178, at 98.

183 *Immigrants Sail in Quarters Not Fit for Swine*, N.Y. TRIB., Dec. 7, 1920, at 5.

184 Giffin, *supra* note 178, at 98-99 (quoting MONTHLY LAB. REV., Jan. 1921, at 187-94).

185 *Id.* at 99.

have received [Wilson's] decision and it has been communicated to Moscow. I am going to Washington shortly, and it is probable that I will be asked to surrender Mr. Martens, and that arrangements will then be made for his deportation."[186] Recht had his answer by the end of the month when Soviet Foreign Commissar Grigori Chicherin, who had appointed Martens to his position in January 1919, wired Martens ordering him to return to Russia on his own accord.[187] Martens's staff voted to go with him.[188]

Recht surrendered Martens to Wilson on January 3, 1921, who immediately released Martens on his own recognizance.[189] On January 22, Martens, his family, and 46 members of the Bureau staff sailed from New York aboard the *Stockholm*, a Swedish-American liner.[190] Martens landed at Reval, now Tallinn, Estonia, on February 7 or 8,[191] then Moscow on February 13.[192] Among the Bureau officials who traveled with him was Gregory Weinstein, Martens' secretary and general manager of the Bureau, who was also under a deportation order.[193]

With Ludwig Martens no longer in the country, Recht's role became somewhat ambiguous, not least because he moved his offices from 42nd Street to 110 West 40th St., the building that had once housed the Soviet Bureau and the Deportees' League. Called to testify on February 1, 1921, before a Senate Judiciary Subcommittee investigating charges of illegal practices by the U.S. Department of Justice, Recht spent a substantial amount of time trying to clarify whom he represented and whom he did not.[194]

Recht testified that he was attorney for Martens, for the Soviet Bureau and its staff, and, through a defense committee, for nearly all of the people detained on Ellis Island following the January 2, 1920, raids. He denied that he was attorney for what one senator called "the communist organization in the

---

186 *Martens to Inform Moscow*, N.Y. TIMES, Dec. 17, 1920, at 4.

187 Giffin, *supra* note 178, at 99.

188 *Martens' Staff Vote to Go With Him to Russia*, N.Y. Trib., Dec. 30, 1920, at 2.

189 *Martens Surrendered [To] Secretary Wilson by His Counsel Today*, N.Y. Herald, Jan. 3, 1921, at 1.

190 Giffin, *supra* note 178, at 99.

191 *Martens Lands at Reval*, N.Y. EVE. WORLD, Feb. 8, 1921, at 3.

192 Associated Press, *Martens Reaches Moscow*, BUFFALO COMMERCIAL, Feb. 16, 1921, at 1. On Feb. 19, Martens cabled Recht to say he had arrived safely in Russia. *Martens in Russia*, BROOKLYN DAILY EAGLE, Feb. 21, 1921, at 18; *Attorney Recht Receives Cablegram from Red "Ambassador,"* N.Y. TRIB., Feb. 22, 1921, at 7.

193 *Martens Requests Labor Department Rush Deportation*, BUFFALO COURIER, Jan. 4, 1921, at 2.

194 *Illegal Practices*, *supra* note 170, at 365.

United States." Rather, he said his work was representing "what we might call political minorities, without distinction as to the principles." Asked directly whether he represented the Soviet Government, Recht seemed to hedge. "I represented Mr. Martens, as his personal attorney." He also noted that several other lawyers represented Martens, including George Gordon Battle, former Sen. Thomas W. Hardwick, Dudley Field Malone, and others. Recht firmly denied that he represented the Communist Party of the United States or any local party organization.[195]

When Attorney General Palmer testified before the subcommittee on February 18, he seemed to praise Recht for his testimony.

> [He] struck me as probably the most intelligent, clear thinking, and plain-spoken man of all those who testified before the committee, and therefore his testimony, I have no doubt, will be taken, as it ought to be taken if its face value is to be accepted, very seriously. He was, as he said very frankly, counsel for practically all the persons who were arrested for deportation in the city of New York.

Palmer took issue with Recht's assertion that the secretary of labor should have announced that Communist Party members would be subject to arrest, noting that such an announcement "would have simply warned evaders of the law in advance in order that they might hide from Government officials." In his testimony, Palmer identified Recht as "at present a representative of the Russian Soviet Republic in this country." To back that up, he introduced a letter purporting to be from Martens to Recht:

> Dear Comrade Recht:
>
> In view of my sailing, I wish to make some arrangements and leave certain instructions which you should carry out during my absence or until you receive further instructions from the commissariat of foreign affairs of the Soviet Government.
>
> 1. You are hereby authorized to act as my personal representative and to act for me in all matters of importance.
> 2. You are authorized, if necessary and if so instructed by the commissary of foreign affairs in Moscow, to receive all legal papers and in every way act as an attorney representing the Russian Socialist Federated Soviet Republic.

---

195 *Id.* at 365-367.

3. You are authorized to take action in the cases of needy and worthy Russians who may appeal to you for aid, in accordance with instructions which will be sent to you.

In all such cases this letter will be sufficient authorization for you.

L. Martens
Representative of the Russian Socialist Federated
Soviet Republic in the United States[196]

Recht responded that he was Martens's attorney and only represented the Soviet government "in the sense that bills owed by or to the Moscow government may be handled through me. I do not have, however, any such plenipotentiary powers as Mr. Palmer would ascribe to me," he said, "for Mr. Martens didn't have authority to appoint a new ambassador in this country to succeed him."[197] In a letter to the subcommittee, Recht suggested that the letter Palmer put in the record "had been incorrectly translated from English to Russian and again into English."[198] He also denied Palmer's implication that his "appointment" was shrouded in secrecy.[199]

By the time Martens returned to Russia, the civil war had turned conclusively in favor of the Bolshevik army, although it would be more than a year before all of the fighting ended. The United States officially refused to recognize the Soviet government, however, claiming two-thirds of the Russian people did not recognize that government.[200] Nevertheless, in what might have been a gesture of recognition that Martens represented Russia in some fashion, the Department of Labor cancelled the arrest and deportation warrants against Martens and Weinstein.[201] Despite rumors to the contrary,[202] Martens never returned to the United States but rather enjoyed a successful career in the Soviet Union. He retired in 1941 and died in 1948.[203]

---

196 *Id.* at 576. *See also Martens Left Red Agent Here, Palmer Says,* N.Y. TRIB., Feb. 19, 1921, at 1.

197 *Recht Is Martens's Lawyer, He Explains,* N.Y. TRIB., Feb. 19, 1921, at 2.

198 *Recht Charges Palmer with Misrepresentation,* N.Y. TRIB., Feb. 20, 1921, at 22.

199 *Martens Aid* [sic] *Denies Secret Appointment,* N.Y. HERALD, Feb. 23, 1921, at 4.

200 *Washington Won't Recognize Soviet,* N.Y. HERALD, Feb. 19, 1921, at 4.

201 *Deportation Order Canceled After Martens Goes Home,* BROOKLYN DAILY EAGLE, Feb. 26, 1921, at 2.

202 *Say Martens is Soon to Return to U.S.,* BROOKLYN DAILY EAGLE, Feb. 27, 1921, at 35; *Claims Martens to Soon Return to this Country,* BUFFALO TIMES, Feb. 27, 1921, at 41.

203 Giffin, *supra* note 178, at 99. Both Martens and Weinstein, represented by Recht, sued to recover property left behind in the United States. Weinstein unsuccessfully sought return of books and papers allegedly seized during the raids. In re Weinstein, 271 F. 5

Socialist Legislators (1919, 1920)

Morris Hillquit

Seymour Stedman

In 1919 and 1920, Morris Hillquit would take the lead in two cases involving legislative bodies attempting—and largely succeeding—in expelling duly elected Socialist members. In 1919, Hillquit and his law partners, Jacob Hillquit and Alexander Levene, joined progressive lawyer Gilbert E. Roe, to oversee a recount of votes in New York City's Eighth Aldermanic District, where Socialist Algernon Lee was allegedly ousted along with another Socialist, Edward F. Cassidy.[204] Neither would occupy his seat on the Board of Aldermen for some 21 months of their 24-month term.

Finally, on September 19, 1921, Supreme Court Justice Isidore Wasservogel issued a peremptory writ of mandamus directing the board to determine by means of a recount the validity of Lee's and Cassidy's claims to have won the 1919 election.[205] The board was given until November 3 to comply. When a minority report of the board's Committee on Privileges and Elections revealed that both Lee and Cassidy were actually elected by comfortable majorities, the Tammany-dominated board voted nevertheless to prevent them from taking their seats by refusing to file the committee report.[206]

Two days later, Appellate Division unanimously sustained Wasservogel's original order, cutting off any further Tammany appeals and mandating the immediate filing of the report.[207] The next day, Hillquit obtained an order from the Supreme Court requiring six Tammany and one Republican member of the committee to show cause why they should not be held in contempt of court for violating Wasservogel's order.[208] Lee and Cassidy were finally seated, but their victory was Pyrrhic at best. Both were defeated in the November 7 election, and

---

(S.D.N.Y. 1920), *aff'd,* Weinstein v. Atty. Gen. of the United States, 271 F. 673 (1921). Martens also sued for recovery of books and papers, as well as a red flag, that had been presented to him by Russian organizations around the country. *Martens Sues for Red Flag,* N.Y. TRIB., Mar. 19, 1921, at 2.

204 *Election Figures Stand Under Official Canvass,* N.Y. TRIB., Nov. 16, 1919, at 7; *Two Socialists Pave Way for Ballot Recount,* N.Y. TRIB., Nov. 18, 1919, at 6.

205 *Aldermen Directed to Decide as to Lee,* N.Y. HERALD, Sept. 20, 1921, at 7.

206 *Hylan Aldermen Defy Court and Bar Socialists,* N.Y. Trib., Oct. 26, 1921, at 7; *Aldermen Bar Out Elected Socialists,* N.Y. HERALD, Oct. 26, 1921, at 1; *Citation of Aldermen for Contempt Sought To-day,* N.Y. TRIB., Oct. 27, 1921, at 2.

207 *Socialist Victory Blow to Tammany,* N.Y. HERALD, Oct. 28, 1921, at 5.

208 *Aldermen Named in Contempt Order,* N.Y. HERALD, Oct. 29, 1921, at 3.

their terms of office expired on December 31.[209] Perhaps they took some solace from Appellate Division's retroactive award of salaries due to the two men in May 1923.[210]

Shortly after that 1919 aldermanic election, a similar situation was taking shape in Albany. As Hillquit was regaining his strength at Saranac Lake, he learned that five Socialist Party members elected to the New York State Assembly—two from Manhattan, two from Queens, and one from Brooklyn—had been temporarily suspended on January 7, 1920, pending an investigation by the Judiciary Committee, for membership in an organization whose ideals were inimical to the U.S. government. "A day or two later," Hillquit wrote in his autobiography, "I was visited by a representative of the Socialist Party who had come to consult me about the situation and inquire whether I felt well enough to take charge of the defense. I did."[211]

The Judiciary Committee hearing was set to begin on January 20, 1920. Joining Hillquit on the defense team were Seymour Stedman, Gilbert Roe, and Walter Nelles, as well as S. John Block, counsel for the Socialist Party in New York City, and former Socialist assemblyman William Karlin. Also participating on the defense team were two of the ousted assemblymen, Charles Solomon of Brooklyn and Samuel Orr of the Bronx.[212]

The defense team's formal answer to the charges argued that the five ousted assemblymen were duly elected and qualified to hold office, and the Assembly and its Judiciary Committee had no jurisdiction to inquire into whether they possessed qualifications other than those prescribed by law. The resolution of January 7, denying them seats pending investigation, was illegal and void, the brief said. Further, the five denied every charge contained in the resolution, except for their affiliation with the Socialist Party, a lawful and legitimate political party. Finally, the brief argued, the investigation had been instituted lawlessly, in bad faith, and with malice, by a conspiracy among certain members of the Assembly.[213]

---

209 *Socialist Vote Cut Down Half; Panken Polls Only 84,000,* N.Y. TRIB., Nov. 10, 1921, at 6; *Democrats Gain 14 Seats in Board of Aldermen,* N.Y. TRIB., Nov. 10, 1921, at 3.

210 Lee v. Graubard, 199 N.Y.S. 563 (N.Y. App. Div. 1923); Cassidy v. Sullivan, 199 N.Y.S. 566 (N.Y. App. Div. 1923).

211 LOOSE LEAVES, *supra* note 1, at 251.

212 *Socialists Plan New Lusk Attack,* N.Y. TIMES, Jan. 12, 1920, at 1; *Sweet Blocks Move to Seat Socialists,* N.Y. TIMES, Jan. 20, 1920, at 3.

213 Answer, In the Matter of the Investigation by the Assembly of the State of New York, February 1920, at 1–3, in Gilbert E. Roe Papers, Box H12, Folder Assemblymen Case, in La Follette Papers, Wisconsin Historical Society.

Testimony during the Judiciary Committee hearings—often referred to as a "trial" in the press—dragged on through the rest of January and all of February, resulting in some two thousand pages of transcript. Hillquit was forced to return to Saranac Lake toward the end of January, leaving Stedman in charge, but said he would "remain in daily and intimate touch with the proceedings before the committee and would return in about a week." According to a statement issued on January 23:

> This is the first work Mr. Hillquit has undertaken for a year and a half, and it has been understood among his colleagues from the beginning that he would not remain in Albany continuously to subject himself to the intense strain involved. He has had two weeks of travel and hard work and sustained them exceedingly well.[214]

Stedman played an active role in the give-and-take, at one point sparring with committee counsel John B. Stanchfield over the admissibility of a certain Hebrew book purchased from one Samuel Miller.

> Stedman: It isn't competent or direct evidence. We don't know this man "Miller." Who is going to dispute what he said?
>
> Stanchfield: In response to my eloquent and distinguished friend from the west, let me suggest that he must have overlooked the fact that there is the express charge that these five men here involved had been a party to a conspiracy to subvert our law and to overturn the government by force.
>
> Stedman: In reply to the distinguished gentleman whose consciousness of himself is never absent, let me say that we are not charged here with conspiracy. This is a new thing—conspiracy. I suppose we will have another offense by tomorrow morning.[215]

On another occasion, Stedman objected to the admission of evidence collected during the investigation of Ludwig C. A. K. Martens, the self-styled Soviet ambassador to the United States. Stedman demanded that if the testimony were to be entered at all, it should be read in its entirety. When the reading commenced and seemed likely to continue for days, Stedman reached an agreement with Stanchfield to print the testimony and present a copy to the defense. Then both sides could read into the record those excerpts that suited them.[216] Another time, Stedman defended the Socialist Party from charges that it advocated sabotage, reading from a 1914 campaign book to show that no one

---

214 *Ousted Socialists Will Lose Hillquit,* N.Y. SUN, Jan. 24, 1920, at 6; *Hillquit Sent Back to Woods by His Doctors,* N.Y. DAILY NEWS, Jan. 24, 1920, at 2.

215 *Hot Clashes at Assembly Trial of 5 Socialists,* CHI. TRIB., Jan. 23, 1920, at 5.

216 *U.S., Soviet Quiz Data are Used in Socialist Trial,* CHI. TRIB., Jan. 29, 1920, at 7.

practicing sabotage was allowed to become a member. Asked why the clause was stricken out three years later, Stedman replied that the I.W.W. element was no longer enrolled in the party and that sabotage was a "dead issue."[217] Stedman even took the stand to testify for the defense.[218]

Hillquit returned to Albany three weeks later, on February 17, in time to open the defense case from the witness stand. Examined by Stedman over two days, Hillquit explained the theory and practice of socialism, its evolution in the United States and Europe, and the attitude of the various factions within the movement. He praised Wilson's Fourteen Points and the League of Nations, and he defined the "social revolution" advocated by socialists as a peaceful transition from the capitalist to the socialist form of producing and distributing wealth. He also denied that the socialists were pacifists. "The socialists' opposition to war is not based chiefly on humanitarian grounds," he said, "but on the contention that wars are usually based on commercial rivalry. The great war just ended served only the capitalists." Hillquit testified that socialists would not oppose a war of independence and, in response to a question from the committee, said American socialists would have no hesitancy whatever in joining forces with the rest of their countrymen to repel the Bolsheviks in the event of an invasion, an event he described as "bordering on the impossible."

Hillquit said socialists had "no idea of establishing a Soviet government here, as has been charged," and that the Soviet system in Russia was only a temporary expedient until a new form of democracy could be established. He also defined the Internationale as an exchange for ideas on the philosophy and practice of socialism and said that its functions were purely advisory. He said he had never heard of a "citizen of the Internationale," noting that the Internationale "has never claimed authority to direct the policies of the various affiliated parties or attempted to enforce its views on separate nations." Nor did socialists desire to create a universal war for the purpose of bringing about international socialism, he declared. [219]

Hillquit was thoroughly cross-examined by Martin Conboy, counsel to the committee, who pushed Hillquit to interpret a speech and an article by Victor Berger in which the Milwaukee socialist intimated that the proletariat would

---

[217] *Unite Behind T.R. Jr. to Seat Five Socialists,* CHI. TRIB., Jan. 30, 1920, at 1.

[218] *2 Chicagoans on Stand at Trial of Socialists,* CHI. TRIB., Feb. 21, 1920, at 4.

[219] *Two Suspended Socialists Open Guns on Sweet,* N.Y. TRIB., Feb. 16, 1920, at 2; *Clergymen to Aid in Defense of Socialists,* N.Y. DAILY NEWS, Feb. 17, 1920, at 7; *Hillquit to Take Stand in Defense of Five Socialists,* N.Y. TRIB., Feb. 17, 1920, at 5; *Hillquit Is Witness for Ousted Five,* N.Y. TRIB., Feb. 18, 1920, at 1; *Hillquit Denies Socialists Plot U.S. Revolution,* N.Y. DAILY NEWS, Feb. 18, 1920, at 6; *Hillquit Denies Party Planned Soviet for U.S.,* N.Y. DAILY NEWS, Feb. 19, 1920, at 4.

ultimately have to "shoot" to seize power. Hillquit acknowledged that "a little shooting" might be necessary to defend socialism's political gains from the lawless reaction of privileged minorities, but insisted that some of Berger's wording was "unfortunate" and "altogether too strong for the meaning which they ... are intended to carry." Another committee counsel, Arthur E. Sutherland, cross-examined Hillquit regarding Eugene Debs, whose Espionage Act conviction had recently been affirmed by the U.S. Supreme Court. Hillquit declined to defend "every word ... contained in [Debs's] speech" but said, "[As] a rule, I fully indorsed his statements and sentiments on the subject of the war, as expressed, I suppose in that speech and other speeches." Hillquit was excused shortly before 6 p.m. on his third day on the stand.[220]

All of the testimony in the case ended on February 27; three of the five defendants had taken the stand on their own behalf.[221] Closing arguments took place in early March, and briefs were submitted later that month. Conboy closed for the prosecution with a vicious denunciation of the socialists as traitors. "The Socialist Party of America is not a loyal organization disgraced occasionally by the traitorous act of a member," Conboy said, "but a disloyal party composed of perpetual traitors."[222]

Hillquit published the full stenographic record of his closing address, in which he attempted to summarize the issues from the socialist point of view. He began with a formal, legalistic argument stressing the limits of the committee's mandate, and the fact that the House resolution authorizing the inquiry contained no charges of misconduct against any of the assemblymen except their affiliation with the Socialist Party. The statement of additional charges added by the committee itself "should be disregarded from beginning to end; should be thrown out of your minds, and from your consideration, together with all the testimony based on it." With respect to the evidence, Hillquit argued that it was so one-sided as to "distort the vision of those who read it" and render it "absolutely worthless and worse."

Asserting that nearly all of the charges were actually charges against the Socialist Party itself, he proceeded to instruct the committee on socialism and contrast it with capitalism. He then took on each of the charges in turn, conceding that the Socialist Party was a revolutionary party, but denying that it sought to achieve its goals through violence. He insisted that the Socialist Party was a real political party, not merely "masquerading" as one, and denied that it controlled its elected members any more than any other political party. He

---

220 *Hillquit Would Back Ballots with Bullets,* N.Y. TRIB., Feb. 20, 1920, at 5.

221 *Socialists Close Defence Abruptly,* SUN & N.Y. HERALD, Feb. 28, 1920, at 4.

222 *Ousted Socialists Called Traitors,* SUN & N.Y. HERALD, March 5, 1920, at 5.

denied that the party was unpatriotic and disloyal, even as it opposed the war. And he vehemently rejected the charge that the Socialist Party owed its allegiance "wholly and solely to an alien, invisible empire, known as the Internationale," or that it sought to introduce a Soviet system of government in the United States.

He concluded with a resounding condemnation of the proposed expulsion:

> For the first time since the existence of this Republic ... for the first time in the history of any country of parliamentary government, has a case of this kind come up, a case involving the outlawry of an entire political party, a case in which the majority parties would take it upon themselves to bar a minority party because they disagree with such minority .... [If] you unseat these Assemblymen, that stain upon our democracy will never be washed off, never be removed. That precedent once created will work towards the undoing of the entire constitutional, representative system so laboriously built up.[223]

Stedman had the last word for the defense. Addressing the committee, Stedman declared, "You take your chance in presenting your view to the people. We take ours, feeling that the mass intellect of this country, with all the facts before it, will ultimately arrive at the correct solution."[224]

During Sutherland's cross-examination of Stedman, an apparent disagreement over tactics arose between Nelles and Hillquit. When Sutherland requested a copy of the record in the case of Kate Richards O'Hare, who had been convicted of Espionage Act violations during the war, Nelles offered to produce it. Hillquit refused to allow it, claiming that it was wholly irrelevant and that he would not assist the prosecution in traveling so far afield. Sutherland said he sought to show that Debs had declared in his famous Canton, Ohio, speech in June 1918, that O'Hare had been convicted on the testimony of a "hired" government witness, and that the presiding judge had refused to permit 30 farmers to testify that she had not made the remarks attributed to her in the indictment. Judiciary Chair Louis Martin said he would subpoena the record, and Hillquit said he would comply with the subpoena.[225]

All of the defense arguments were summed up in a 122-page brief filed March 15, 1920, listing Hillquit, Stedman, Roe, Block, Karlin, and Nelles as counsel. Nelles had told reporters the previous day that the brief would enter a general

---

223 MORRIS HILLQUIT, SOCIALISM ON TRIAL (1920). *See also Hillquit Warns of Recoil from Socialist Trial,* N.Y. TRIB., March 4, 1920, at 6; *Hillquit Scores 'Expert' at Trial of Ousted Five,* N.Y. DAILY NEWS, March 4, 1920, at 6.

224 *Defense Winds Up in Trial of Five Socialists,* CHI. TRIB., March 6, 1920, at 3.

225 Associated Press, *Continue Trial of Suspended Assemblymen,* MONTPELIER (Vt.) EVENING ARGUS, Feb. 24, 1920, at 5.

denial to all charges advanced against the Socialists and would recommend reseating the five expelled members.[226] The brief's conclusion echoed Hillquit's closing: "To unseat these Socialists will not prevent return to the normal condition of an actual free and democratic republic, enduring political differences and trusting the common sense of the mass of its people. But it will leave an ugly stain on our democracy."[227]

The Judiciary Committee issued a majority report on March 30, calling for the expulsion of the five Socialists on the grounds that they were disloyal to the United States and the state of New York, affiliated with the disloyal Socialist Party, and intent upon the overthrow of the government by force. The majority report, signed by seven of the 13 members of the committee, also called for new legislation denying the Socialist Party the status of a political party. Five other members, who filed four separate minority reports, called for reseating the ousted Socialists on the ground that the Assembly lacked legal authority to disqualify them on the charges presented.[228] Debate on the expulsion recommendation began the following day and lasted into the early morning hours of April 1. The date was significant—and the length of debate shrewdly calculated— because New York election law precluded any special election to fill vacancies arising after March 31.[229] After 22 hours of debate and maneuvering, the Assembly voted to expel all five Socialists by margins of 70% to 80%.[230]

Despite his initial determination that he lacked the authority to call a special election, Gov. Alfred Smith found an exception in the law that provided for special elections whenever they were made necessary by the governor's calling a special session of the legislature. Smith did just that and called for elections to fill any vacancies on September 16.[231] All five Socialists were reelected.[232] When the Assembly convened for the special session, however, it again voted to oust three

---

[226] *Accuses Sweet of Bi-Partisan Trade on League Probe*, BUFFALO COURIER, March 14, 1920, at 42.

[227] Brief for the Socialist Assemblymen, In the Matter of the Investigation of the Qualifications of Louis Waldman, August Claessens, Samuel A. DeWitt, Samuel Orr, and Charles Solomon to Seats in the Assembly, Before the Judiciary Committee of the Assembly of the State of New York 121-22 (March 15, 1920).

[228] *Expel the Five Socialist Assemblymen, Urges Majority Report, Charging Treason; Roosevelt to Oppose Ouster Motion*, N.Y. TIMES, March 31, 1920, at 1; *Majority Report Ousts Socialists*, SUN AND N.Y. HERALD, March 31, 1920, at 5.

[229] *Democratic Filibusters Delay Vote on Expulsion of Socialists in Stormy Debate in Assembly*, N.Y. TIMES, April 1, 1920, at 1.

[230] *Assembly Expels All Five Socialists by Big Vote after a Thrilling Session*, BROOKLYN DAILY EAGLE, April 1, 1920, at 1.

[231] *Special Elections Refused Socialists*, SUN & N.Y. HERALD, April 13, 1920, at 1.

[232] *Five Socialists Assemblymen Are Reelected*, SUN & N.Y. HERALD, Sept. 17, 1920, at 22.

of the Socialists; the other two were seated but resigned in protest. The Assembly cheered their resignations.[233] It was over.

The Rand School (1921)

Morris Hillquit

In August 1921, Morris Hillquit was called in to defend the Rand School and his colleague Algernon Lee from prosecution under the so-called Lusk Laws requiring that private schools be licensed by the State Board of Regents. State Sen. Clayton R. Lusk had chaired a legislative committee charged with investigating seditious activities in 1919; the socialist Rand School had been one of its key targets. The legislature enacted a series of statutes based on the committee's recommendation, and the school licensing bill was vetoed by Gov. Al Smith, but later passed again by the legislature and signed by Gov. Nathan L. Miller in March 1921.

Lee, who served as Rand's educational director, declared on September 3, 1921, that he was prepared to open the fall term without a license in order to test the constitutionality of the law. Hillquit, who would represent Lee in any legal action, said he was prepared to attack the law on free speech and other grounds.[234] The following day, the state Attorney General's office stated that, if Lee carried out his threat, "action will be taken at once to stop the Rand School on the ground that its operation without a license violates a statute."[235] Nevertheless, Rand opened as scheduled on September 26, but no legal action was taken against Lee or the school.

Instead, Attorney General Charles D. Newton announced that the state would ask Appellate Division to consider the constitutionality of the law based on a stipulated statement of facts prepared by his office and Hillquit. A month later, Newton asked the court to enjoin the further operation of the school, and Hillquit sought the dismissal of that action.[236] In his brief, Hillquit said the entire statute was unconstitutional and should be struck down. He argued that it was so broad that, under its provisions, no instruction could be given in painting, singing, dancing or any other craft without obtaining a license,

---

233 *Assembly Again Expels Three Socialists,* N.Y. Times, Sept. 22, 1920, at 1; *Ouster Means More Socialists in Legislature, Leaders Say,* N.Y. TRIB., Sept. 22, 1920, at 2.

234 *Rand School Will Defy License Law,* N.Y. HERALD, Sept. 4, 1921, at 1.

235 *Rand School Must Obtain License or Face Prosecution,* N.Y. TRIB., Sept. 5, 1921, at 7.

236 *Rand School Opens Without a Single Thrill or a License,* N.Y. TRIB., Sept. 27, 1921, at 11; *Rand School Unmolested Till Court Rules on Law,* N.Y. TRIB., Sept. 28, 1921, at 6; *State Seeks Closing of Rand Socialist School,* N.Y. TRIB., Oct. 25, 1921, at 17; *A Good Test of a Bad Law,* N.Y. EVE. WORLD, Oct. 26, 1921, at 22.

violating the First and Fourteenth Amendments. Arguments in the case were held on May 4, 1922.[237]

On July 14, 1922, Appellate Division upheld the validity of the law, ruling that the American Socialist Society could be prohibited from operating the Rand School without a license. The court held that the legislature had the authority to prevent the teaching of doctrines hostile to the safety of the government and that the law in question was well within the proper exercise of the state's police powers. Under the pressure of great danger, the rights of individuals could be subjected to restraint and enforced by reasonable regulation.[238] Hillquit immediately declared he would appeal the decision,[239] but the issue soon became moot. Gov. Smith would be reelected in November 1922, the Lusk Laws were repealed in early 1923, and the state's action against Rand was suspended.[240]

Benjamin Gitlow (1925)

Charles Recht

The first of the so-called Palmer Raids took place on November 7, 1919. Historian David Kennedy writes that Attorney General A. Mitchell Palmer, who had replaced Thomas W. Gregory in March, had been the target of one mail bomb attack in April that was foiled by the Post Office and another in June that demolished part of Palmer's Washington, D.C., residence. Palmer created a new anti-radical unit, the General Intelligence Division of the Bureau of Investigation, and appointed a young J. Edgar Hoover to run it. Congress gave Palmer a half-million dollars to carry out the necessary operations.[241]

On November 7, Palmer's raiders conducted simultaneous raids against the Union of Russian workers in a dozen cities.[242] Under Palmer's orders, U.S. attorneys throughout the country had been preparing cases against more than 200 radicals who were arrested, and deportation hearings were set to begin on November 11 in many cities.[243] Over the weekend, Charles Recht issued a

---

237 *Rand School Tests Lusk Law To-Day,* N.Y. HERALD, April 20, 1922, at 26; *Rand School Fights in Appellate Court,* N.Y. HERALD, May 5, 1922, at 24; *Socialist School Fights for Life in Appellate Court,* N.Y. TRIB., May 5, 1922.

238 New York v. Am. Socialist Soc'y, 195 N.Y.S. 801 (N.Y. App. Div. 1922).

239 *Socialists to Fight Court Ban on Rand School,* N.Y. TRIB., July 15, 1922, at 1; *Rand School Loses Fight on Lusk Law,* N.Y. TIMES, July 15, 1922, at 1.

240 JULIAN F. JAFFE, CRUSADE AGAINST RADICALISM: NEW YORK DURING THE RED SCARE, 1914–1924 (1972).

241 KENNEDY, *supra* note 163, at 288-89.

242 *Id.* at 290.

243 *U.S. Moves to Deport Reds; Plot to Start Strike Bared,* N.Y. TRIB., Nov. 10, 1919, at 1.

lengthy statement protesting the raids. "The spectacular raids are simply a continuation of the stupid procedure by the Lusk committee and its cohorts with the ulterior motive of creating public excitement, and with a view of further appropriations for their ridiculous work," Recht said.[244]

Responding to the sensational reports of revolutionary and anarchic literature found in the raids, Recht said the literature seized "was of the same type as has been published and read for more than seventy years, ever since social and economic problems have been formulated and advocated." Recht charged that the group responsible for "this hysterical outburst" either could not understand the literature or "maliciously perverted its meaning for their selfish purposes. It is an indictment of their own intelligence and integrity."[245]

> The methods used by the raiders were worthy of the palmiest days of Czarist Russia. People were herded by hundreds into patrol wagons and then released. The force and the violence used by the raiders is an outrage to public decency and belied the pretenses to law and order of which they continually prate. The people subjected to these indignities are the ones charged with advocating force and lawlessness, but there is not an iota of proof and there will not be produced a particle of evidence to justify the charge.
>
> On the other hand, the agents of the Department of Justice and those conducting the raid were most brutal in their methods. Even the people who were released were badly beaten, so that they had to get medical attention. They were also subjected to the additional outrage of having been photographed, measured, finger printed and put through the process of avowed criminals. And this by people who scream from the housetops their love of order and their desire to protect liberty and American institutions.
>
> It is hardly believable that the public will continue to be fooled by these sensational stories, such as the May Day plots, the Fourth of July bomb plots and others, which, strange to say, have never been uncovered and no one ever caught. There is no doubt but that there is much unrest. That anyone would be foolish enough to believe that any individual or group of individuals causes unrest is hardly possible.
>
> In other countries attempts to suppress dissatisfaction by forceful and brutal methods have failed. They will fail here, too, for the simple reason that most people are law-abiding and will not tolerate wanton raids and unlawful methods, for if they can be used with impunity against one

---

244 *Id.* at 3.

245 *Id.*

> group the same thing can be done to any other not meeting with the approval of the Administration.
>
> It is unfortunate that at a time when clear, level-headed action and intelligent discussion are so necessary, a Democratic Administration should use all its power to prevent such discussion by using Cossack methods.[246]

Of the 1,000 or so men seized in the New York City Palmer Raids and examined until 4 a.m. the next day, 35 were formally charged with criminal anarchy by fomenting a conspiracy to overthrow the government. One of those, Benjamin Gitlow, a communist leader in his Bronx district, had been elected to the state Assembly as a Socialist member in 1917. A raid on Gitlow's Brooklyn home yielded two revolvers and six boxes of cartridges.[247] Before his election, Gitlow had been head of the Retail Clerks Union in New York.[248] Recht would be part of the defense team that included Walter Nelles, who would take Gitlow's case all the way to the U.S. Supreme Court.[249]

Gitlow had been one of the leaders of the Left Wing of the Socialist Party that broke from the party in early 1919 to form the Left Wing Section of the Greater New York Locals of the Socialist Party. They began publishing their own newspaper, the *New York Communist*, with John Reed as editor.[250] They also adopted "The Left Wing Manifesto," which was published in the July 5, 1919, issue of *The Revolutionary Age*, a weekly magazine edited by Gitlow and James Larkin, who was also arrested. The manifesto became the focus of the government's post-raid publicity because its strident call for "complete destruction of private control of natural resources and capital and complete destruction of ... the institutions invested with power to enforce rule of one man over another."[251]

Encouraged by the success of the case against the Finns Carl Paivio and Gust Alonen, Assistant District Attorney Alexander I. Rorke looked ahead to five more trials—this time targeting the Left Wing and their manifesto under the state criminal anarchy law. Besides Gitlow, defendants would include Isaac E. Ferguson, James Larkin, Charles E. Ruthenberg,[252] and Harry Winitsky. The defendants decided to be tried separately; the prosecutors decided Gitlow would be first because he had the closest, most easily proved connection to the

---

246 *Id.*

247 *Id.*

248 SIDNEY LENS, RADICALISM IN AMERICA 270-71 (1969).

249 *See* People v. Gitlow, 195 A.D. 773 (1921), and Gitlow v. New York, 268 U.S. 652 (1925).

250 LENS, *supra* note 248, at 271.

251 *U.S. Moves to Deport Reds; Plot to Start Strike Bared*, N.Y. TRIB., Nov. 10, 1919, at 1.

252 Nelles had previously submitted an *amicus curiae* brief in Ruthenberg's Conscription Act case.

manifesto.[253] Nelles had represented Gitlow at his arraignment[254] and would re-join Gitlow's defense team following his trial.

Gitlow and others were brought before Chief Magistrate William McAdoo, who charged them, set bail at $15,000, and sent them off to The Tombs after receiving an affidavit from Archibald E. Stevenson, special counsel to the Lusk Committee, and Samuel Berger, deputy attorney general. The affidavit said that Gitlow and Larkin "wilfully and feloniously printed, issued and caused to be circulated a publication known as 'The Revolutionary Age,' which advises, advocates and teaches the doctrine that organized government should be overthrown by force and violence or by unlawful means." Gitlow declined to comment.[255]

There was some confusion as to who actually held the prisoners: the Lusk Committee, the attorney general, or the immigration authorities. Recht had obtained a writ of habeas corpus from Judge Leonard A. Giegerich, but found himself unable to serve it, declaring that the prisoners were being kept incommunicado. "I was told by the Lusk committee that the prisoners belonged to the federal government, and by the [government] that they didn't know anything about them," Recht said. "When our process server went to the Lusk committee's headquarters at the Prince George Hotel they refused to admit him. I expect to try tomorrow."[256]

At a hearing before McAdoo on November 12, Nelles moved to dismiss the charges against all of the prisoners on the ground that the law under which they were held was unconstitutional. "The statute which defines the alleged crime [of criminal anarchy] is in violation of the constitution both of the state and of the nation," he said. Nelles and Recht also moved to reduce the $15,000 bail.[257] "These men are poor," Recht had told McAdoo, "and cannot raise the amount of the bail. They have been maltreated as prisoners and were not permitted their rights under due process of law."[258] McAdoo denied both motions, expressing the view that the Communist Party, as it was now called, was organized solely to destroy the government.

'Our government is at war with Russia,' McAdoo told Recht at one point.

'We are not legally at war with Russia,' Recht replied. 'In fact, our troops have been withdrawn from Russia.'

---

253 Marc Lendler, *Gitlow v. New York*: Every Idea an Incitement 35 (2012).

254 *N.Y. "Red" Leaders Held in $15,000 Bail*, Phila. Inquirer, Nov. 11, 1919, at 16.

255 *Red Agitators to be Driven Out of City*, N.Y. Trib., Nov. 11, 1919, at 1.

256 *Id.* at 2.

257 *Radicals Plead Anti-Anarchy Law Is Invalid*, N.Y. Trib., Nov. 13, 1919, at 2.

258 *7 Brooklynites Held Following Radical Raids*, Brooklyn Times Union, Nov. 12, 1919, at 9.

'We do not recognize the government of Russia and to the United States, Russia is but a state of chaos and anarchy,' McAdoo answered.

Recht repeated, 'We are not at war with Russia.'

'Who killed the 111 American soldiers whose bodies are being brought back from Russia?'

'I don't know.'

'Well, it was the Soviet Guards of Russia. Now let's get back to the law.'

McAdoo insisted that "The Communist Party has declared a state of war against the United States ... and the establishment of the Communist Party in the state of New York is the highest crime known to the law." Both Gitlow and Larkin were remanded to The Tombs, while McAdoo sent the case to the grand jury empaneled at an extraordinary trial term of the Supreme Court with a strong statement of condemnation: "I am of the opinion beyond any doubt, reasonable or otherwise, that these defendants in their writing, concocting, ... printing and circulation of the manifesto, are clearly guilty as charged in the complaint."[259]

The following week, Nelles and Recht secured a second writ of habeas corpus from Justice Giegerich, and arguments on the merits were set for the morning of November 19.[260] On that date, Recht argued that nothing Gitlow and Larkin had said or done constituted criminal anarchy and that the communists were no more radical than members of the Sinn Fein movement in Ireland. Magistrate Francis McCloskey reserved his decision until December 2. At least Gitlow and Larkin were able to await the decision in freedom; friends and supporters "interested in the cause" had pooled their resources to come up with $30,000 in cash and Liberty Bonds for their bail. Recht contributed $500 of his own money.[261]

Before McCloskey's decision was due, however, Gitlow, Larkin and two others were indicted on November 26, 1919, by the grand jury. Gitlow would be tried separately beginning January 21, 1920,[262] with the legendary Clarence Darrow now leading the defense team.[263]

---

[259] LENDLER, *supra* note 253, at 18-21.

[260] *Gitlow and Larkin Again Seek Release; Martens is Grilled*, BROOKLYN DAILY EAGLE, Nov. 17, 1919, at 1.

[261] *15 Teachers Summoned as 'Red' Suspects*, N.Y. Trib., Nov. 20, 1919, at 1; *Woman Put Out as Red Teacher*, N.Y. HERALD, Nov. 20, 1919, at 6.

[262] People v. Gitlow, 195 A.D. 773 (N.Y. App. 1921); 1921 N.Y. App. Div. LEXIS 4835 (Prior History).

[263] JOHN A. FARRELL, CLARENCE DARROW: ATTORNEY FOR THE DAMNED 308 (2011).

Gitlow's indictment consisted of three counts. The first count charged that, on July 5, 1919, Gitlow "feloniously advocated advised and taught the duty, necessity and propriety of overthrowing and overturning organized government by force, violence and unlawful means by certain writings then and there procured, prepared, composed, circulated and distributed" by Gitlow, principally "The Left Wing Manifesto," published in *The Revolutionary Age*, a communist weekly. The second count alleged essentially the same facts, but rather than target Gitlow's felonious "advocacy," focused on his felonious "publishing" of the Manifesto.

The third count charged that the defendants were

> evil-disposed and pernicious persons and of most wicked and turbulent dispositions and unlawfully, wickedly and maliciously intending and contriving to disturb the public peace and to excite discontent and disaffection and to excite the good citizens of the United States to hatred and contempt of the government and the Constitution of this State, and to solicit, incite, encourage, persuade and procure divers persons to commit acts of violence upon the persons and property of divers of the good citizens aforesaid and to raise and make insurrections, riots, routs, unlawful assemblies and breaches of the peace within the State, and to obstruct the laws and government thereof and to oppose and prevent their due execution, and to procure and obtain arms and ammunition for the more effectual carrying into effect their said most wicked and unlawful intentions and contrivances.[264]

That prolix third count was ultimately withdrawn, although it fairly illustrated the "steamed up" mood of the country,[265] and Gitlow was tried separately from other Left Wing adherents on the first two counts, which alleged violations of Sections 160 and 161 of the New York penal code.[266]

The trial began on January 22, 1920, with New York Supreme Court Justice Bartow Weeks presiding. Although Recht had handled Gitlow's initial trial in a magistrate's court, as well as jury selection in his New York Supreme Court trial, Gitlow's Communist Labor Party had brought in Clarence Darrow at the last minute to handle the actual defense. Despite having Darrow, perhaps the preeminent criminal defense lawyer of his time and a long-time defender of such radicals as Big Bill Haywood of the I.W.W., leading his defense, Gitlow insisted on taking responsibility for writing and publishing the Manifesto.[267]

---

[264] People v. Gitlow, 1921 N.Y. App. Div. LEXIS 4835, at ***1-3 (Prior History).

[265] FARRELL, *supra* note 263, at 308.

[266] People v. Gitlow, 1921 N.Y. App. Div. LEXIS 4835, at ***4 (Prior History).

[267] *Id.*

Gitlow refused to deny that he advocated the overthrow of the government by illegal means. As these were the only defenses appropriate for a trial court, Darrow presented no defense case at all.[268] "I want to say ... so that it may save time, that my client was the business manager and on the board of this paper, and there will be no attempt on his part to deny legal responsibility for it," Darrow told the court.[269]

Darrow dissuaded Gitlow from taking the witness stand, where he would be subjected to cross-examination, but he had no success in persuading the court to truncate the prosecution's case on account of Gitlow's admission of the only salient facts at issue. Weeks allowed the prosecutor to call witnesses to Gitlow's actions, as well as the "violence inherent in his revolutionary doctrine." At the conclusion of the prosecution's case, Darrow announced that there would be no defense witnesses, but that Gitlow himself would address the jury.[270] His "Red Ruby" speech was hardly calculated to obtain an acquittal:

> Socialist philosophy has always been a revolutionary philosophy and people who adhered to the socialist program and philosophy were always considered revolutionists, and I as one who maintain that, in the eyes of the present-day society, I am a revolutionist ... I am not going to evade the issue. My whole life has been dedicated to the movement which I am in. No jails will change my opinion.[271]

In his closing argument, Darrow portrayed Gitlow as a harmless intellectual, within the tradition of revolutionaries like George Washington, John Brown, and Jesus Christ. "For a man to be afraid of revolution in America would be to be ashamed of your own mother," he said.[272] "This country, with its institutions, belongs to the people who inhabit it," Darrow said. "Whenever they shall grow weary of the existing government, they can exercise their constitutional right to amend it, or their revolutionary right to dismember or overthrow it." Acknowledging his quoting Lincoln's first inaugural address, Darrow declaimed, "If Lincoln would have been here today, Mr. Palmer ... would send his night-riders to invade his office and the privacy of his home and send him to jail.[273]

---

[268] LENDLER, *supra* note 253, at 36-43.

[269] FARRELL, *supra* note 263, at 309.

[270] *Id.*

[271] Benjamin Gitlow, *The "Red Ruby": Address to the Jury*, Communist Labor Party pamphlet (1920), at 4.

[272] *Id.* at 43-48.

[273] FARRELL, *supra* note 263, at 309-10.

In his lengthy charge to the jury, Weeks insisted that,

> you are not sitting here to determine any question of the rights of free speech. That question, so far as this court is concerned, is fully disposed of by the opinions of the courts of this state .... While the right to publish is thus sanctioned and secured, the abuse of that right is excepted from the protection of the Constitution and authority to provide for and publish such abuse is left to the legislature. The punishment of those who publish articles which tend to corrupt morals, induce crime, or destroy organized society, is essential to the security of freedom and the stability of the state.[274]

Weeks went through all of Darrow's written requests for instructions, granting some, denying more, then asked if there were any others. Darrow responded, "I would like to except to that portion of the court's charge where he instructs the jury that the question of free speech is not involved," but he did not pursue the point. Rather, he continued to request other changes in the instructions, leaving the constitutional question he raised unanswered.[275] Darrow did object to Weeks's definition of "advocate," but when Weeks offered to charge Darrow's definition, he admitted to not giving it much thought. The word "incite" did not appear in the colloquy, although it did appear in Darrow's proposed requests for instructions.[276] Weeks rejected any incitement requirement: "It makes no difference whether the language was calculated to incite, if the language did advise, advocate and teach the doctrine."[277]

It took the jury three hours to convict Gitlow, and it didn't take much longer for Darrow to go back to Chicago, where he continued to defend radicals caught up in the Palmer Raids.[278] Recht handled Weeks's presentencing interrogation of Gitlow, and on February 11, 1920, he was sentenced to the maximum five to ten years at hard labor at Sing Sing.[279] A new defense team, including Recht, would take the case up on appeal.[280]

Gitlow's first step was a petition for a certificate of reasonable doubt, which sought Gitlow's release on bond. The petition was filed March 26, 1920, by Charles Recht, but the brief was written by Charles Whitman, a Republican and

---

274 Transcript of Record at 145-46, Gitlow v. New York, 268 U.S. 652 (1925) (No. 770) (Charge to the Jury).

275 *Id.* at 157.

276 *Id.* at 164.

277 *Id.* at 156.

278 *Id.* at 310.

279 LENDLER, *supra* note 253, at 46.

280 The rest of the team included Swinburne Hale, Walter Nelles, and Murray C. Bernays. People v. Gitlow, 1921 N.Y. App. Div. LEXIS 4835, at ***10 (Prior History).

the respected former governor of New York. Whitman may have appeared to be the lawyer most likely to get Gitlow out of jail. Whitman's principal argument was that Gitlow had been prosecuted under a law designed for anarchists, not communists, who wanted to replace an existing government with another, rather than destroy government altogether. Justice John McAvoy's opinion, which closely tracked the government's brief, held that the legislature had defined anarchism in the statute and that there was no reasonable doubt that the manifesto satisfied that definition. McAvoy denied the petition, and Gitlow remained in jail.[281]

Gitlow returned to the cadre of leftist lawyers for his appeal to the Appellate Division of the New York Supreme Court. Swinburne Hale was lead counsel, with Nelles and Murray C. Bernays with him on the brief. Recht was also listed as attorney for Gitlow. Opposing were John Caldwell Myers, deputy assistant district attorney, of counsel, with Robert S. Johnstone and Alexander I. Rorke on the brief. District Attorney Edward Swann was also listed for the state. The judges who heard the case were Frank C. Laughlin, John P. Clarke (presiding), Walter C. Smith, Alfred R. Page, and Edgar S. K. Merrell.[282]

Recht wrote the brief, while Hale presented the oral argument. Recht's brief tracked Walter Nelles's sense of the case articulated in November 1919. In a letter to the editor of the *New York Tribune*, shortly after Gitlow's arraignment, Nelles had written:

> Sir: You published this morning an editorial ridiculing my argument in the case of the so-called 'Reds' arraigned before Magistrate McAdoo that the New York criminal anarchy statute is invalid. Will you have the fairness to print my argument?
>
> It was this: The [U.S.] Supreme Court has held that the expression of principles cannot be made criminal except when it creates a clear and present danger of overt criminal conduct.[283] The principle attributed to the so-called 'Reds' creates no such danger. It is a wrong principle. It is not persuasive. So long as we have not, by oppression, created a wide prevalence of despondency as to the social justice order under our government, expression of the view that our government should be overthrown will not result in a formidable action directed toward that end.
>
> Walter Nelles,
> New York, Nov. 14, 1919[284]

---

281 *Id.* at 79-81.

282 People v. Gitlow, 195 A.D. 773, 187 N.Y.S. 783, 1921 N.Y. App. Div. LEXIS 4835***10.

283 *See* Schenck v. United States, 249 U.S. 47, 52 (1919).

284 *Innocuous Anarchy*, N.Y. TRIB., Nov. 17, 1919, at 8.

Recht tried to sell that point by suggesting that the principle of "clear and present danger" was correct, but misapplied in the famous Espionage Act cases from which it had sprung. Since no such danger was presented by the manifesto, any law purporting to criminalize it would be unconstitutional. "The mere spreading of any doctrine as a doctrine cannot constitutionally be declared a crime," Recht wrote. "Speaking or writing can be dealt with as a crime only when in such close relation to substantive evil condemned as criminal as to constitute an active, immediate factor toward the prohibited end."[285]

Justice Laughlin, who wrote the unanimous opinion filed April 1, 1921, would have none of it.

> The Constitution... places no restraint upon the power of the Legislature to punish the publication of matter which is injurious to society according to the standard of the common law. *It does not deprive the State of the primary right of self-preservation.* ... I am of the opinion that the common-law theory of proximate causal connection between the acts prohibited and the danger apprehended therefrom ... has no application here.

Justice Laughlin went on to hold that the legislature could "forbid the advocacy ... of a doctrine designed and intended to overthrow government" without waiting "until it can be shown that there is a present or immediate danger that it will be successful."[286]

Recht again sought to have the court construe the act as limited in application to its original purpose, that is, to punish anarchists who advocated the destruction of all government by assassination, notably of President McKinley, whose death precipitated the law, and other violent means. Gitlow could not be convicted under such an interpretation, he reasoned, because he advocated creating a government, albeit a proletarian dictatorship.[287] Specifically, Recht tried to use canons of statutory construction to limit the meaning of "or by any unlawful means" to the use of force, which he maintained Gitlow did not necessarily advocate.

> [If] a peaceable mass demonstration of all or a large part of the people of any country should prevail upon all the officers of government to cease functioning, and a new set of officials chosen under a new constitution thereafter functioned in fact, without opposition, there ...

---

[285] LENDLER, *supra* note 253, at 82-84.

[286] People v. Gitlow, 195 A.D. 773, 788-790 (N.Y. Sup. Ct. App. Div. 1921).

[287] *Id.* at ***24-25, 195 A.D. 773, 784, 187 N.Y.S. 783, 792.

> would have been an overthrow, not affirmatively lawful perhaps, but not unlawful in its means.[288]

Justice Laughlin utterly rejected the appellant's statutory construction argument:

> [The] verdict of the jury is an answer to this argument in so far as it implies that the appellant and those associated with him did no more than to advocate that ... through a peaceable mass demonstration of the proletariat, all the officers of our State and National governments may be prevailed upon to cease functioning and that a new set of officers may be chosen under a new Constitution without the use or exertion of force or violence. The defendant and his fellow-Socialists of the Left Wing knew perfectly well that such results could not be peaceably accomplished, and moreover they are not advocating a change in the Constitution or a new Constitution or government. They are plainly advocating the destruction of all existing government. The only practical difference between the doctrines advocated by them and the doctrine of anarchy pure and simple is that they intend to utilize the existing government temporarily while organizing the proletariat for mass strike.[289]

Recht also argued that their client was prejudiced by testimony given by a Winnipeg attorney who testified to the effects of a mass strike on that city. In particular, he objected to Weeks's instruction to the jury: "You have heard the evidence of what did occur at Winnipeg. Was that a violation of law?" Laughlin ruled that "it was perfectly plain that the court meant and the jury must have understood, that they were to determine whether such a mass strike if it occurred here would have been lawful .... It is obvious," he said, "that it would be unlawful," finding the evidence competent and not prejudicial.[290]

A variety of additional exceptions were raised by Gitlow's team, but Laughlin shrugged each of them off as "trivialities," most of which were not preserved for appeal by the failure to object during the trial. None were found prejudicial to Gitlow, and the judgment below was affirmed on April 1, 1921.[291] All of the communist defendants were ultimately convicted. Winitsky and Larkin, who defended themselves with Nelles's assistance, also lost on appeal. Both were ultimately pardoned by Gov. Al Smith in 1923. Ferguson and Ruthenberg successfully argued on appeal that they were not legally responsible for publishing the manifesto; new trials were ordered, but never held.[292]

---

[288] *Id.* at ***45, 195 A.D. 773, 794-95, , 187 N.Y.S. 783, 800.

[289] *Id.* at ***46, 195 A.D. 773, 795, 187 N.Y.S. 783, 800.

[290] *Id.* at ***47-50, 195 A.D. 773, 795-97, 187 N.Y.S. 783, 800-801.

[291] *Id.* at ***50-66, 195 A.D. 773, 797-805, 187 N.Y.S. 783, 801-807.

[292] *Id.* at 68.

Only Gitlow's case reached the U.S. Supreme Court. According to Marc Lendler, it was the newly formed American Civil Liberties Union that persuaded Gitlow to appeal his conviction, rather than accept a pardon, in order to get a test case before the U.S. Supreme Court.[293] Lendler suggests that this persuasion may not have occurred until 1923, however, after Gitlow had exhausted his appeals in New York state courts.[294]

Walter Nelles led the team that took *Gitlow* to the New York Court of Appeals, with Joseph R. Brodsky and I. E. Ferguson supporting. The new district attorney, Joab H. Banton, led the state's team, with Myers of counsel. Chief Judge Frank H. Hiscock and Associate Judges Frederick Crane, John W. Hogan, Chester B. McLaughlin, William S. Andrews, Cuthbert W. Pound, and Benjamin N. Cardozo heard the appeal. The case was argued on June 6, 1922, and decided on July 12.

Crane's majority opinion was perfunctory with regard to the constitutional issue. "The Constitution, federal or state, does not authorize publications ... advocating the destruction of the government by violence or unlawful means," he wrote. "The legislature of this state, therefore, was within its powers when it enacted [the Criminal Anarchy statute] ."[295] Hiscock's concurrence offered no constitutional analysis at all, focusing instead on whether publishing the manifesto fell within the prohibitions of the statute.[296] Pound's dissent, joined by Cardozo, also avoided the constitutional issue, echoing Whitman's argument that Gitlow was convicted of advocating the dictatorship of the proletariat, not criminal anarchy.[297]

None of the decisions below offered the definitive constitutional test of the Criminal Anarchy law that the ACLU sought. Only a U.S. Supreme Court decision could resolve the issue. The ACLU would put Nelles and Walter Pollak, a partner in the firm of Engelhard, Pollak, Pitcher, Stern, and Clarke, in charge of steering the case through that process. Unlike Recht and Hale, they would have no ideological need to defend the manifesto, but could focus squarely on the constitutional issues. There were two: whether and, if so, how, the federal constitution protected free speech against infringement by state law, and did the New York statute under which Gitlow was convicted infringe that guarantee?

---

293 LENDLER, *supra* note 253, at 76 (quoting Walter Pollak, who argued the case in the U.S. Supreme Court as writing in 1925, "We [the ACLU], who were anxious for a decision on these laws by the highest court, persuaded Gitlow to make the appeal.").

294 *Id.* at 79. Lendler notes that the nature of the first appeal suggests that it was not originally designated a test case, but was rather designed to overturn the conviction by whatever approach seemed the most promising. *Id.*

295 People v. Gitlow, 234 N.Y. 132, 138 (1922).

296 *Id.* at 145 (Hiscock, J., concurring).

297 *Id.* at 158.

Nelles was tapped to file the petition for a writ of error, the first step in getting the case before the High Court. Nelles submitted his application for writ of error to Justice Louis D. Brandeis on July 22, 1922,[298] followed by a list of eleven purported errors dated August 10.[299] Nine days later, Brandeis referred the application to the full Court and ordered that the New York attorney general be so notified.[300] Lindler notes that, in his original submission, Nelles tried to finesse the question of which constitutional clause was at issue. When Brandeis expressed doubt that the record was sufficient, Nelles amended his petition to specify that the issue was the due process clause of the Fourteenth Amendment,[301] specifically whether the amendment "incorporated" the First Amendment, thus making it applicable to the states.

Nelles's Assignment of Errors listed the constitutional issue first—that is, that New York's "so-called Criminal Anarchy laws" violated the due process clause. A variation of that theme appears in the fifth numbered "error"; most of the others involved some form of the proposition that the operative standard was "incitement," not "advocacy."[302] There was no defense of the manifesto or its ideology.

The Supreme Court brief, filed April 4, 1923, was written for the ACLU by Pollak and Nelles. Also named on the brief are Albert DeSilver, another important figure in the ACLU, and Charles S. Ascher. It got right to the point: "The case brings to this Court for the first time the question of the constitutionality of making advocacy *per se*, and without regard to circumstances, a crime."[303]

The first point in Pollak's argument asserted that the "'liberty' protected by the Fourteenth Amendment includes the liberty of speech and of the press, a process known as incorporation."[304] Pollak cited three cases in which the Court had ruled in a manner consistent with that theory, although without explicitly deciding the point.[305] Pollak's second point argued that the New York statute under which Gitlow was convicted unduly restrained liberty of expression.

---

298 Transcript of Record at 137-38, Gitlow v. New York, 268 U.S. 652 (1925) (No. 770) (Petition for Writ of Error).

299 *Id.* at 139-43 (Assignment of Errors).

300 *Id.* at 139 (Order of Mr. Justice Brandeis Referring Application to the Full Court).

301 LENDLER, *supra* note 253, at 107.

302 Transcript of Record at 139-43, Gitlow v. New York, 268 U.S. 652 (1925) (No. 770) (Assignment of Errors).

303 Brief for Plaintiff-in-Error at 1-2, Gitlow v. New York, 268 U.S. 652 (1925) (No. 19) (Statement of Facts).

304 *Id.* at 9 (Outline of Argument).

305 Brief for Plaintiff-in-Error at 15-16, Gitlow v. New York, 268 U.S. 652 (1925) (No. 19) (Argument, Point I(b)) (citing Patterson v. Colorado, 205 U.S. 454 (1907); Fox v. Washington, 236 U.S. 273 (1915); and Gilbert v. Minnesota, 254 U.S. 325 (1920).

Specifically, he asserted that such restraints could only be imposed where "its exercise bears a causal relation with some substantive evil, consummated, attempted, or likely," that is, "incitement to crime." Since the Criminal Anarchy law contained no such qualification, he argued, it was unconstitutional.

Pollak surveyed the recent Espionage Act decisions of the Court, distinguishing them from Gitlow's case on both the facts and the law. He pointed out that the Espionage Act decisions accounted for circumstances—especially the ongoing war—that could give rise to serious danger. And he asserted that the New York law punished, not incitement, but "the mere utterance—'advocacy'—of certain doctrines, whether or not such utterance was reasonably calculated to persuade persons to the acts condemned, or to any unlawful conduct whatever, and whether or not a causal connection between the utterance and a substantive evil can be deduced from surrounding circumstances."[306]

Most of the balance of Pollak's argument consisted of an erudite recounting of the history of sedition law in both England and the United States, comparing the New York law with those disfavored statutes. He concluded with the requested action from the Court: "Since the statute is unconstitutional, the conviction of the plaintiff-in-error should be reversed and the indictment dismissed."[307]

The state's principal brief, by Attorney General Carl Sherman and District Attorney Joab H. Banton, filed April 8, 1923, appeared to misconstrue the thrust of Pollak's argument. Pollak's brief contrasted "advocacy" and "incitement," arguing that New York's law punished the former, while only the latter was actionable. Sherman's brief contrasted "advocacy" with "heresy," that is, punishment for believing in the doctrine of anarchy itself. In any event, it asserted that such advocacy—for example, advocating the overthrow of government—was a sufficient abuse of freedom of speech to be criminalized.[308]

Sherman's brief did address Pollak's argument that advocacy could only be restrained where "its exercise bears a causal relation to some substantive evil consummated, attempted or likely," the so-called "necessity of imminent danger," but dismissed the argument as false and absurd.[309] This brief did not address the question of incorporation, but a second brief—filed April 9, possibly requested by the Court—focused on that issue. It perfunctorily denied that, notwithstanding the adoption of the Fourteenth Amendment, the First

---

306 Brief for Plaintiff-in-Error at 19-24, Gitlow v. New York, 268 U.S. 652 (1925) (No. 19) (Argument, Point II).

307 *Id.* at 105.

308 Brief for Defendant-in-Error at 7, Gitlow v. New York, 268 U.S. 652 (1925) (No. 19) (The Real Question Involved).).

309 *Id.* at 18 (Argument, Point II, Necessity of imminent danger).

Amendment in any way curtailed the rights of the states to limit the freedom of speech and of the press.[310]

That issue proved to be the most important pronouncement to come out of this case. The U.S. Supreme Court declined to credit Sherman's conclusory argument, nor did it take issue with Pollak's claim. "For present purposes," wrote Justice Edward T. Sanford in the majority opinion, published June 8, 1925, "we may and do assume that freedom of speech and of the press—which are protected by the First Amendment from abridgment by Congress—are among the fundamental personal rights and 'liberties' protected by the due process clause of the Fourteenth Amendment from impairment by the States."[311] That principle was never disputed again.

> Gitlow did not fare as well.
>
> By enacting the present statute the State has determined, through its legislative body, that utterances advocating the overthrow of organized government by force, violence and unlawful means, are so inimical to the general welfare and involve such danger of substantive evil that they may be penalized in the exercise of its police power[312]

Sanford wrote. "We cannot hold that the present statute is an arbitrary or unreasonable exercise of police power of the State unwarrantably infringing the freedom of speech or press; and we must and do sustain its constitutionality."[313] Gitlow's conviction would stand.

Justice Oliver Wendell Holmes wrote the dissenting opinion for himself and Justice Louis D. Brandeis. Quoting his own "clear and present danger" test, Holmes said it was

> manifest that there was no present danger of an attempt to overthrow the government by force on the part of the admittedly small minority who shared the defendant's views. It is said that this manifesto was more than a theory, that it was an incitement. Every idea is an incitement. It offers itself for belief and if believed it is acted on unless some other belief outweighs it or some failure of energy stifles the movement at its birth. The only difference between the expression of an opinion and an incitement in the narrower sense is the speaker's enthusiasm for the result. Eloquence may set fire to reason. But whatever may be thought

---

[310] Brief for Defendant-in-Error at 7, Gitlow v. New York, 268 U.S. 652 (1925) (No. 19) (Argument, Point III).).

[311] Gitlow v. New York, 268 U.S. 652, 666 (1925).

[312] *Id.* at 668.

[313] *Id.* at 670.

> of the redundant discourse before us it had no chance of starting a present conflagration.[314]

Reaction to the Gitlow decision was mixed. Roger Baldwin considered it a crushing defeat, concluding in the ACLU *Annual Report* that "the repressive measures passed during and since the war were strengthened by the U.S. Supreme Court in the *Gitlow* case." Pollak and Nelles saw it as a "near miss" and looked forward enthusiastically to the next case. Those with a longer view, primarily scholars like Charles Warren and Zechariah Chaffee, saw in the incorporation decision a "new liberty" and "victory out of defeat," respectively.[315]

---

314 *Id.* at 673 (Holmes, J., dissenting).

315 SAMUEL WALKER, IN DEFENSE OF AMERICAN LIBERTIES: A HISTORY OF THE ACLU 79-80 (1990).

Epilogue

Having reintroduced the three most important lawyers of the Old Left establishment in the first quarter of the twentieth century—as well as a number of their colleagues: Clarence Darrow, Dudley Field Malone, Roger Baldwin, Walter Nelles, Swinburne Hale, Rose Weiss, and many others—I should now take a brief look at some of their successors. In so doing, I hope to demonstrate that American lawyers' representation of radical thinkers and actors remains deeply ingrained in our legal tradition.

One might trace the Second Red Scare to the signing of the Molotov-Ribbentrop Pact between the Soviet Union and Nazi Germany in 1939 and the anxiety it caused in the United States.[1] The very next year, Congress enacted the Alien Registration Act of 1940, better known as the Smith Act. Not unlike the Sedition Act of 1798 discussed in the prologue, the Smith Act made it a crime

> (1) to knowingly or willfully advocate, abet, advise, or teach the duty, necessity, desirability, or propriety of overthrowing or destroying any government in the United States by force or violence, or by the assassination of any officer of any such government;
>
> (2) with the intent to cause the overthrow or destruction of any government in the United States, to print, publish, edit, issue, circulate, sell, distribute, or publicly display any written or printed matter advocating, advising, or teaching the duty, necessity, desirability, or propriety of overthrowing or destroying any government in the United States by force or violence; [or]
>
> (3) to organize or help to organize any society, group, or assembly of persons who teach, advocate, or encourage the overthrow or destruction of any government in the United States by force or violence; or to be or become a member of, or affiliate with, any such society, group, or assembly of persons, knowing the purposes thereof.[2]

---

[1] Geoffrey R. Stone, Perilous Times 250 (2004). *See also* Daniel Levin, *Smith Act*, Encyclopedia of American Civil Liberties 1488, https://books.google.com/books?id=TXoKAgAAQBAJ&printsec=frontcover#v=snippet&q=Levin&f=false.

[2] 54 Stat. 670 (1940).

The first prosecution under the act took place in 1941 and involved 29 members of the Trotskyite Socialist Workers Party in Minneapolis.[3] Attorney General Francis Biddle would later admit that the defendants had been guilty of nothing more than rhetorical excess.[4] The principal defense attorney for the 29 was one of the indicted men, Albert Goldman, who had been encouraged to attend the law school of Northwestern University by the leadership of the Communist Party. Goldman would become part of the International Labor Defense developed by the party and from there gravitate toward Trotskyism and the Socialist Workers Party. Indeed, Goldman was Leon Trotsky's personal attorney at the Dewey Commission hearings in 1937, which cleared Trotsky of all charges levied against him at the infamous Moscow Trials.[5]

Goldman's opening statement at the trial, as summarized by Donna T. Haverty-Stacke, fits neatly into the American tradition:

> Goldman urged the jurors to "know the difference between … a political movement … and a conspiracy hatched in the darkness of night for the purpose of committing a crime." The SWP was created in the open, he explained, and although it was based on principles with which [the prosecutor] and the jury may not agree, that did not make it an illegal conspiracy. The position of the defense, Goldman told the jury, was that the accused had a First Amendment right to free speech that allowed them to hold and advocate their beliefs, however unpopular they may be.[6]
>
> The real issues, he insisted, were "Did we advocate the overthrow of the Government by force and violence? Did we incite people for the violent overthrow of the government? That is the heart of the question." The party's prediction that there would be violent class struggle at some time in the future did not constitute such advocacy, he argued, because the SWP's followers could not create something that would come about of its own volition (class struggle) and because they actually preferred a peaceful transition to socialism. The prosecution's accusations to the contrary, he claimed, not only represented a clear violation of the defendants' First Amendment rights to free speech but also embodied a fundamental misunderstanding of the political beliefs it condemned.

---

[3] Dunne v. United States, 138 F.2d 137 (8th Cir. 1943). *See also* DONNA T. HAVERTY-STACKE, TROTSKYISTS ON TRIAL, FREE SPEECH AND POLITICAL PERSECUTION SINCE THE AGE OF FDR (2015).

[4] STONE, *supra* note 1, at 255.

[5] Joe Allen, Defender of the Movement, SocialistWorker.org, Jan. 21, 2011, at https://www.counterpunch.org/2011/01/21/defender-of-the-movement/.

[6] HAVERTY-STACKE, *supra* note 3, at 90.

> Goldman closed by insisting that the evidence the defense would bring forth during the trial would show that the defendants had a constitutional right to express their beliefs—a position he hoped the jury would support with a verdict of not guilty.[7]

The Minneapolis trial ultimately resulted in 18 convictions affirmed by the U.S. Court of Appeals for the Eighth Circuit.[8]

Certainly, the best-known postwar prosecution of American leftists was the 1951 espionage trial of Julius and Ethel Rosenberg. The Rosenbergs were part of a Soviet spy ring that was partly responsible for America's losing its monopoly over nuclear weaponry. By the time of the trial, the Soviet Union had firmly established its hegemony over Eastern Europe, while in Asia, the Chinese Communist Party had ousted its Nationalist rivals to take over that vast country. The United States was in no mood to tolerate nuclear espionage.

The Rosenbergs' trial began on March 6, 1951, before Judge Irving Kaufman of the U.S. District Court for the Southern District of New York. The Rosenbergs were defended by Emmanuel Bloch, well known at the time as a defender of left-wing radicals, including alleged members of the Ware Group, a covert organization of the Communist Party USA, and Steve Nelson, who headed the CPUSA in the Pittsburgh area. Bloch was a member of the National Lawyers Guild, an organization of left-leaning lawyers that got its start in the 1930s as part of the labor movement. The NLG still exists today, having championed other victims of the postwar "anticommunist hysteria" and the McCarthy era, as well as later civil rights and anti–Vietnam War movements.[9]

In his summation to the Rosenberg jury, Bloch expressed the spirit that animates the lawyers of the left—old and new:

> If you want to convict these defendants because you think that they are Communists and you don't like communism and you don't like any member of the Communist Party, then, ladies and gentlemen, I can sit down now and there is absolutely no use in my talking. There was no use in going through this whole rigmarole of a three weeks' trial. That is not the crime.
>
> But believe me, ladies and gentlemen, I am not here, other defense counsel are not here as attorneys for the Communist Party and we are not here as attorneys for the Soviet Union. I can only speak for myself and my father. We are representing Julius and Ethel Rosenberg, two

---

[7] *Id.* at 92-93.

[8] 138 F.2d at 152.

[9] *See* NATIONAL LAWYERS GUILD at https://www.nlg.org/.

> American citizens, who come to you as American citizens, charged with a specific crime, and ask you to judge them the way you would want to be judged if you were sitting over there before twelve other jurors.[10]

The Rosenbergs were found guilty and ultimately executed, despite what has been called "heroic efforts" by Bloch and his associates to save their lives.[11]

The constitutionality of the Smith Act was reviewed by the U.S. Supreme Court in 1951 and again in 1957. The charges were similar, but the results could not have been more different. The 1951 decision in *Dennis v. United States* affirmed the conviction of Eugene Dennis, then general secretary of the Communist Party USA, for violating the Smith Act by conspiring to advocate the overthrow of the United States government.[12] Dennis was defended by George W. Crockett Jr., Abraham J. Isserman and Harry Sacher. Crockett had been a defender of communists and other radicals during the early part of his career; later, he became known for his work in civil rights as a lawyer and, later, as a judge.[13] All were members of the National Lawyers Guild, and all were cited for contempt at the conclusion of the trial.[14]

Dennis and his co-conspirators were convicted and their convictions affirmed by a 6-2 majority consisting of Chief Justice Fred M. Vinson, who wrote the opinion, and Justices Stanley F. Reed, Harold H. Burton, Sherman Minton, Felix Frankfurter and Robert H. Jackson; Justices Hugo L. Black and William O. Douglas dissented. Six years later, a very different Supreme Court reversed the Smith Act convictions of Oleta Yates and eleven other leaders of the Communist Party in California. The *Yates* defense team was led by Benjamin Margolis, a founding member of the NLG, who had become famous for defending the so-called Hollywood Ten in 1947 and for stonewalling the House Committee on Un-American Activities

---

[10] *Summation of Emmanual Bloch for the Defense*, FAMOUS TRIALS, https://www.famous-trials.com/rosenberg/2021-blochsummation.

[11] *See* United States v. Rosenberg, 195 F.2d 583 (2d Cir. 1952), 200 F.2d 666 (2d Cir. 1952) & 346 U.S. 273 (1953).

[12] 341 U.S. 494 (1951). Perhaps the most interesting aspect of the *Dennis* case is the decision of Learned Hand, then chief judge of the Second Circuit, affirming the convictions. Hand's 1917 opinion in *Masses Publ. Co. v. Patten* is held up today as a paragon of First Amendment jurisprudence. *See* STONE, *supra* note 1, at 398-402.

[13] Ruth Martin, *"They feel the beams resting upon their necks": George W. Crockett and the Development of Equal Justice Under Law, 1948-1969*, 39 MICH. HIST. REV. 51, 52 (2013).

[14] NATIONAL LAWYERS GUILD FOUNDATION, A HISTORY OF THE NATIONAL LAWYERS GUILD 1937-1987, at 28 (1987). *See also* United States v. Sacher, 1949 U.S. Dist. LEXIS 3228, *aff'd*, 182 F.2d 416 (2d Cir. 1950), *aff'd*, 343 U.S. 931 (1952) (affirming contempt citations).

in 1952.[15] The *Yates* 7-0 decision—Chief Justice Earl Warren and Justices Hugo L. Black, Felix Frankfurter, William O. Douglas, Harold H. Burton, Tom C. Clark and John M. Harlan—reinterpreted the Smith Act to permit the kind of advocacy that led to the *Dennis* convictions.[16] While Justice Harlan's opinion did not go as far in protecting radical speech as later cases would, it effectively ended Smith Act prosecutions.[17]

It did not end the attack on leftists, however, or the vigorous defense by American lawyers. In 1961, for example, the Supreme Court affirmed 5-4 a decision requiring the CPUSA to register as a communist organization under the Subversive Activities Control Act, over the dissents of Chief Justice Warren and Justices Black, Douglas, and Brennan. John Abt, chief counsel for the CPUSA and Joseph Forer, another founder of the NLG, defended the party. Both the Guild and the American Civil Liberties Union filed *amicus* briefs in an unsuccessful effort to reverse the lower court's decision.[18]

This was by no means the ACLU's first or only intervention in the civil liberties cases of the Second Red Scare and Cold War period, but the ACLU was far more reluctant than the National Lawyers Guild to be identified with communists. While it did participate in the unsuccessful effort to thwart HUAC and blacklisting, it had also supported the Trotskyite prosecutions in 1941. Only gradually did the ACLU come to oppose later Smith Act prosecutions and finally condemn *Dennis* on First Amendment grounds.[19] As the Cold War morphed into a hot war in Vietnam, the ACLU found itself torn between mounting a vigorous defense in traditional free speech and draft cases and avoiding the increasing number of civil disobedience cases that grew out of the anti-war movement.

One erstwhile member of the ACLU board, however, would become to the New Left what Hillquit, Stedman and Recht had been to the Old Left: a true believer and powerful advocate. William Kunstler, who was also an active member of the NLG, did not share the ACLU's willingness to represent neo-Nazis and other right-wing radicals. He was a leftist through and through and became the left's best-known lawyer in the '60s and '70s. Nor did Kunstler blanch at civil or not-so-civil disobedience cases. His clients included Black Power activists H. Rap Brown and Stokely Carmichael; war resisters Fathers

---

[15] John McTernan, *Ben Margolis: A Lifetime of "Contempt" for Injustice and Oppression*, 56 GUILD PRAC. 1 (1999).

[16] Yates v. United States, 354 U.S. 298 (1957).

[17] STONE, *supra* note 1, at 415.

[18] CPUSA v. Subversive Activities Control Board, 367 U.S. 1 (1961).

[19] SAMUEL WALKER, IN DEFENSE OF AMERICAN LIBERTIES: A HISTORY OF THE ACLU 184-88 (1990).

Daniel and Philip Berrigan; surviving student protesters at Kent State; four of the infamous Chicago Seven, including David Dellinger, Tom Hayden, Abbie Hoffman, and Jerry Rubin; Dennis Banks, Russell Means, and other members of the American Indian Movement; and the list goes on and on.[20]

Even as this book was being edited in March 2025, the president of the United States launched an unprecedented assault on law firms and lawyers who represented persons or positions adverse to the government now in power. Some of those targets have "bent the knee" to salvage their privileges and skittish clientele, while others have challenged the president in court. One such challenge, a complaint filed by conservative lawyer Paul Clement for the law firm of Wilmer Cutler Pickering Hale and Dorr (WilmerHale), begins with a paragraph that captures the very essence of this book:

> "[T]he right to counsel is the foundation for our adversary system," *Martinez v. Ryan*, 566 U.S. 1, 12 (2012), and the "courage" of attorneys who take on unpopular clients has long "made lawyerdom proud," *Sacher v. United States*, 343 U.S. 1, 4 (1952). John Adams famously embodied these principles by defending eight British soldiers in the "Boston Massacre" trial, an effort he described as "one of the best pieces of service I ever rendered my country." [citation omitted] And British monarchs' practice of punishing attorneys "whose greatest crime was to dare to defend unpopular causes"—which threatened to reduce lawyers to "parrots of the views of whatever group wields governmental power at the moment"—helped inspire the Bill of Rights. *Cohen v. Hurley*, 366 U.S. 117, 138-40 (1961) (Black, J., dissenting). It is thus a core principle of our legal system that "one should not be penalized for merely defending or prosecuting a lawsuit." *F. D. Rich Co. v. United States ex rel. Indus. Lumber Co.*, 417 U.S. 116, 129 (1974).[21]

Once again, I return to the central point of this book, as articulated in the introduction: that the legal representation of radical thinkers, speakers, and actors has been an integral feature of the American legal system from colonial times to the present. And that the lawyers who undertook that representation deserve to be remembered, if only because their courage will be needed again and again and again.

---

[20] David J. Langum, William M. Kunstler: The Most Hated Lawyer in America 3-4 (1999).

[21] Complaint for Declaratory and Injunctive Relief at 7, Wilmer Cutler Pickering Hale and Dorr LLP v. Executive Office of the President et al., Civil Case No. 1:25-cv-00917 (D.D.C. March 28, 2025).

Bibliography

Archives and Databases

Ancestry. https://www.ancestry.com/.

David Leip's Atlas of U.S. Presidential Elections. https://uselectionatlas.org/.

GG Archives. https://www.ggarchives.com/Immigration/Deportation/DeportationOfTheIWW-1919.html.

Marxist Internet Archive. https://www.marxists.org/.

Munn, James Buell Collection. New York University Archives.

National Archives. "The Amistad Case." Updated June 2, 2021. https://www.archives.gov/education/lessons/amistad#background.

Newspapers.com. https://www.newspapers.com/.

Our Campaigns. https://www.ourcampaigns.com/.

Recht, Charles Papers. Tamiment Library, New York University.

Roe, Gilbert E. Papers, in La Follette Papers. Wisconsin Historical Society.

Books

Alexander, James. *A Brief Narrative of the Case and Trial of John Peter Zenger, Printer of the New York Weekly Journal.* N.p., 1736. Reprint, Harvard University Press, 1972.

American Socialist Society. *The Trial of Scott Nearing and the American Socialist Society.* Rand School of Social Science, 1919.

Burstyn, Joan N., ed. *Past and Promise: Lives of New Jersey Women.* Syracuse University Press, 1996.

Carlson, Peter. *Roughneck: The Life and Times of Big Bill Haywood.* W. W. Norton, 1983.

Crain, Esther. *The Gilded Age in New York, 1870-1910.* Black Dog & Leventhal, 2016.

Dubin, Michael J. *United States Congressional Elections, 1788-1997: The Official Results of the Elections of the 1st Through 105th Congresses.* McFarland, 1998.

Early, Frances H. *A World Without War: How U.S. Feminists and Pacifists Resisted World War I.* Syracuse University Press, 1997.

Eastman, Max. *The Trial of Eugene Debs.* Liberator Publishing, 1918.

Easton, Eric B. *Defending the Masses: A Progressive Lawyer's Battles for Free Speech.* University of Wisconsin Press, 2018.

Farrell, John A. *Clarence Darrow: Attorney for the Damned.* Doubleday, 2011.

Flynn, Elizabeth Gurley. *The Rebel Girl.* Masses & Mainstream, 1955.

Haverty-Stacke, Donna T. *Trotskyists on Trial: Free Speech and Political Persecution Since the Age of FDR.* New York University Press, 2015.

Hawley, Lowell S., and Ralph Bushnell Potts. *Counsel for the Damned.* J. B. Lippincott, 1953.

Hillquit, Morris. *From Marx to Lenin.* Hanford Press, 1921.

Hillquit, Morris. *History of Socialism in the United States.* Funk & Wagnalls, 1903.

Hillquit, Morris. *History of Socialism in the United States.* 2nd ed. Funk & Wagnalls, 1910.

Hillquit, Morris. *Loose Leaves from a Busy Life.* Da Capo Press, 1934.

Hillquit, Morris. *Loose Leaves from a Busy Life.* 2nd ed. Da Capo Press, 1971.

Hillquit, Morris. *Present-Day Socialism.* Rand School of Social Science, 1920.

Hillquit, Morris. *Recent Progress of the Socialist and Labor Movements in the United States.* Charles H. Kerr, 1907.

Hillquit, Morris. *Report of the Socialist Party of the United States to the International Socialist Congress at Copenhagen.* Socialist Party National Headquarters, 1910.

Hillquit, Morris. *Socialism on Trial.* B. W. Huebsch, 1920. Reprint, Kessinger Publishing, 2008.

Hillquit, Morris. *The Story of the British Labor Party.* Socialist Party National Headquarters, 1923.

Hillquit, Nina. "Morris Hillquit: Pioneer of American Socialism." Unpublished manuscript, n.d.

Jackson, Kenneth T., ed. *The Encyclopedia of New York City.* New-York Historical Society; Yale University Press, 1995.

Jaffe, Julian F. *Crusade Against Radicalism: New York During the Red Scare, 1914–1924.* Associated Faculty Press, 1972.

Johnson, Christopher H. *Maurice Sugar: Law, Labor, and the Left in Detroit 1912-1950.* Wayne State University Press, 1988.

Kennedy, David M. *Over Here: The First World War and American Society.* 2nd ed. Oxford University Press, 2004. https://doi.org/10.1093/oso/9780195173994.001.0001.

La Follette, Belle Case, and Fola La Follette. *Robert M. La Follette: June 14, 1855-June 18, 1925.* Macmillan, 1953.

Langum, David J. *William M. Kunstler: The Most Hated Lawyer in America.* New York University Press, 1999.

Lawrence, Jerome, and Robert Edwin Lee. *Inherit the Wind.* Random House, 1955.

Lendler, Marc. *Gitlow v. New York: Every Idea an Incitement.* University Press of Kansas, 2012. https://doi.org/10.1353/book.125187.

Lens, Sidney. *Radicalism in America.* 2nd ed. Thomas Y. Crowell, 1969.

Levin, Daniel. "Smith Act." In *Encyclopedia of American Civil Liberties* Vol. 3, *R - Z,* edited by Paul Finkelman. Routledge (2006).

Nearing, Scott. *The Debs Decision.* Rand School of Social Science, 1919.

Nelles, Walter, ed. *Espionage Act Cases with Certain Others on Related Points* [...]. National Civil Liberties Bureau, 1918.

New York University, and W. J. Maxwell, eds. *General Alumni Catalogue of New York University.* New York University, 1916.

O'Neill, William L. *The Last Romantic: A Life of Max Eastman.* 2nd ed. Routledge, 1991.

Papke, David Ray. *The Pullman Case: The Clash of Labor and Capital in Industrial America.* University Press of Kansas, 1999. https://doi.org/10.2307/jj.2990344.

Pasley, Jeffrey L. *The Tyranny of Printers: Newspaper Politics in the Early American Republic.* University of Virginia Press, 2001.

Pratt, Norma Fain. *Morris Hillquit: A Political History of an American Jewish Socialist.* Greenwood, 1979.

Rabinowitz, Victor, and Tim Ledwith, eds. *A History of the National Lawyers Guild: 1937-1987.* National Lawyers Guild Foundation, 1987.

Rand School of Social Science. *Must We Arm? Hillquit-Gardner Debate.* Rand School of Social Science, 1916.

Rand School of Social Science. *Should Socialism Prevail? A Debate* [...]. Rand School of Social Science, 1916.

Recht, Charles. *American Deportation and Exclusion Laws.* Greenwood, 1919.

Recht, Charles. "Objection Overruled." Unpublished manuscript, n.d.

Stone, Geoffrey R. *Perilous Times: Free Speech in Wartime; From the Sedition Act of 1798 to the War on Terrorism.* W. W. Norton, 2004.

Trachtenberg, Alexander, ed. *The American Socialists and the War: A Documentary History* [...]. Rand School of Social Science, 1917.

Twain, Mark. *The Gilded Age.* American Publishing Co., 1873.

Walker, Samuel. *In Defense of American Liberties: A History of the ACLU.* Oxford University Press, 1990.

Scholarly Articles

Allen, Joe. "Defender of the Movement." *CounterPunch,* January 21, 2011. https://www.counterpunch.org/2011/01/21/defender-of-the-movement/.

Brumberg, Stephen F. "New York City Schools March Off to War." Paper presented at the annual meeting of the American Educational Research Association, April 6, 1988. Available through Educational Resources Information Center (ERIC).

Ehrlich, Walter. "The Origins of the Dred Scott Case." *Journal of Negro History* 59, no. 2 (1974): 132–42. https://doi.org/10.2307/2717325.

Ehrlich, Walter. "Was the Dred Scott Case Valid?" *Journal of American History* 55, no. 2 (1968): 256–65. https://doi.org/10.2307/1899556.

Feigenbaum, William M. "Seymour Stedman: Socialist Candidate for Vice-President." *New Age* (Buffalo), June 17, 1920. Reprint, marxisthistory.org, n.d. http://www.marxisthistory.org/history/usa/parties/spusa/1920/0617-feigenbaum-stedman.pdf.

Giffin, Frederick C. "The Martens Mission." *International Social Science Review* 73, no. 3/4 (1998): 91–102. https://www.jstor.org/stable/41882275.

Hillquit, Morris. Review of *The Labor Injunction,* by Felix Frankfurter and Nathan Greene. *St. Johns Law Review* 5, no. 1 (1930): 164–65. https://scholarship.law.stjohns.edu/lawreview/vol5/iss1/41/.

Martin, Ruth. "'They feel the beams resting upon their necks': George W. Crockett and the Development of Equal Justice Under Law, 1948–1969." *Michigan Historical Review* 39, no. 2 (2013): 51–75. https://www.jstor.org/stable/10.5342/michhistrevi.39.2.0051. https://doi.org/10.1353/mhr.2013.0038.

McTernan, John. "Ben Margolis: A Lifetime of 'Contempt' for Injustice and Oppression." *Guild Practice* 56, no. 1 (1999): 1–3.

Moglen, Eben. "Considering 'Zenger': Partisan Politics and the Legal Profession in Provincial New York." *Columbia Law Review* 94, no. 5 (1994): 1495–1524. https://doi.org/10.2307/1123158.

Sayer, John. "Art and Politics, Dissent and Repression: The Masses Magazine Versus the Government, 1917-1918." *American Journal of Legal History* 32, no. 1 (1988): 42–78. https://doi.org/10.2307/845994.

Sterling, David L. "In Defense of Debs: The Lawyers and the Espionage Act Case." *Indiana Magazine of History* 83, no. 1 (1987): 17–42. https://www.jstor.org/stable/27791041.

Trasciatti, Mary Anne. "Athens or Anarchy? Soapbox Oratory and the Early Twentieth-Century American City." *Buildings & Landscapes: Journal of the Vernacular Architecture Forum* 20, no. 1 (2013): 43–68. https://doi.org/10.5749/buildland.20.1.0043.

Volokh, Eugene. "Thomas Cooper, Early American Public Intellectual." *New York University Journal of Law & Liberty* 4, no. 2 (2009): 372–81. https://www.law.nyu.edu/sites/default/files/ECM_PRO_062712.pdf.

Warne, Colston E. "The Co-operative Society of America—A Common Law Trust." *University Journal of Business* 1, no. 4 (1923): 373–92. https://www.jstor.org/stable/2354626. https://doi.org/10.1086/506686.

Cases

Index

C

G

H

N

O

P

X

Y

Z

www.ingramcontent.com/pod-product-compliance
Lightning Source LLC
LaVergne TN
LVHW020414220926
848484LV00018B/2569/J
* 9 7 9 8 8 8 1 9 0 3 0 2 2 *